LEGENDARY LOCALS

OF

THE SANTA CLARITA VALLEY

CALIFORNIA

DR. ALAN POLLACK, KIM STEPHENS,
AND E.J. STEPHENS

LEGENDARY LOCALS

ISBN 978-1-4671-0027-4

Legendary Locals is an imprint of Arcadia Publishing
Charleston, South Carolina

Printed in the United States of America

Library of Congress Control Number: 2012935057

For all general information, please contact Arcadia Publishing:
Telephone 843-853-2070
Fax 843-853-0044
E-mail sales@arcadiapublishing.com
For customer service and orders:
Toll-Free 1-888-313-2665

Visit us on the Internet at www.arcadiapublishing.com

Dedication
To the legendary locals of the Santa Clarita Valley, past, present, and future.

On the Cover: From left to right:
(TOP ROW) Crystl Bustos, Olympic athlete (Courtesy of Crystl Bustos, see page 82); Lyman and Lillian Curtis, St. Francis Dam victims (Courtesy of Keith Buttelman, see page 42); Kenny Smith, television sports commentator (Courtesy of mediabistro.com, see page 76); William S. Hart, silent film cowboy star (Courtesy of scvhistory.com, see page 93); and Gene Autry, singing cowboy, pictured with actress Peggy Stewart, (Courtesy of classiccinemagold.com, see page 106).

(MIDDLE ROW) William Jenkins, Santa Clarita Valley pioneer (Courtesy of scvhistory.com, see page 28); Mark Paul Gosselaar, actor (Courtesy of fanpop.com, see page 125); Thomas and Martha Mitchell, Santa Clarita Valley pioneers (Courtesy of scvhistory.com, see page 22); Alexander Mentry, oilman (Courtesy of scvhistory.com, see page 23); and Theodore Roosevelt, US president (Courtesy of scvhistory.com, see page 34).

(BOTTOM ROW) Lou Henry Hoover, US first lady (Courtesy of scvhistory.com, see page 35); Tim McCoy, cowboy actor (Courtesy of Santa Clarita Valley Historical Society, see page 109); Tiburcio Vasquez, outlaw (Courtesy of scvhistory.com, see page 21); W.C. Fields, comic actor (Courtesy of scvhistory.com, see page 103); and Tippi Hedren, actor and animal activist (Courtesy of Philippe Halsman, see page 124).

LEGENDARY LOCALS OF

THE SANTA CLARITA VALLEY

CALIFORNIA

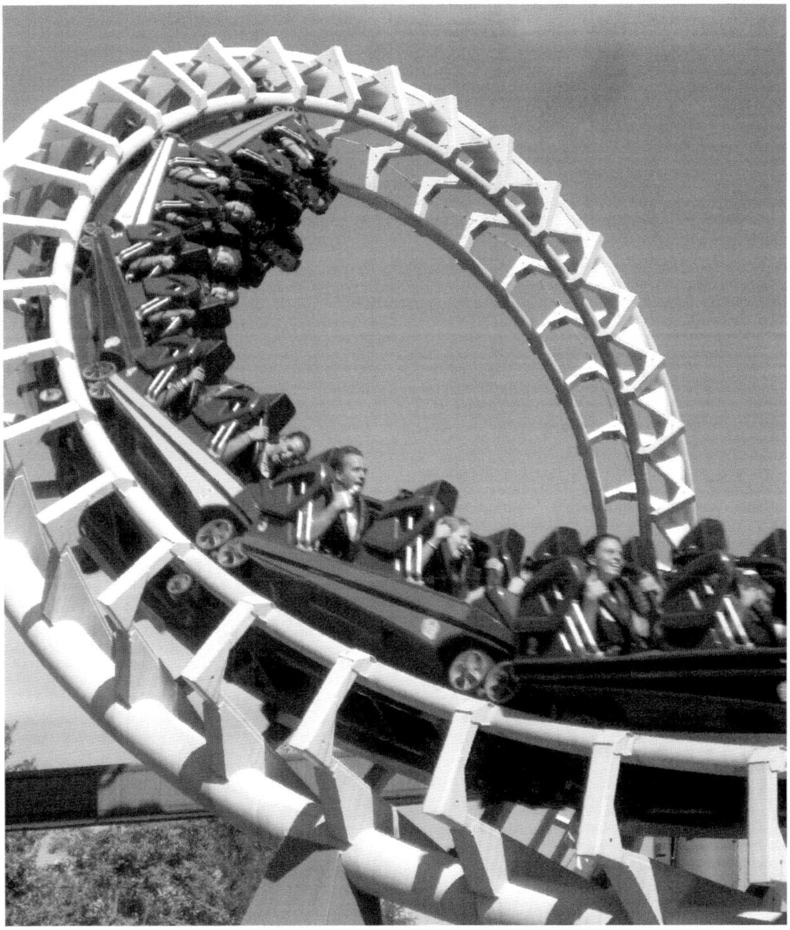

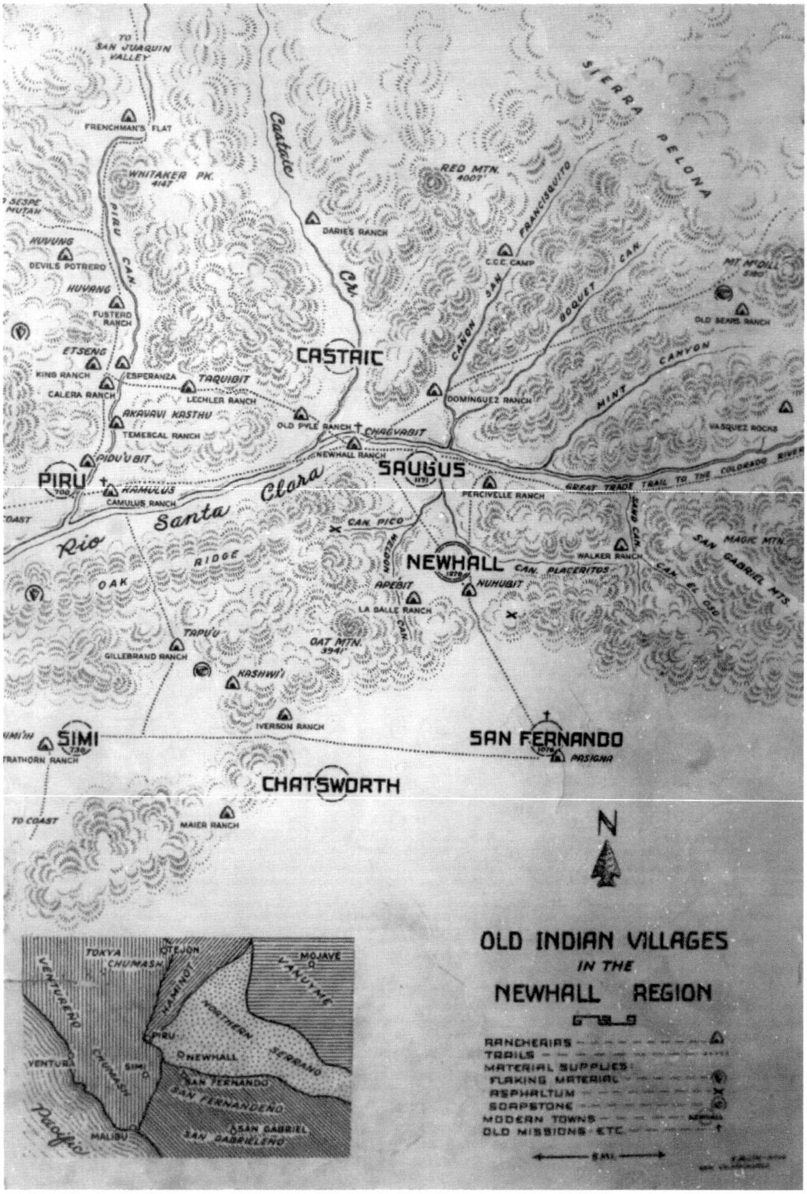

Page 1: **Six Flags Magic Mountain**
A legion of local legends helps make the Santa Clarita Valley (SCV) one of *Money* magazine's 50 Best Places to Live in America. An hour north of downtown Los Angeles, the SCV boasts near-perfect weather, beautiful scenery, and a range of entertainment options, including Six Flags Magic Mountain theme park in Valencia (previous page).

Page 2: **Santa Clarita Valley Map**
This Depression-era map is centered on the Santa Clarita Valley, highlighting the former sites of Tataviam villages. The Tataviam culture existed in the valley for centuries before being rapidly supplanted by the Spanish during the late 1700s. (Courtesy of the Santa Clarita Valley Historical Society.)

CONTENTS

ACKNOWLEDGMENTS

A book highlighting the colorful characters of the Santa Clarita Valley would not be possible without the scores of great chroniclers who, via ink-stained fingers, tell us the tales of the legends who came before and of those who stand alongside us now. We would especially like to thank Leon Worden of SCVTV and scvhistory.com for committing his life to forever capturing the stories of the Santa Clarita Valley. We also wish to thank the Santa Clarita Valley Historical Society for providing images throughout the book. A heaping helping of gratitude goes to our editors at Arcadia Publishing, Tiffany Frary and Erin Vosgien. All images are courtesy of scvhistory.com unless otherwise noted.

We would also like to thank the following people and organizations: Charlie and Christina Belardinelli; b-westerns.com; John Boston; Gary Condie; *The Daily News*, Los Angeles, California; the Heritage Haunt; findagrave.com; Carl Goldman and Jeri Seratti, KHTS 1220 AM; the incomparable Tippi Hedren; Roger Horn; imdb.com; Jack and Irene Lilley; the *Los Angeles Times*; Ed Marg Jr.; Sally Moore, Halfway House Café; Tony Newhall; the docents at the Saugus Train Station; Pat Saletore, executive director, Santa Clarita Valley Historical Society; *The Santa Clarita Valley Signal*, Santa Clarita, California; Cary Quashen; Julie Ann Ream; Carol and Frank Rock; Phil Scorza; Linda Therrien, Vasquez Rocks Natural Area and Nature Center; usasoftball.com; Kevin Turner; Andre, Renaud, and Sue Veluzat, Melody Ranch Motion Picture Studio; Jim Walker; Stephanie Weiss; Bill West; Laurene Weste; and Jeff and Pam Wheat. And thanks to Corner Bakery, Freshworks, Panera Bread, and Starbucks for all the free wi-fi.

Alan would like to dedicate this book to his dad, Samuel, for his courageous battle with Alzheimer's disease, and to the memory of his mother, Jean, and dog, Dakota ("Puppy").

Kim and E.J. wish to thank their friends and family for their unwavering support and dedicate this book to their children, Mariah and Dylan, who bring joy and laughter to each day.

In an area as populous as the Santa Clarita Valley, it is possible that some truly legendary personalities slipped through the cracks and were not listed in this book. Send their stories to scvlocallegends@gmail.com, and they may be included in a future edition.

INTRODUCTION

What do the following people have in common?

Cowboys, Native Americans, gunfighters, farmers, shepherds, soldiers, range warriors, miners, wildcatters, ranchers, saloon keepers, stagecoach drivers, railroaders, town drunks, teetotalers, engineers, land speculators, explorers, missionaries, actors, and lots of common folk?

You may have answered that these were the colorful souls who once populated the Old West, or perhaps the cast of characters in a B-Western.

You would be right on both counts, but there would also be a third possible answer: the Santa Clarita Valley. That is because all the elements that made up the era we know as the Old West were once in the valley, and there's a good chance that the Western you had in mind was actually filmed here.

The Santa Clarita Valley (SCV) stretches north to south from the Angeles National Forest to the San Fernando Valley. The city of Palmdale lies at its eastern edge, and the Heritage Valley in Ventura County borders it on the west. Surrounded by the San Gabriel and Santa Susana Mountains, the SCV encircles the city of Santa Clarita—comprising the districts of Valencia, Newhall, Saugus, and Canyon Country—along with the communities of Castaic, Stevenson Ranch, Val Verde, Agua Dulce, and Acton.

The 275,000 residents of the SCV live in an area that has proven pivotal time-and-again to the story of Southern California. The SCV hosted the first documented gold discovery in California; the state's first successful oil well and refinery; the linking of Northern and Southern California by rail, which prevented the state from splitting in two; and the birth of a bustling ranching and land development enterprise.

While many cities boast a lineage from the Old West, few have the SCV's two-tiered history of actually being part of the era and later being the site of its portrayal. That's because the early history of the movie industry played out in the SCV's rugged hills and canyons, which provided the perfect backdrops for many of the first Westerns.

But the true history of the valley exists in tales told of the diverse personalities who left their mark on the landscape.

These stories begin with a group of Shoshone-speaking people who migrated here from the Great Plains about 1,700 years ago, displacing the previous inhabitants. They were known as the Tataviam, or "people of the sunny slope," so named for their habit of setting up dome-shaped huts on the sunny southern slopes of the local mountains. The Tataviam built around 25 settlements, with their main village of Chaguayabit located at present-day Castaic Junction. The Tataviam way of life continued over the centuries, relatively unchallenged and unaltered, until August 8, 1769. On that particular Tuesday, a band of leather-clad Spanish soldiers under the command of Don Gaspar de Portolá crossed over the San Gabriel Mountains from the south into the valley.

The coming of the Europeans brought new laws, the Roman Catholic religion, and the Spanish language. Father Juan Crespí, the expedition's diarist, is credited with christening the region when he named the valley's Santa Clara River.

The arrival of the Spaniards marked the beginning of the end of the traditional way of life for the natives. In time, most of the Tataviam, along with other Native American tribes, were displaced from their homeland and herded to the nearby San Fernando Mission to work and learn the ways of the Europeans.

The padres' domination of the region ended just over 50 years later when Mexico gained its independence from Spain. In time, Mexico secularized the missions, granting land to the natives, who were unfamiliar with the concept of land ownership and proved easy marks for shady speculators.

In 1839, the Mexican government granted Antonio Del Valle a spread of over 48,000 acres in the SCV that became known as the Rancho San Francisco. After Antonio's death, a portion of the land was renamed Rancho Camulos and passed to his son, Ygnacio.

Novelist Helen Hunt Jackson visited Rancho Camulos in 1882 while doing research for her novel, *Ramona*. Her purported use of Camulos as a backdrop in the book painted a romantic vision of the Mission and Rancho period of Old Spanish California, making Camulos—the "home of Ramona"—into a major tourist attraction. Many of these visitors decided to put down roots in California, helping transform nearby Los Angeles from a sleepy pueblo of 5,000 souls in the 1880s into a burgeoning city of more than 100,000 within a generation.

Camulos's owner, Ygnacio Del Valle, spent much of his time 40 miles to the south in Los Angeles. Hell-bent on cleaning up the lawless town, he helped organize a group of lawmen known as the California Rangers, headed by Maj. Horace Bell. Bell was assisted by William W. Jenkins, who later worked in the fledgling oil industry in SCV's Pico Canyon and was involved in a decades-long range war in Castaic. Another of Bell's Rangers was Cyrus Lyon, who later purchased a stagecoach stop with his brother Sanford, located in present-day Newhall.

In 1865, a portion of the rancho was sold to Thomas Bard, who was unsuccessful in his bid to find oil and quickly gave up on the property. Bard later struck it rich in neighboring Ventura County, where he became one of the founders of Union Oil. Ironically, the first successful oil strike in the West happened just outside the rancho when Alexander Mentry drilled the famous Pico No. 4 well in 1876 in Pico Canyon. It pumped continuously until 1990, and a pipeline was later stretched from the site to the Pioneer Oil Refinery—California's first—in downtown Newhall.

Most school children learn that the first discovery of gold in California was at Northern California's Sutter's Mill in 1848. In fact, there was an earlier discovery in 1842 in the SCV's Placerita Canyon. Legend has it that a man named Francisco Lopez fell asleep under an oak tree and dreamed of gold. When he awoke, he dug up some wild onions nearby and found gold flakes clinging to the roots. The tree later became known as the "Oak of the Golden Dream," and is today a historic landmark.

In 1847, explorer and soldier John "The Pathfinder" Fremont passed through the SCV on his way to accept the surrender of Mexican troops under the command of Gen. Andrés Pico. This action, known as the "Capitulation of Cahuenga," effectively ended the Mexican-American War in California. Three years later, California became the 36th state.

One of the valley's most colorful personalities during this era was Mexican-American War hero Edward F. Beale. In 1857, Beale was put in charge of building a wagon road from Fort Defiance in Arizona to the mouth of the Mojave River. As part of the expedition, Beale took along 25 Egyptian camels, which became the basis for the legendary "Camel Corps" at nearby Fort Tejon. In 1863, Beale deepened a cut first dug by Phineas Banning through the San Fernando Pass to 90 feet. Named Beale's Cut, this passageway provided stagecoach access between the SCV and San Fernando Valley.

The valley's next wave of new arrivals rode in by rail.

Failing to hit pay dirt, Gold Rush pioneer Henry Mayo Newhall turned to auctioneering, which brought him his first fortune. He later became a board member of the powerful Southern Pacific Railroad and, capitalizing on insider information, bought up old Spanish ranchos in Central and Southern California, knowing they would rise in value once tracks were laid. One of these parcels was a huge chunk of the Santa Clarita Valley. His namesake town of Newhall (today a district of Santa Clarita) was founded in 1876 when he deeded land to the railroad for $1 to establish a town and train station. Newhall died six years later after falling from a horse. The following year, his widow and sons founded the Newhall Land and Farming Company, which is still a major land developer today.

New Yorker John Lang moved to Soledad Canyon (near present-day Canyon Country) and became the boss of Lang Station, where in 1876, Northern and Southern California were first linked by rail. Lang once reportedly shot a record-setting 2,350-pound grizzly bear that wandered into the canyon.

In 1888, Newhall was a two-block-long Wild West town with more saloons than churches. In rode Henry Clay Needham, a rabid prohibitionist, who arrived with the grand intention of setting up an alcohol-free colony. Needham was eventually forced to give up this scheme, but his fanaticism nearly earned him the Prohibitionist Party's nod for president in 1932.

Not all of the valley's characters were as virtuous, especially the legendary outlaw Tiburcio Vasquez. Born in Monterey, California, in 1835, Vasquez began his life of crime as a teenager rustling cattle and holding up stagecoaches. In 1873, he led a brazen robbery in the Northern California town of Tres Pinos, killing three men. After the raid, Vasquez became a wanted man and posses chased him south, where he hid out for a time among the SCV's otherworldly geologic formation that today bears his name, Vasquez Rocks.

These same rocks and other rugged Santa Clarita Valley vistas later played an important role in the birth of the movie industry. Due to its varied scenery and proximity to Hollywood, the valley hosted many early Western stars like Hoot Gibson, Tim McCoy, Tom Mix, Harry Carey, John Wayne, and Newhall's most famous resident, William S. Hart.

"Two Gun Bill" Hart was a silent movie actor whose Westerns were known for their realism. During his 11-year film career, he was one of the most famous actors on the planet. After his retirement, Hart built a hilltop mansion in Newhall where he lived until his death in 1946.

Cowboy film star Tom Mix established one of his early "Mixville" movie sets in Newhall. His most notable local film was *Three Jumps Ahead* (1923), in which he appears to jump Beale's Cut on the back of Tony the Wonder Horse. Beale's Cut also appeared in the 1939 John Ford–John Wayne classic, *Stagecoach*.

For a time, singing cowboy Gene Autry owned Melody Ranch, the most famous of the many film studios that dot the SCV. Countless Western movies and television shows, most notably *Gunsmoke*, were filmed at Melody, and most of the genre's biggest stars once strolled along its dusty streets and boardwalks. Melody Ranch burned to the ground in the wildfires of 1962 but was painstakingly resurrected by the Veluzat family in 1991. It later became the home of the HBO series *Deadwood* and the site of the annual Santa Clarita Cowboy Festival.

Westerns were not the only genre of films shot in the valley during the early days of Hollywood. Charlie Chaplin, the greatest silent clown of them all, came to the Saugus Train Station in 1923 to film *The Pilgrim*. A dozen years later, he returned to Sierra Highway to shoot the iconic final scene of the Silent Era, which appears at the conclusion of *Modern Times*.

While Chaplin may have represented Hollywood royalty, for a time in the early decades of the 20th century, William Mulholland was the uncrowned ruler of Los Angeles. As the "water czar" of the city, Mulholland's will went unchallenged until the night of March 12, 1928, when the St. Francis Dam in the SCV's San Francisquito Canyon came crashing down. A 180-foot torrent of water cascaded down the canyons to the sea, scouring everything in its path. Between 450 and 600 people are estimated to have died that night in one of the worst disasters in California history.

Shortly after the dam break, the SCV had the dubious honor of being the site of one of the last great train robberies in the West when an ex-rodeo rider named "Buffalo Tom" Vernon derailed a train near the present-day Saugus Swap Meet and made off with $300 for his efforts.

Some believe legendary actor James Dean ate his last meal at a restaurant near Castaic Junction on the morning he died. The same restaurant was later the site of the horrific "Newhall Incident" in 1970, where four California Highway Patrol officers were gunned down in a shootout with two career criminals. Great heroism emerged that night, and from the ashes of the tragedy rose new police procedures that have since saved countless lives.

The SCV of the 21st century is blessed with a treasure trove of interesting characters who enrich the community every day. These stories of artists and activists, entertainers and educators, heroes and homemakers—woven together with tales of the SCV's early pioneers—create a colorful human tapestry that makes the Santa Clarita Valley one of the most fascinating places to live in all of America.

CHAPTER ONE

The Builders

First there was the land.

It was beautiful and verdant, yet restless. Over eons, tremendous subterranean forces lifted mountains, carved valleys, deposited gold and oil underfoot, and created rugged vistas that would much later be used by Hollywood to portray the "Old West."

Then, there were people.

The first to arrive in what would one day be known as the Santa Clarita Valley settled here after a millennia-long migration from Asia. Around 400 A.D., they were displaced by the Tataviam, who became the primary inhabitants of the region for the next 17 centuries. Having no written language, they left few stories to pass down, forever dooming the names and deeds of countless generations to the mists of time.

The Tataviam were quickly supplanted by Spanish colonists and missionaries, who in turn were replaced by the Mexicans. The occasional white mountain man wandered into the area during this time, like Peter Lebeck, who is known solely from an inscription that reads, "IHS [+] PETER LEBECK KILLED BY A x BEAR OCTR 17 1837."

The Mexicans were eventually forced out by the Americans, and as the flags changed, the cattle-based *Californio* rancho culture gave way to Yankee farmers, ranchers, and shopkeepers.

Gold had been discovered when it was still Mexican territory, but it was the Americans who made ripping it from the ground an obsession. Alexander Mentry struck "black gold" in 1876 at a Pico Canyon well that pumped for the next 114 years. His luck finally ran out in 1900 when he was stung by a "kissing bug."

As the pace of life accelerated in the 1900s, so did the speed of turning wheels—on wagons, stagecoaches, and finally steam locomotives. The deafening gallop of the iron horse profoundly changed life in the valley, forever linking the SCV to the rest of the nation.

As the 19th century gave way to the 20th, the automobile became the chosen mode of transport. Former valley footpaths were paved, becoming streets and roads, and the crest-hugging Ridge Route first snaked over the Tehachapis.

Change was slow, but steady, and progress appeared to be on an ever-upward trajectory.

Gaspar de Portolá

Two peoples, with little more in common than the air they breathed, first met in the summer of 1769 in what is today called the Santa Clarita Valley. On August 8, leather-clad Spanish soldiers from Catalonia under the command of Don Gaspar de Portolá crossed over the San Gabriel Mountains from the south, emerging through what is today known as Elsmere Canyon. They must have appeared quite alien to the Tataviam Indians who greeted them that day, but not enough for the natives to prove inhospitable. One of the Spaniards later described the reception in this manner:

> We descended afterwards to a little valley where there was an Indian village. The inhabitants had sent us messengers to the Valle de Santa Catalina, and guides to show us the best trail and pass through the range. These poor fellows had prepared refreshments for our reception, and, as they saw that it was our intention to move on so as not to interrupt the day's march, they made the most earnest entreaties to induce us to visit their village, which was off the road. We had to comply with their requests so as not to disappoint them. We enjoyed their hospitality and bounty, which consisted of seeds, acorns, and nuts. Furthermore, they furnished us other guides to take us to the watering-place about which they gave us information. . . . Near the place in which we camped there was a populous Indian village. The inhabitants lived without other protection than a light shelter of branches in the form of an enclosure. For this reason the soldiers gave to the whole place the name of the Ranchería del Corral.

Two days later, the Portolá expedition left the SCV through the Santa Clara River valley towards their ultimate destination of Monterey, California. What may have seemed like a cordial meeting for the Tataviam was the first step on the Spaniards' path of conquest of the peaceful people and their lands. By the end of the century, most of the Tataviam would be herded to the Mission San Fernando, where they were forced into servitude. The photograph at right is of a statue of Portolá in Pacifica, California.

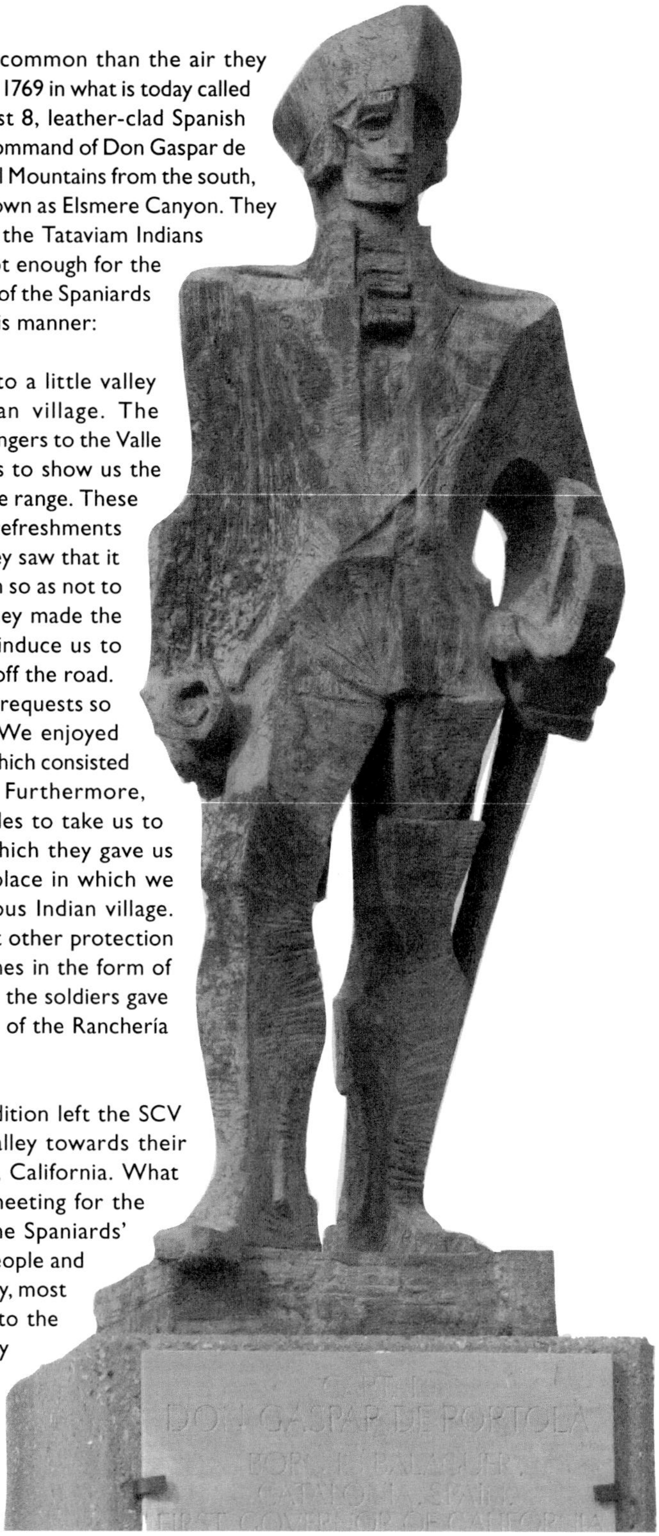

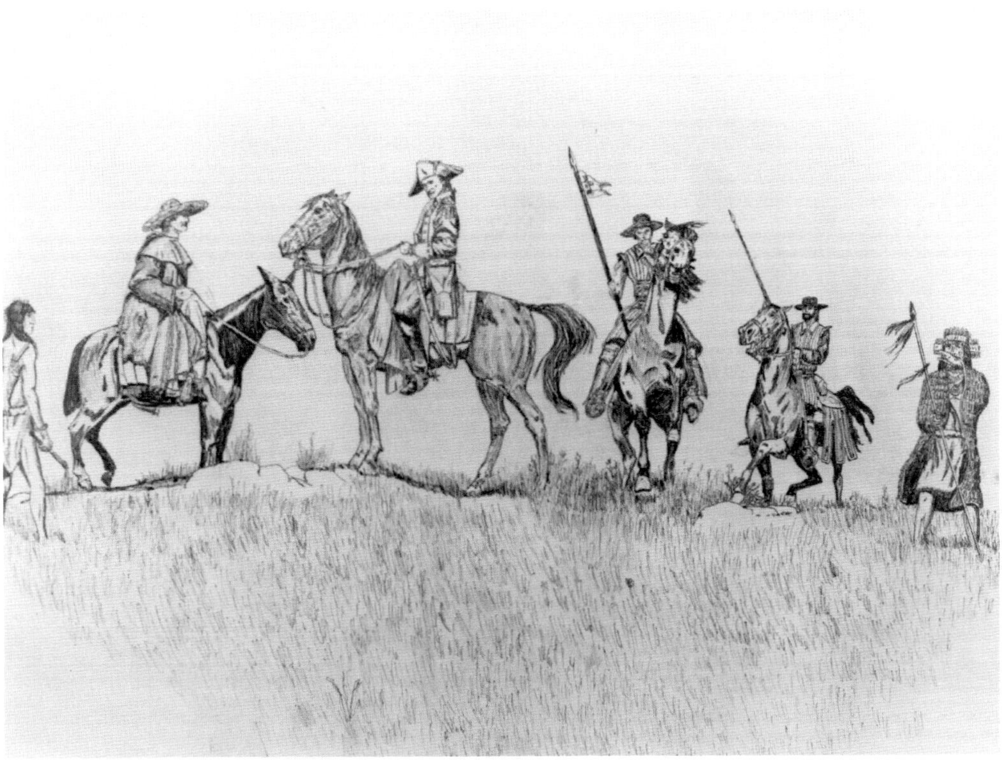

Father Juan Crespí

To the victors go the naming rights. A man who witnessed the sudden culture clash between the Tataviam and the Spaniards was Father Juan Crespí, the expedition's diarist. The Spanish coveted the Tataviam lands and wasted no time naming their future digs. Crespí is credited with christening the valley's main river after Santa Clara (St. Clare). This sketch by Jerry Reynolds depicts a meeting between Portolá and Crespí.

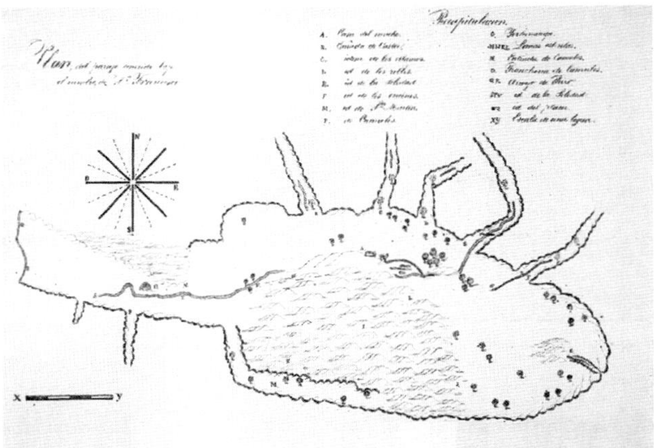

Antonio Del Valle

Antonio Del Valle always seemed to find himself in trouble due to shady political dealings and tawdry affairs with señoritas. But this did not prevent him from successfully petitioning the Mexican governor for the Rancho San Francisco land grant of 48,000 acres in 1839. This "upside-down tick" drawing is a map of the Rancho San Francisco in 1843. (Courtesy Dr. John Johnson, Santa Barbara Museum of Natural History.)

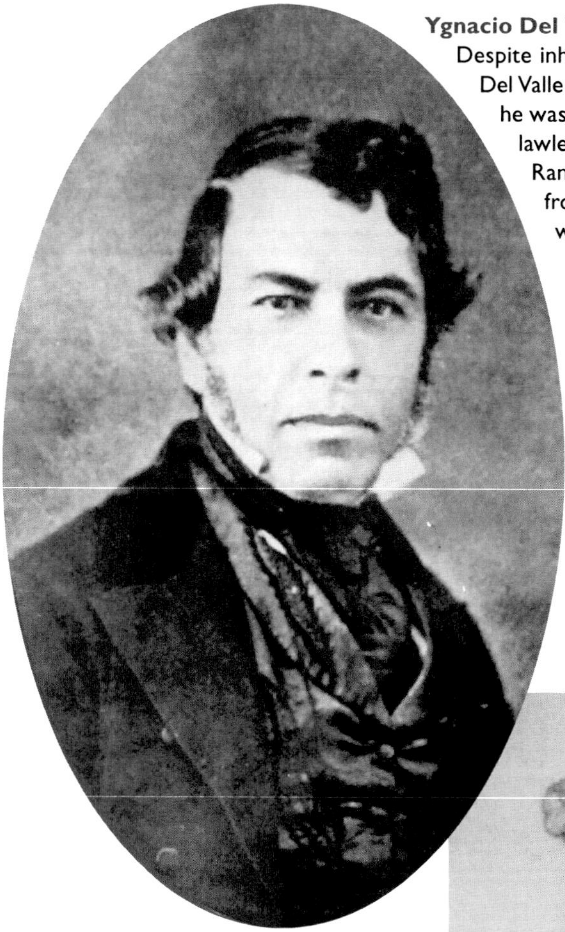

Ygnacio Del Valle

Despite inheriting 13,000 acres of his father's land, Ygnacio Del Valle (seen here) continued to live in Los Angeles where he was *alcalde* (mayor). Ygnacio cleaned up the wild and lawless pueblo by forming the California Rangers. The Rangers blasted their way through town, meting out frontier justice so efficiently that the outlaw element was essentially neutralized within two years.

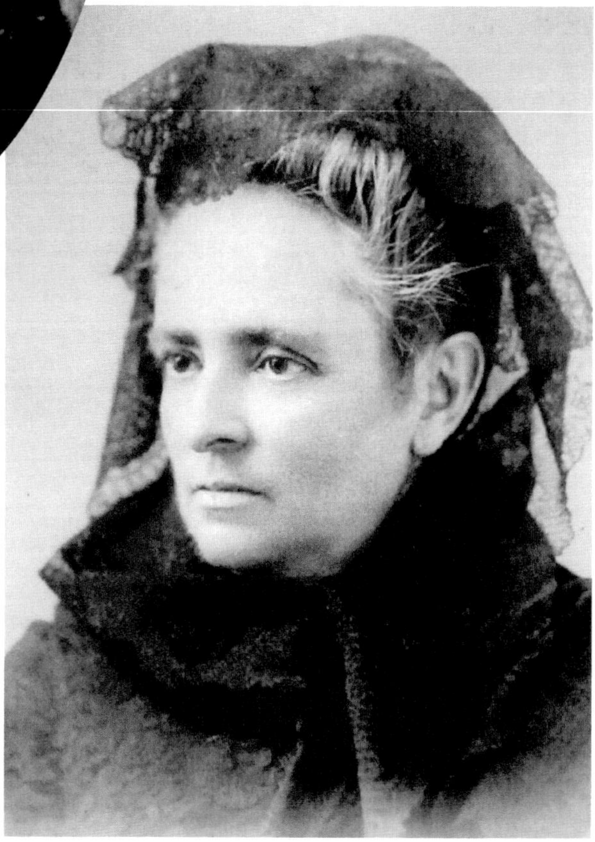

Ysabel Del Valle

Ygnacio Del Valle married 15-year-old Ysabel Varela and together they had a total of 12 children, of which only five lived to adulthood. Ygnacio died in 1880 and was interred at Rancho Camulos until his grieving wife had him exhumed and brought to Los Angeles in 1905. She died soon thereafter, and the couple was buried together in the same coffin.

Francisco Lopez
Talk about a birthday present! Legend has it that on his 40th birthday, Francisco Lopez fell asleep under an oak tree in Placerita Canyon and dreamed of gold. After waking, he dug up wild onions growing under the shade of nearby sycamore trees and found gold flakes clinging to the roots. This photograph is of a mural that graces an underpass near the "Oak of the Golden Dream." (Courtesy Leon Worden.)

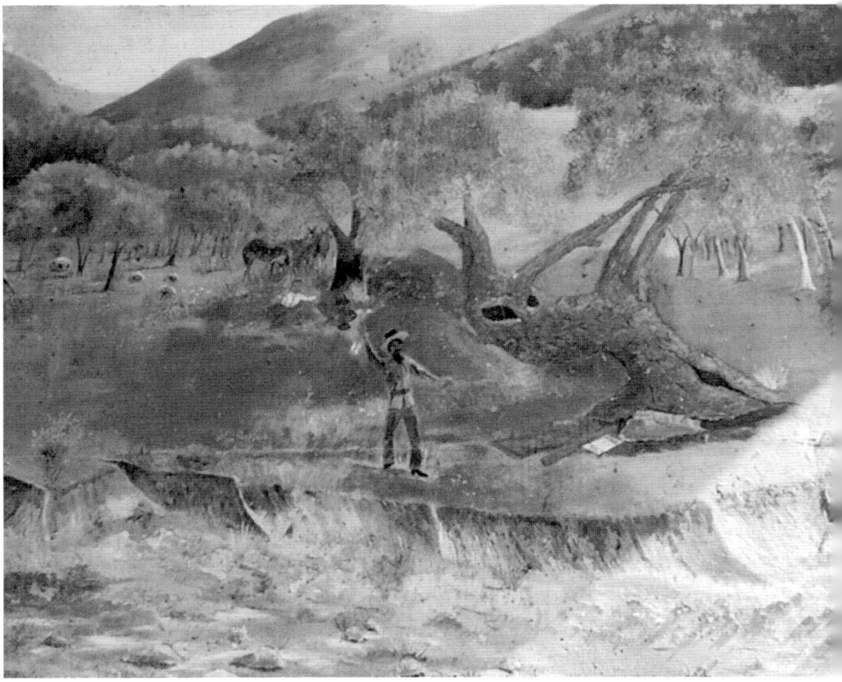

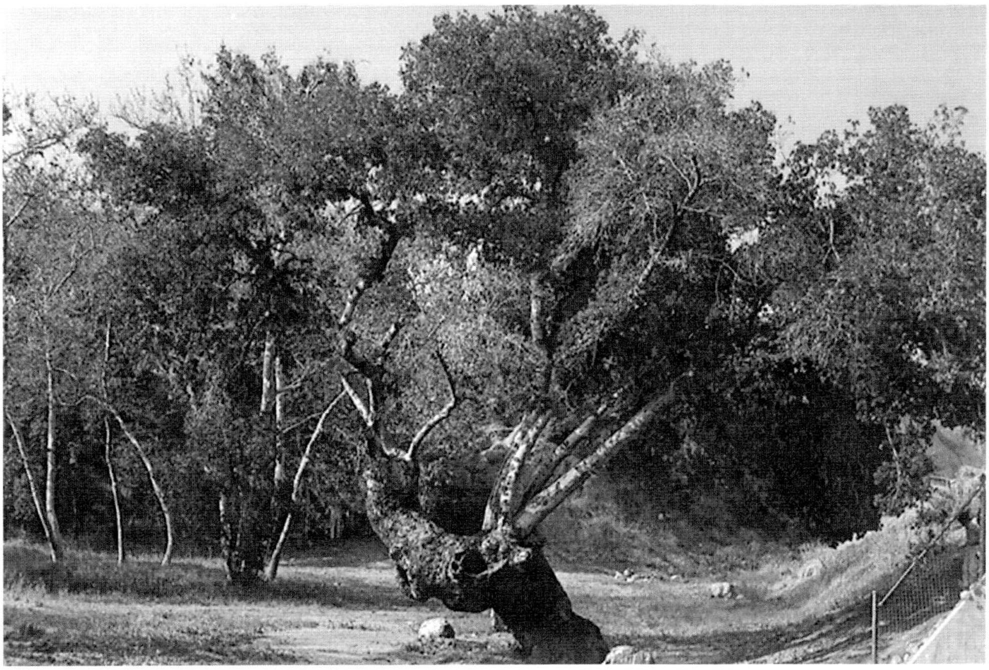

Oak of the Golden Dream
The Placerita Canyon gold discovery made news primarily in Mexico. After a mini-rush, the strike had more or less played out by the time John Marshall discovered gold in 1848 at Sutter's Mill. The oak tree where Lopez had his dream, pictured here, became known as the Oak of the Golden Dream, which today is a historic landmark in Placerita Canyon.

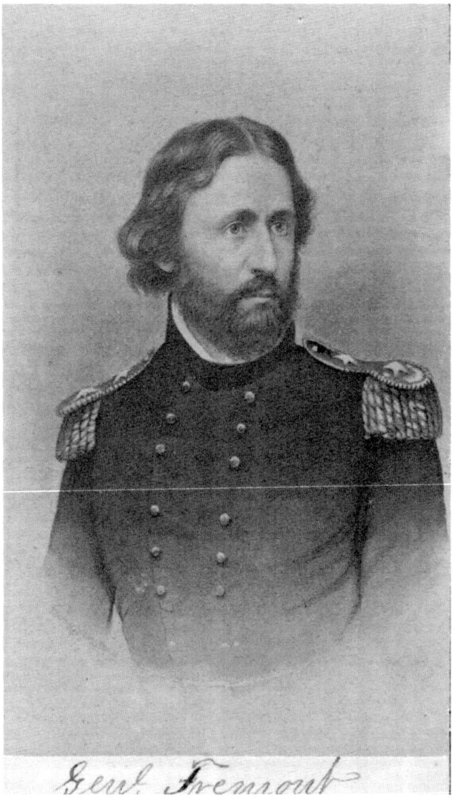

John C. Fremont

Explorer, soldier, and politician John "The Pathfinder" Fremont led an American fighting force during the Mexican-American War. In January 1847, Fremont passed through the Santa Clarita Valley on his way to accept the surrender of Mexican general Andrés Pico. He may have stopped overnight at the home of the Del Valle family (near present-day Magic Mountain) before camping at what is today the intersection of Newhall Avenue and Sierra Highway in Newhall. The following day, Fremont led his troops through the San Fernando Pass to the Campo De Cahuenga (near Universal Studios) where he accepted the surrender of Pico's forces. The "Capitulation of Cahuenga" ended Mexican rule in California. Fremont did not have long to celebrate his victory, as he was court-martialed a short time later for insubordination. The top portrait is from the mid-1800s. The bottom photograph was taken by Matthew Brady in the 1860s.

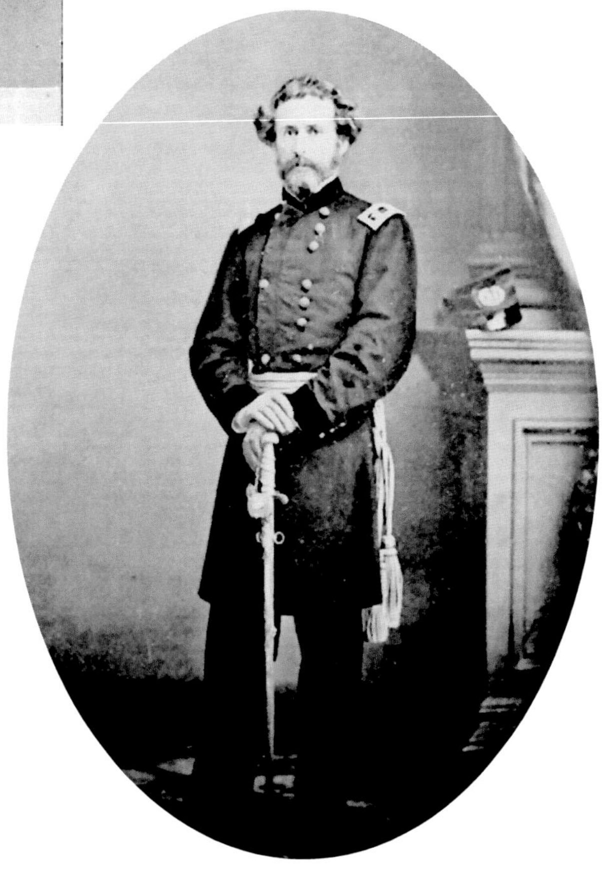

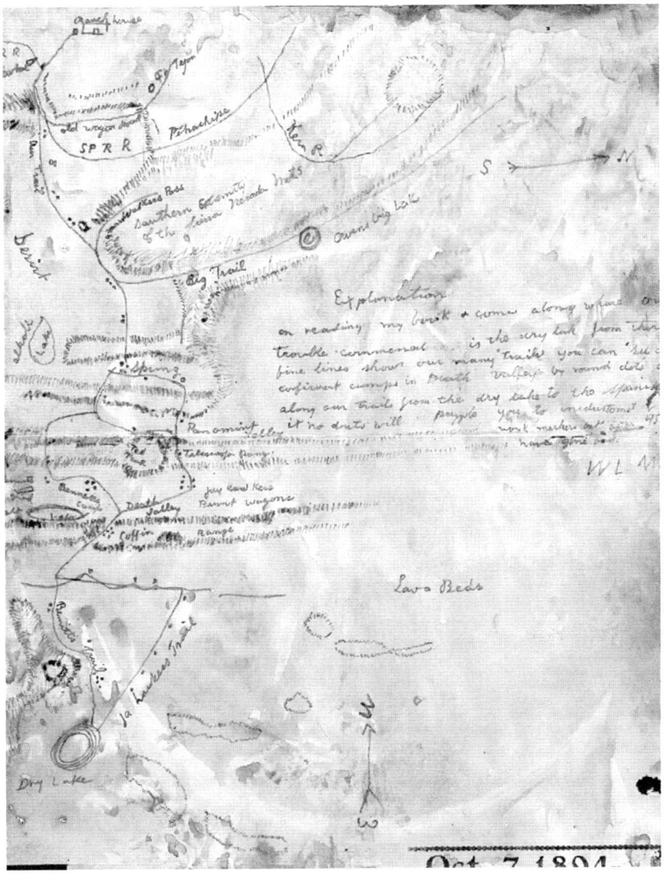

Bennett-Arcan Party

Ten months after Marshall's gold discovery at Sutter's Mill, Pres. James K. Polk announced the California strike to the world in a stunning State of the Union Address in December 1848, setting off the largest migration of humans in world history. While most forty-niners headed to the gold fields by sea or over land using northerly routes, some chose paths through Southern California. One of these groups included a young man by the name of William Manly, who was living in Wisconsin when Gold Rush fever hit. Manly joined up with the Bennett-Arcan Party, which took a "shortcut" through the barren landscape of Death Valley. Running low on food, the group chose Manly and another wagon driver named John Rogers to cross the mountains by foot in search of aid. Manly and Rogers bravely stumbled across 250 miles of barren, uncharted Mojave Desert, subsisting on whatever birds they could shoot. They finally reached Soledad Canyon and entered the Santa Clarita Valley on New Year's Day 1850, where they were met by the vaqueros of the Rancho San Francisco. A kindly, dark-skinned lady (presumably Jacoba Feliz, the widow of Antonio Del Valle) gave the men horses and provisions. They thanked their gracious hosts and headed back to their compatriots. Nearly four weeks after leaving the stranded forty-niners, Manly and Rogers found the Bennett and Arcan families still alive. Upon their arrival, Mrs. Bennett exclaimed, "Good boys! Oh, you have saved us all! God bless you forever! Such boys should never die!" As the group crossed over the Panamint Range into the Mojave Desert, Manly later described the scene as they looked back to the east: "Just as we were ready to leave and return to camp we took off our hats, and then overlooking the scene of so much trial, suffering, and death, spoke the thought uppermost in our minds, saying, 'Good-bye, Death Valley.' " In doing so, they affixed a name to the hottest, driest, and lowest spot in the western hemisphere. The map pictured was drawn by Manly in 1894, showing the route he and Rogers took to the Santa Clarita Valley.

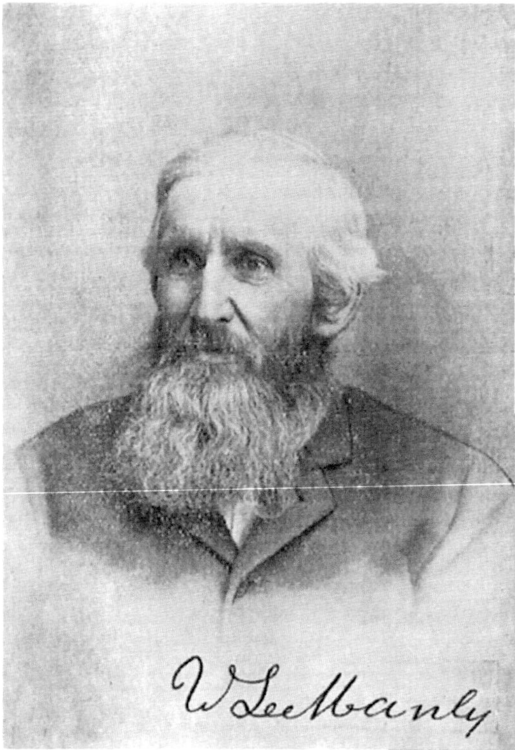

William Manly
When Manly first glimpsed the Santa Clarita Valley, he later described the moment in a manner that could still be used on a chamber of commerce marketing brochure: "When the summit was reached, a most pleasing sight filled our sick hearts with a most indescribable joy . . . [it] was like getting a glimpse of Paradise, and tears of joy ran down our faces." The quote and the portrait of Manly (left) appeared in his 1894 book *Death Valley in '49.*

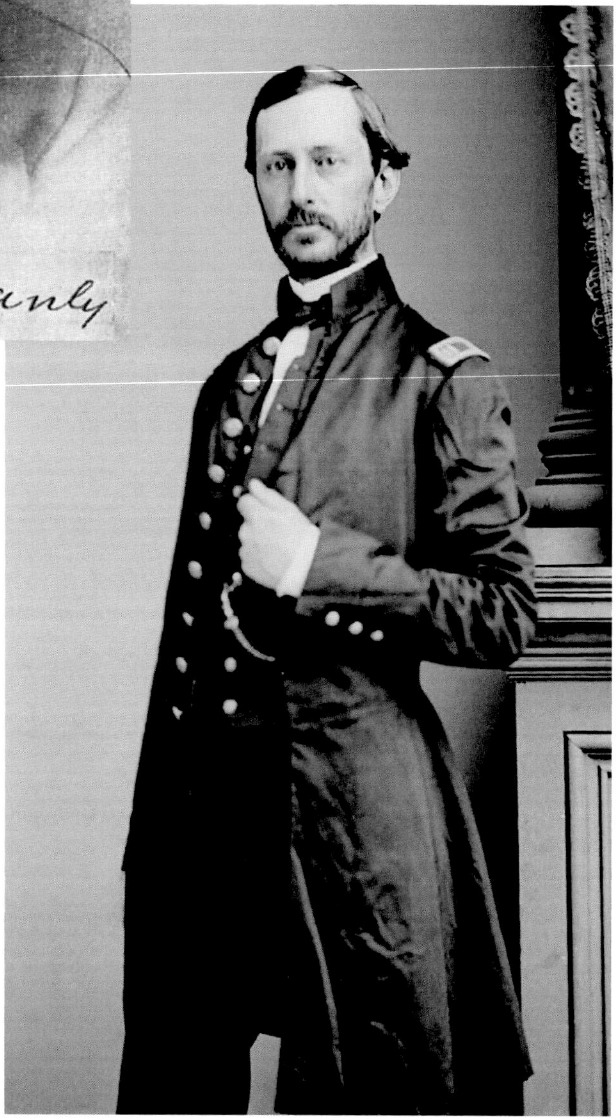

R.S. Williamson
In 1853, Lt. R.S. Williamson scouted a practical route for the transcontinental railroad. His travels took him across the Santa Clarita Valley and over the San Fernando Pass. Williamson failed to find a suitable route, but he was responsible for naming Lake Elizabeth, Hungry Valley, Tick Canyon, and other valley sites. This portrait of Williamson is from the 1860s.

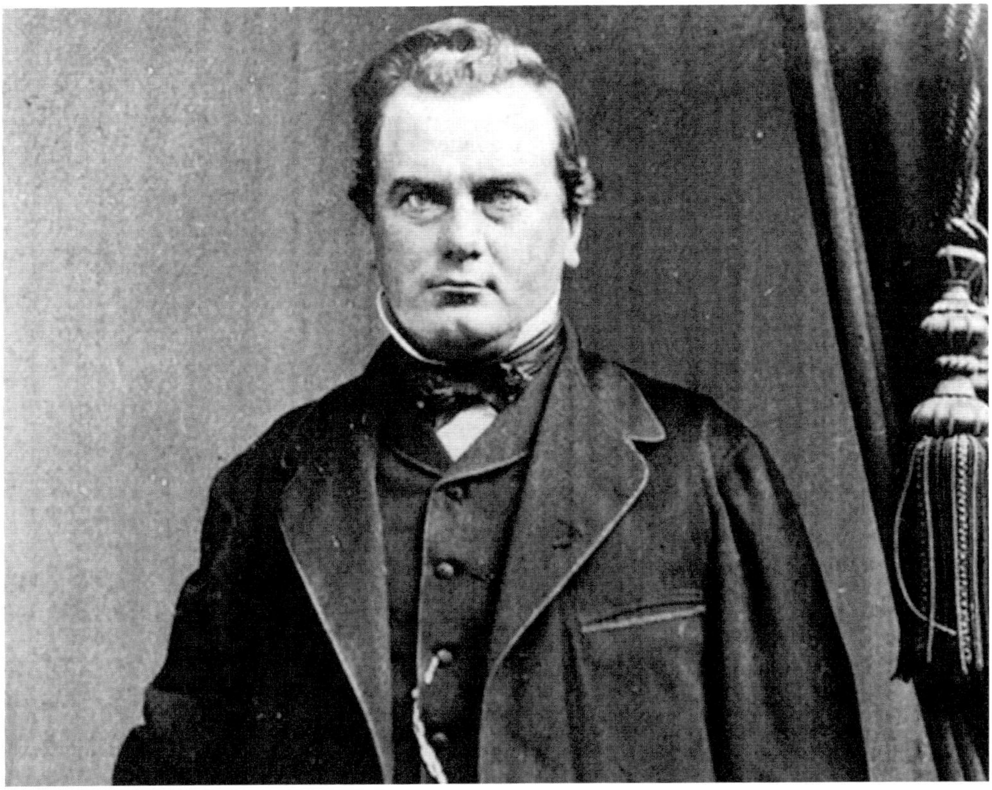

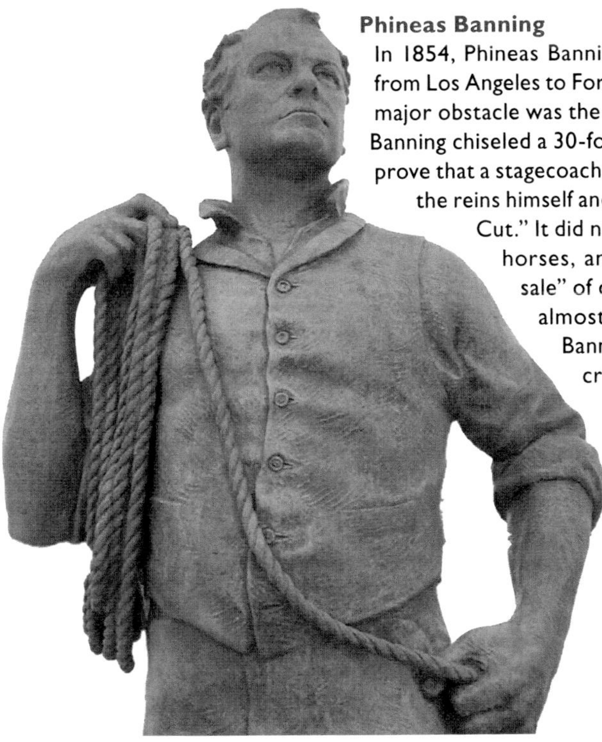

Phineas Banning

In 1854, Phineas Banning wanted to establish a wagon route from Los Angeles to Fort Tejon in the Tehachapi Mountains. The major obstacle was the treacherous San Fernando Pass, where Banning chiseled a 30-foot-deep slit through the mountains. To prove that a stagecoach could navigate the pass, he took hold of the reins himself and led his team through the new "Banning Cut." It did not go well. Banning, the stagecoach, the horses, and the harnesses ended up as a "yard sale" of debris at the base of the grade. One can almost hear the snickers as the unflappable Banning immediately addressed his gathered critics by describing the first pass as, "A beautiful descent, far less difficult than I had anticipated. . . . Gentlemen, you see that my judgment is good." The above photograph of Banning is from the 1860s. At left is a statue of Banning in Wilmington, California.

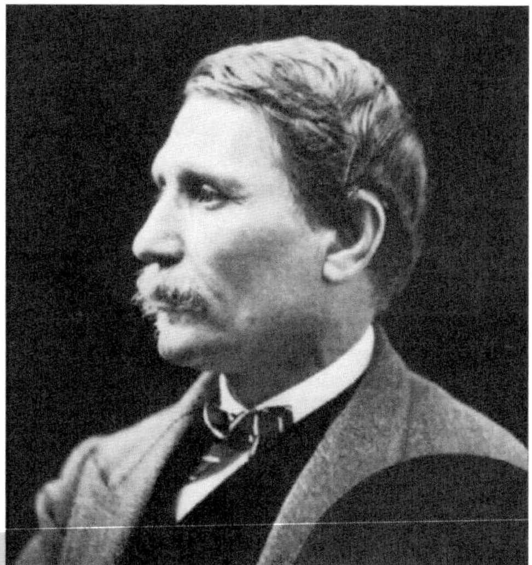

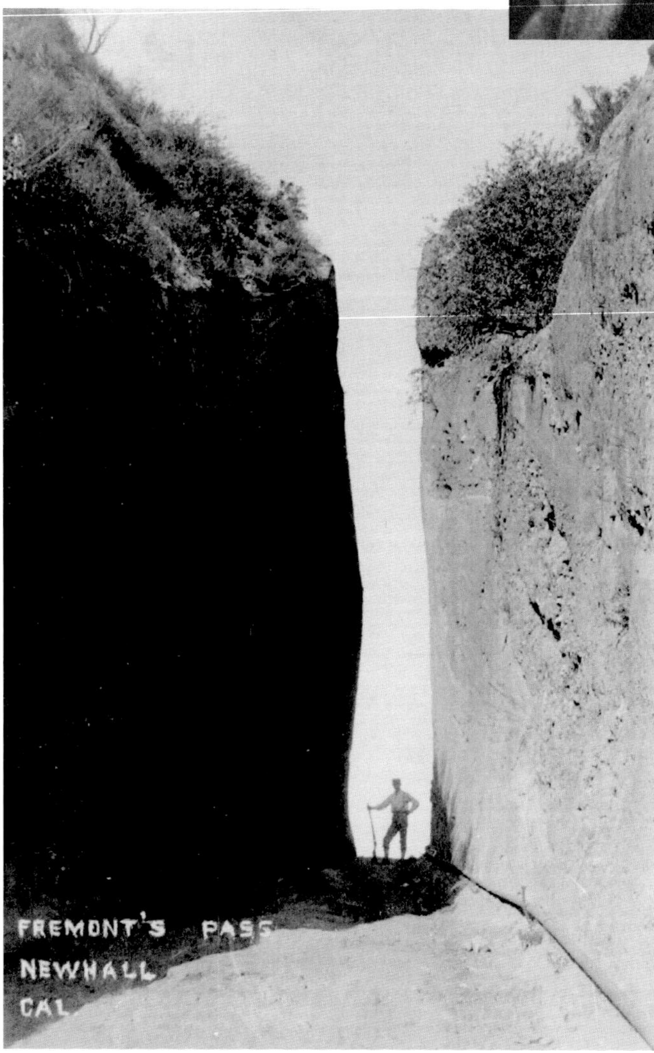

Edward F. Beale

Some guys just can't seem to sit still. Edward Beale got famous fighting in the Mexican-American War. He later crossed the continent in disguise, bringing the first California gold samples back to President Polk. Fired from his Indian agent job for misappropriating funds, Beale then built a road from Arizona to California (which later became a portion of Route 66), taking along 25 camels to test them out in the harsh Southwest climate. In 1863, Beale deepened the cut at the San Fernando Pass (also known as Fremont's Pass) first chiseled by Phineas Banning. Granted a 20-year toll franchise at the renamed Beale's Cut, he was able to purchase the Tejon Ranch in the Antelope Valley with the proceeds, which at the time was the largest private spread in the nation. The photograph above is believed to have been taken in the 1860s. At left is a postcard of Beale's Cut from 1909.

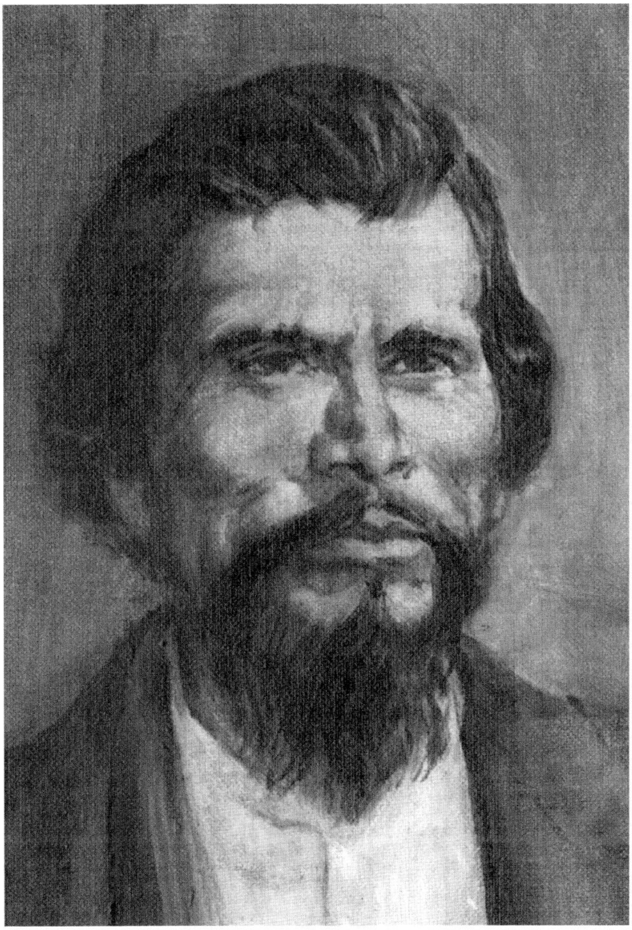

Tiburcio Vasquez

While never attaining the same level of fame as Jesse James or Billy the Kid, Tiburcio Vasquez's exploits were the stuff of legend during the early decades of American rule in California. Vasquez was born in Monterey, California, in 1835 and grew up during the Mexican "Californio" period. As a young man, he, like most of the native inhabitants, felt marginalized by the huge influx of Americans who arrived in California during the Gold Rush. Vasquez began his criminal career in 1854 when he was suspected of murdering a Monterey County constable. He spent most of the 1860s in and out of jail, emerging from San Quentin prison in 1870. Three years later, he was at the head of a gang that raided the town of Tres Pinos, near Hollister, killing three men in the process. Vasquez fled to Lake Elizabeth, near the Antelope Valley, in Southern California. A notorious womanizer, he had an affair there with the wife of a gang member—an act that would lead to his demise. After sacking the town of Kingston in Fresno County in December 1873, a reward of $8,000 was offered by the governor for his live capture, $6,000 if he was brought in dead. After more robberies, Vasquez spent time hiding out among Vasquez Rocks, the fascinating Santa Clarita Valley geological formations that now bear his name. Following additional holdups and trysts with more señoritas, Vasquez was finally apprehended in what is now West Hollywood. He was brought to a Los Angeles jail where throngs of women clambered to see him. He was taken to San Jose to stand trial in January 1875 for a murder that happened during the Tres Pinos raid. During the trial, the Spanish-speaking population treated him like a hero. He was found guilty and sentenced to death by hanging, largely due to the testimony of the gang member he cuckolded at Lake Elizabeth. His body cleared the trap door on March 19, 1875, in San Jose. His final word was reported to be "pronto" (quickly).

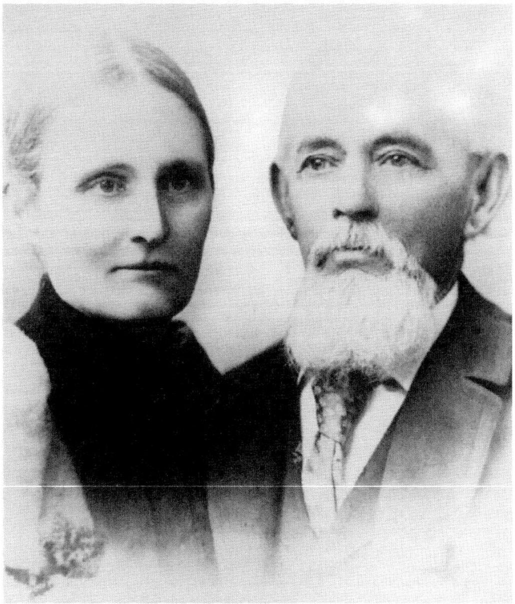

Thomas and Martha Mitchell

Thomas Mitchell did not believe in shopping locally. Settling in Soledad Canyon in 1860, Mitchell traveled over 50 miles to purchase a miner's cabin and freighted it back home. After marrying Martha Taylor, he built an adobe home where the Sulphur Springs School District began in 1872. The one-room school must have been cramped, because the first class had 10 kids, many from the Mitchell family.

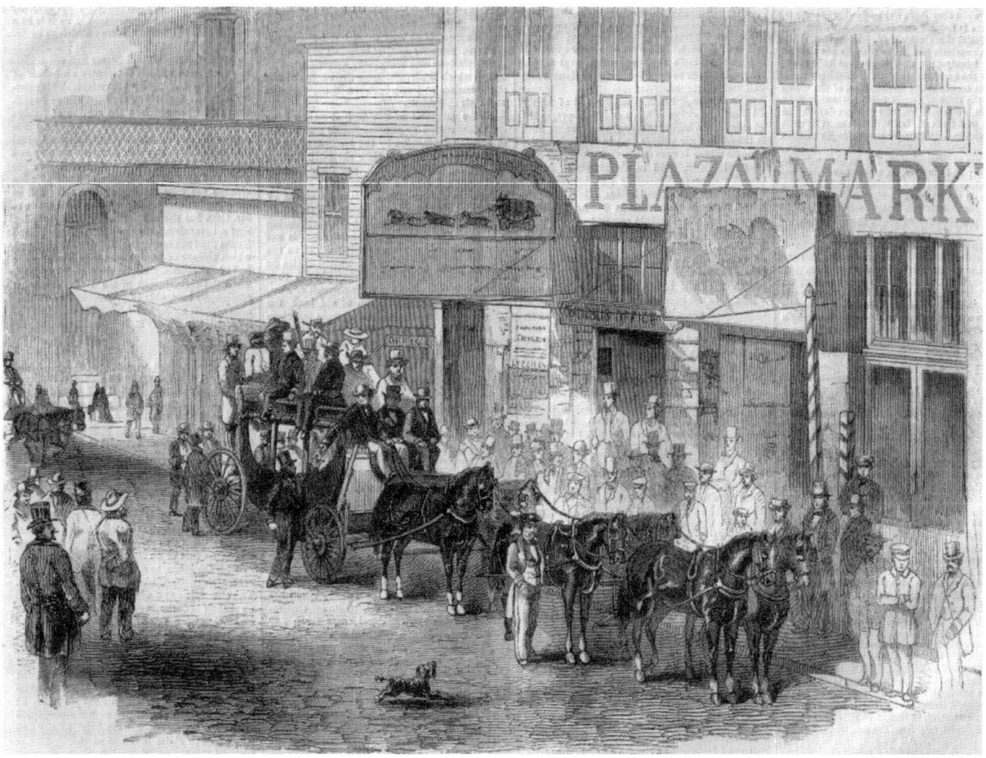

John Butterfield

In 1857, John Butterfield organized the Butterfield Overland Mail route between St. Louis and San Francisco. His stagecoaches traveled through the Santa Clarita Valley over the perilous San Fernando Pass in what was considered the most difficult crossing of the entire route. This photograph, based on an 1858 woodcut from *Harper's Weekly*, shows a Butterfield stage about to leave San Francisco.

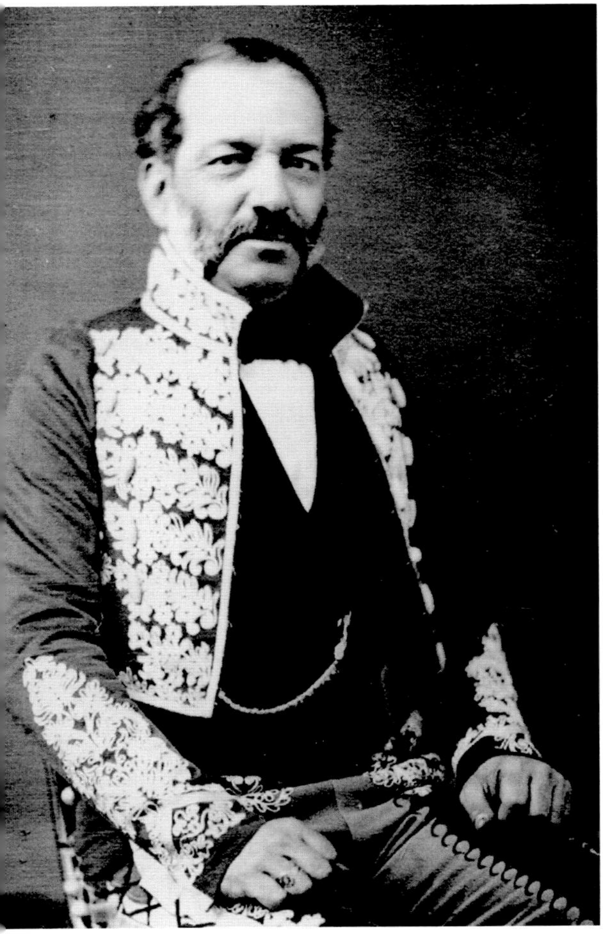

Andrés Pico
Gen. Andrés Pico commanded the Mexican forces in California during the Mexican-American War. In 1865, Pico formed a partnership with a former enemy, Edward Beale, along with Sanford Lyon, to drill oil in what is now known as Pico Canyon. Their company evolved over the years into the Standard Oil Company of California. (Courtesy San Fernando Valley Historical Society.)

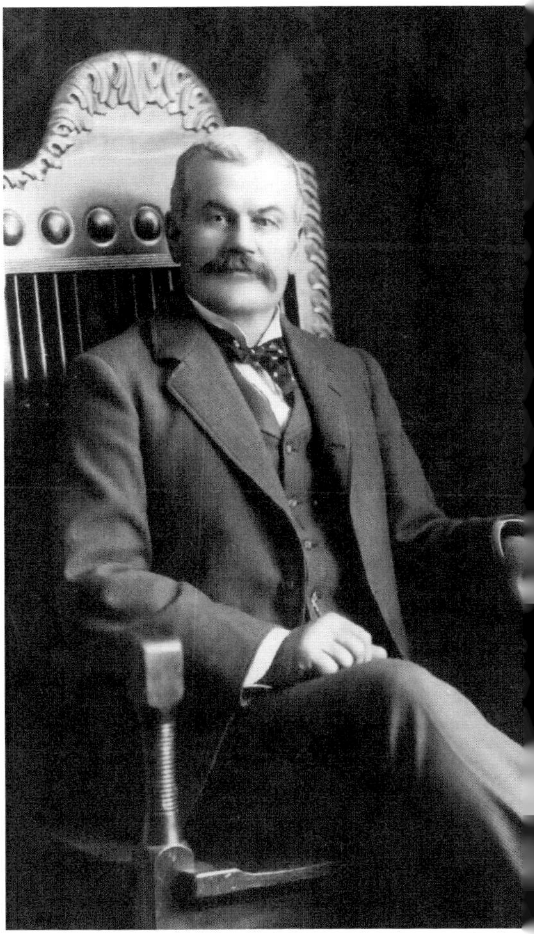

Alexander Mentry
Oilman Alexander Mentry made history in September 1876 when California Star Oil Well No. 4 hit a gusher in Pico Canyon. It was California's first successful oil well and continued to pump for the next 114 years. Mentry died in 1900 when he was stung by a conenose bug, which is variously known as the "kissing bug" or "assassin bug."

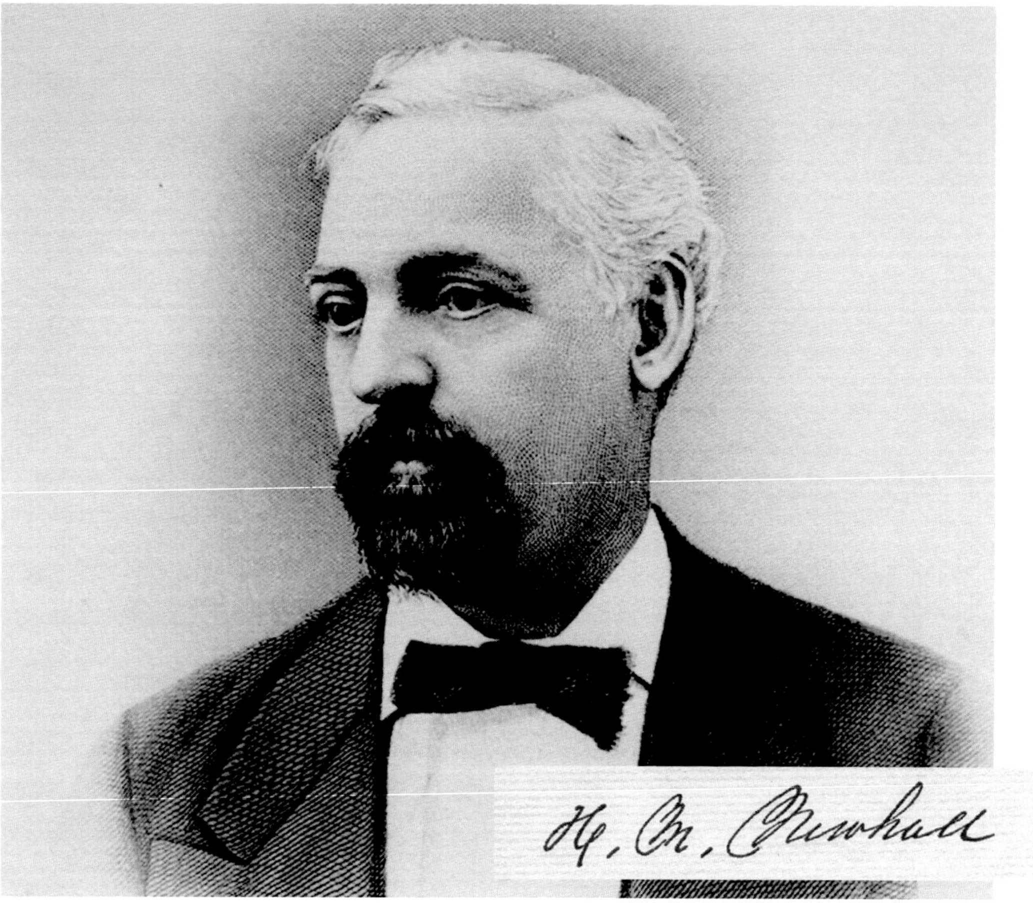

Henry Mayo Newhall

Henry Mayo Newhall was born in Massachusetts in 1825 and later made his way to Philadelphia, where he learned auctioneering. Catching gold fever, he boarded a ship and headed to California. Newhall, like most forty-niners, was unsuccessful in the diggings, so to keep from starving, he was forced to fall back on his previous career by auctioning off his clothes. His fortunes turned when he joined an auction house in San Francisco. In 1851, Newhall took over the company and turned to real estate investing, buying up parcels in San Francisco and surrounding towns. This funded a move into railroading, where he became president of the San Francisco & San Jose line. After the "Big Four" moneymen behind the Central Pacific Railroad (Collis P. Huntington, Charles Crocker, Leland Stanford, and Mark Hopkins) completed the transcontinental railroad in 1869, they turned their sights on the small operators in California, where Newhall's railroad became the target of a hostile takeover. Newhall eventually gave up the fight, trading his line for a spot on the board of directors of the Southern Pacific. He began buying up old Spanish ranchos in Central and Southern California, including what remained of the Rancho San Francisco, which he purchased for $90,000 in 1875. Knowing that the Southern Pacific planned on extending a line through the property, he granted passage to the railroad for $1 and deeded land to establish the town of Newhall, which in 1876 saw its first inhabitants. (The nearby town of Saugus was named after Saugus, Massachusetts, where Newhall was born.) Although Newhall lived primarily in San Francisco, he spent significant time in his namesake village, where he built the elegant Southern Hotel in 1878. In March 1882, Newhall was thrown from his horse while riding in the valley. He was taken to San Francisco, where he died a few days later at the age of 56. The following year, his widow and sons founded the Newhall Land and Farming Company, which is still a major land developer today.

Charles Crocker

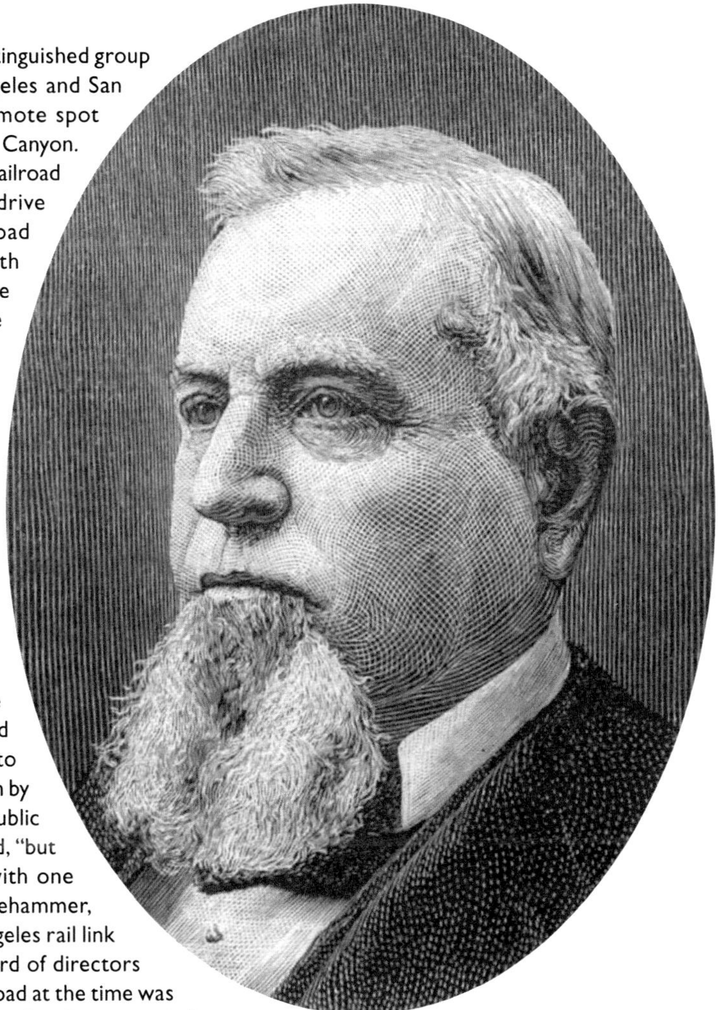

On September 5, 1876, a distinguished group of dignitaries from Los Angeles and San Francisco gathered at a remote spot called Lang Station in Soledad Canyon. They had gathered to watch railroad magnate Charles Crocker drive a golden spike into a railroad tie, uniting Los Angeles with the rest of the nation. At the time, Crocker was one of the richest and most powerful men in the country. As one of the "Big Four" Central Pacific moneymen (along with Collis P. Huntington, Leland Stanford, and Mark Hopkins), Crocker had been present seven years earlier at Promontory Summit, Utah, to witness the linking of the transcontinental railroad. The Big Four had created the Southern Pacific Railroad, and now it was California's turn to be connected north and south by rail. "Gentlemen, I am no public speaker," Crocker announced, "but I can drive a spike." And with one powerful swing of his sledgehammer, the San Francisco to Los Angeles rail link was completed. On the board of directors of the Southern Pacific Railroad at the time was Henry Mayo Newhall, whose San Francisco & San Jose Railroad had been bought out by the Southern Pacific six years earlier. Using inside information, Newhall had previously purchased the Rancho San Francisco in the Santa Clarita Valley and deeded a right-of-way through it to the railroad for the grand sum of $1. Western Development, a subsidiary of the line, paid Newhall another dollar to establish the town that bears Newhall's name (today, a district of the city of Santa Clarita). Crocker's Southern Pacific Railroad would have another "Golden Spike" ceremony five years later at Deming, New Mexico (which was named after Crocker's wife, Mary Ann Deming Crocker), when it was linked with the Atchison, Topeka & Santa Fe line, completing the country's second transcontinental railroad. Crocker was seriously injured in an accident in New York in 1886. When he died two years later, he had a net worth estimated to be between $300 and $400 million. (On February 9, 1971, nearly a century after the golden spike ceremony took place at Lang Station, the site was the epicenter of the deadly Sylmar Earthquake, which registered 6.6 on the Richter scale and claimed 65 lives.)

Chinese Laborers

Hundreds of people lined the tracks at Lang Station on September 5, 1876, to witness the Golden Spike ceremony linking California by rail. According to San Francisco's *Daily Alta California*, "The vicinity of the station is crowded with people. The track for a half mile in extent is lined with the whole force of laborers and spectators, all anxiously awaiting the important consummation." The "important consummation" spoken of was the closing of the quarter-mile gap between the rails needed to complete the line. The closure would be bridged by two teams of unheralded Chinese laborers working from opposite directions in a staged contest pitting the two teams against one another. The Chinese provided most of the muscle behind the building of the railroad, completing the seven-thousand-foot tunnel under the Newhall Pass just days earlier, making the linking at Lang Station possible. One thousand Chinese workers stood along the tracks with picks and shovels raised, awaiting the signal to begin laying the final section of rails. At its sound, "The track-graders and laborers set to work. As fast as the rails were laid on the ties, they were immediately spiked down and the space between the ties filled with earth. In the struggle to close in on the half of the unlaid track, the southern, or Los Angeles party, were winners by a rail, their end being completed three minutes before the San Francisco end. The work occupied but five minutes. The last rail is laid. The cheers are loud and prolonged." Charles Crocker, president of the Southern Pacific, was then presented with a golden spike that he hammered into the tie with a silver hammer. Following Crocker's historic blow, speeches were given by several dignitaries, after which the crowd dispersed and headed to Los Angeles to attend celebratory banquets. The unheralded Chinese laborers remained behind, laying more rails, linking more of the West to the rest of the country.

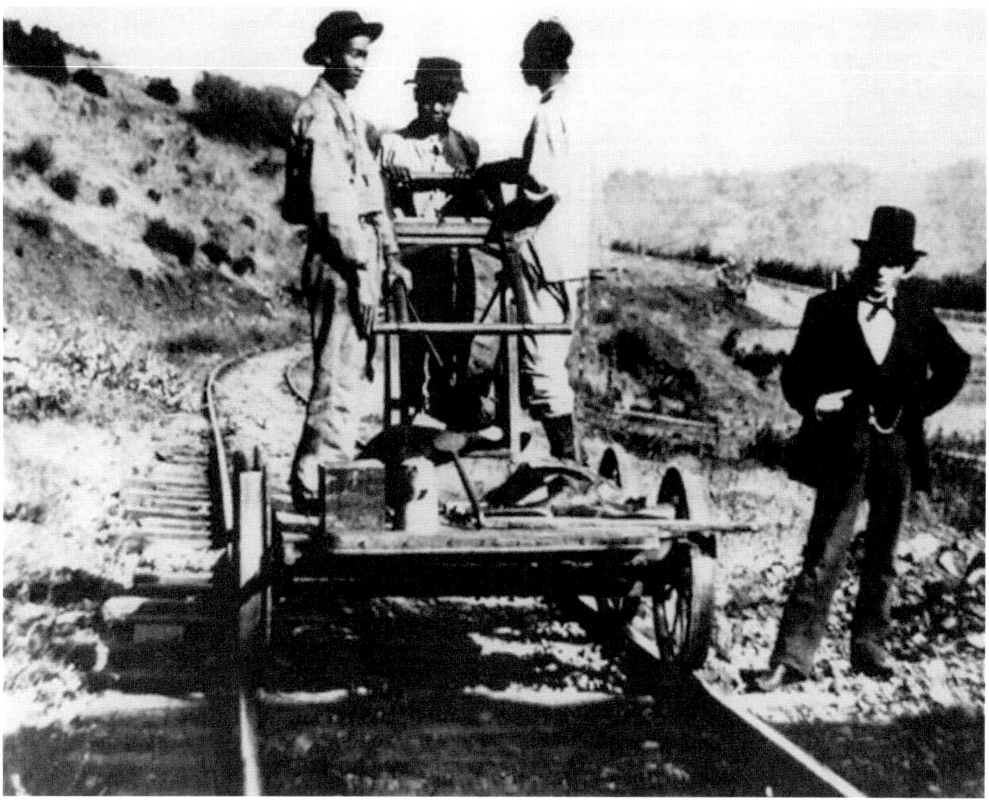

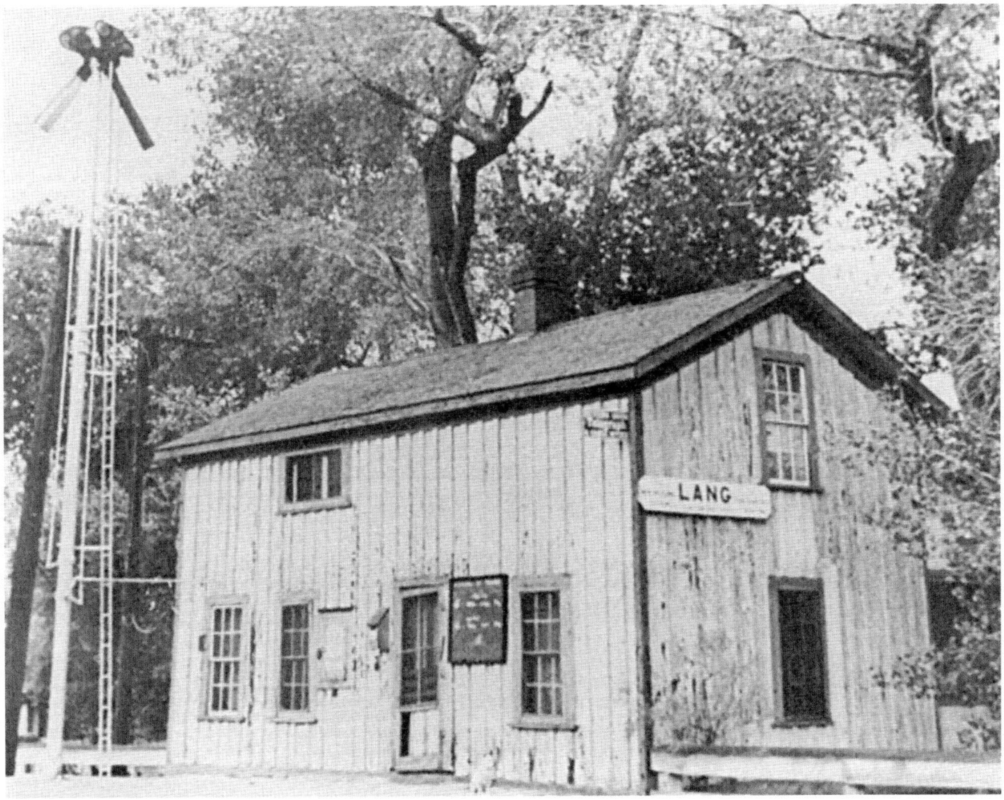

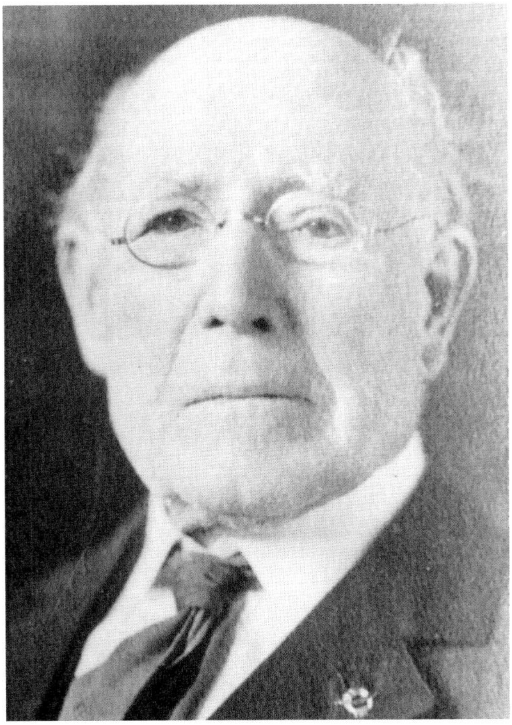

John Lang
In 1871, John Lang purchased 160 acres of Soledad Canyon for $300, where he built a train depot, post office, and a hotel. He was the first master of Lang Station (pictured above) where in 1876 Northern and Southern California were linked together. Three years earlier, Lang shot a record 2,350-pound grizzly bear here that had reportedly made a meal of at least seven people.

John F. Powell
As a young man, John Powell helped free 700 slaves in Africa alongside Dr. Stanley Livingston. After retiring from the military, Powell settled in the Antelope Valley where in 1875 he was appointed justice of the peace. Powell moved to Newhall three years later, where he meted out justice for the next four decades, never having a decision overturned by a higher court.

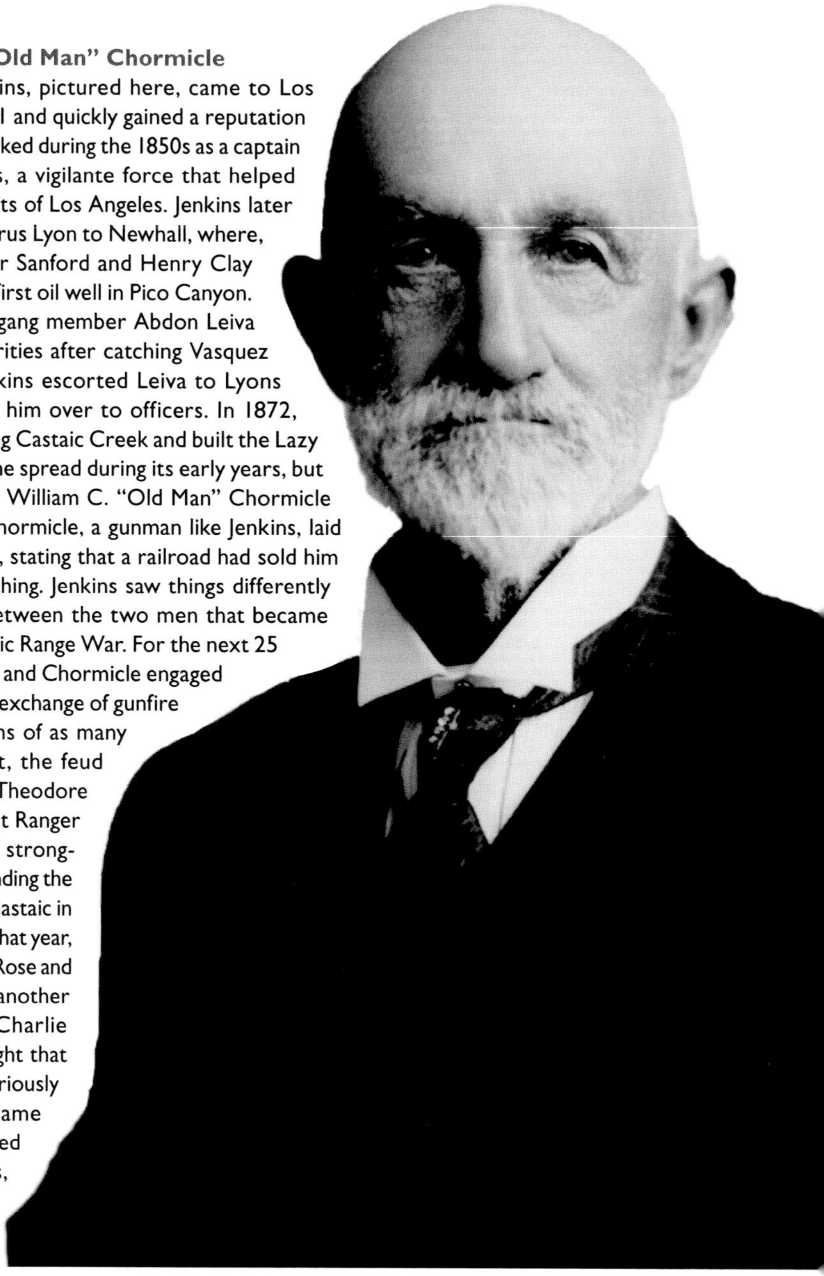

"Wirt" Jenkins and "Old Man" Chormicle

William W. "Wirt" Jenkins, pictured here, came to Los Angeles from Ohio in 1851 and quickly gained a reputation as an able gunman. He worked during the 1850s as a captain in the California Rangers, a vigilante force that helped clean up the lawless streets of Los Angeles. Jenkins later followed fellow ranger Cyrus Lyon to Newhall, where, along with Lyon's brother Sanford and Henry Clay Wiley, he helped sink the first oil well in Pico Canyon. When Tiburcio Vasquez gang member Abdon Leiva gave himself up to authorities after catching Vasquez in bed with his wife, Jenkins escorted Leiva to Lyons Station where he turned him over to officers. In 1872, Jenkins staked a claim along Castaic Creek and built the Lazy Z ranch. All was well on the spread during its early years, but everything changed when William C. "Old Man" Chormicle came to town in 1890. Chormicle, a gunman like Jenkins, laid claim to the Lazy Z ranch, stating that a railroad had sold him the land Jenkins was ranching. Jenkins saw things differently and a feud was ignited between the two men that became known as the Great Castaic Range War. For the next 25 years, followers of Jenkins and Chormicle engaged in a Hatfield-McCoy style exchange of gunfire that resulted in the deaths of as many as 40 men. At one point, the feud was so heated that Pres. Theodore Roosevelt asked US Forest Ranger Robert Emmett Clark to strong-arm the combatants into ending the conflict. When Clark left Castaic in 1916, the battle resumed. That year, Chormicle henchman Billy Rose and Jenkins encountered one another while herding cattle in Charlie Canyon. During the gunfight that followed, Rose shot and seriously wounded Jenkins. That same year, someone fatally gunned down Chormicle. Jenkins, who was suspected, "died with his boots on" from an illness in 1919.

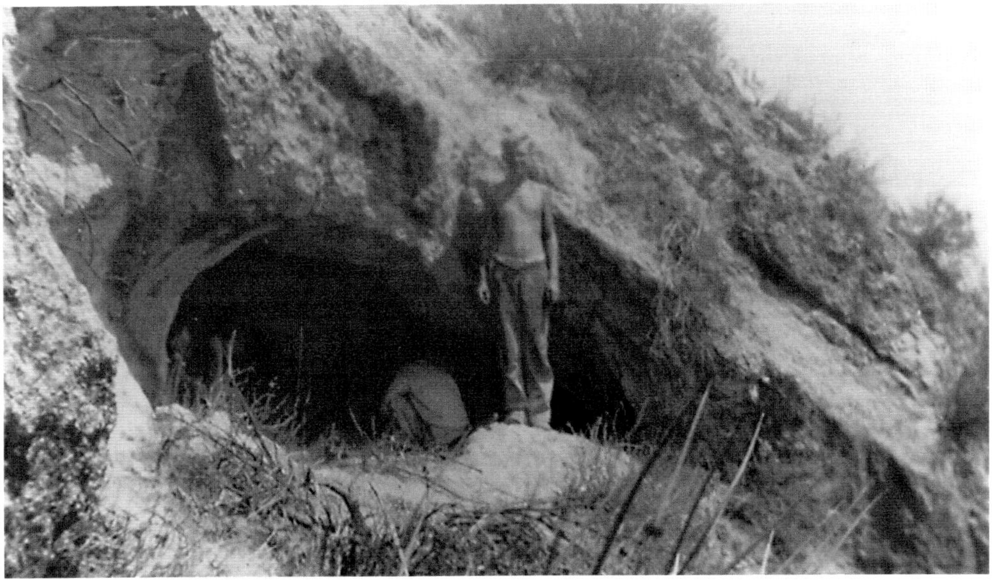

McCoy Pyle

In May 1884, McCoy Pyle was hunting along a cliff in the present-day location of the Chiquita Canyon landfill when he noticed a cave 50 feet below (now known as Bowers Cave). Peering inside, Pyle discovered a treasure trove of artifacts left behind by the Tataviam. The awestruck Pyle hauled the artifacts back to his home. This 1962 photograph shows two unidentified explorers at the entrance to Bowers Cave.

Stephen Bowers

Newspaperman and antiquities dealer Rev. Stephen Bowers got word of McCoy Pyle's discovery and bought the entire collection for $1,500. Bowers sold most of the collection to Harvard University's Peabody Museum of American Ethnology. A few years after the sale, Pyle was working as a deputy constable at Castaic Junction, where he perished in a shootout. The photograph below shows a display of some of the artifacts discovered by Pyle.

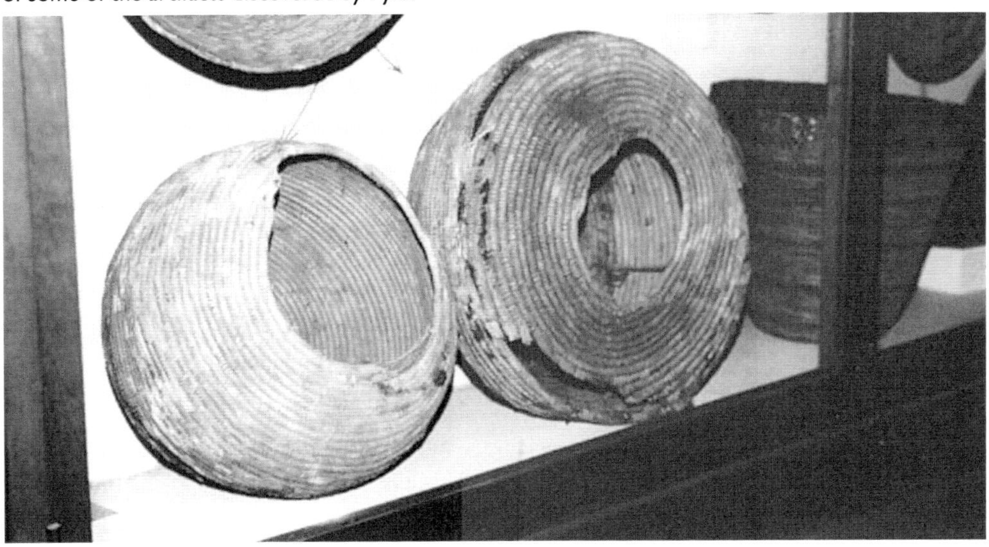

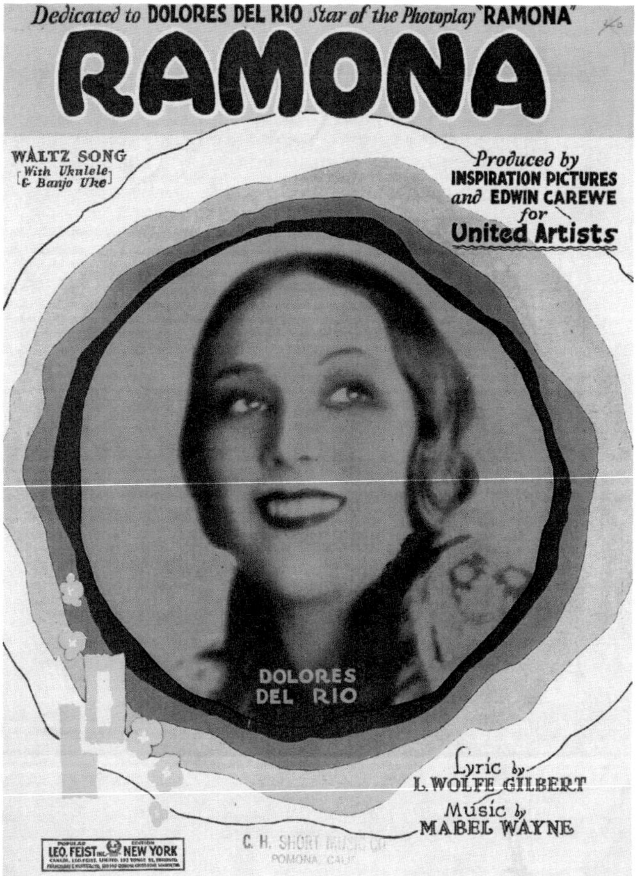

Ramona

As author Dydia DeLyser states in the introduction to her book *Ramona Memories*, "The most important woman in the history of Southern California never lived. Nor has she yet died." The fictional woman's name was Ramona, and she was the subject of an enormously popular 1884 novel of the same name written by Helen Hunt Jackson. *Ramona* is the story of a privileged young señorita who gets rejected by her own culture when she marries a Native American man named Alessandro. Though largely forgotten today, *Ramona* was one of the 19th century's best-loved novels. Hunt intended the novel to be something of an *Uncle Tom's Cabin* for Native Americans, dramatizing the harsh oppression of California's Mission Indians at the hands of white Californians. It gave birth to the "Ramona myth," in which Ramona, who never lived, took on a life of her own. Although not specifically mentioned in the book, Rancho Camulos was believed to be the setting for Ramona's home. The rancho quickly became a place of pilgrimage, and for years the Southern Pacific railroad made stops at Camulos's own train station to accommodate all the tourists wishing to visit Ramona's house. This did not always sit well with the Del Valles, who complained about tourists who pocketed souvenirs, trampled gardens, and entered the home uninvited, often asking to see a torn altar cloth that Ramona mended. The phenomenon continued long after Jackson's death in 1885. Many years later, showman Robert E. Callahan penned a sequel to *Ramona* and founded one of California's first theme parks in Culver City, known as Mission Village. After being displaced by the Santa Monica freeway, remnants of the park were moved to Sierra Highway near Canyon Country and became Callahan's Old West. Many of the items from the park are now found at Heritage Junction in Newhall, including Ramona's Chapel. Pictured is the cover of the sheet music from the 1928 remake of *Ramona*, which was directed by Edwin Carewe and starred Delores del Rio.

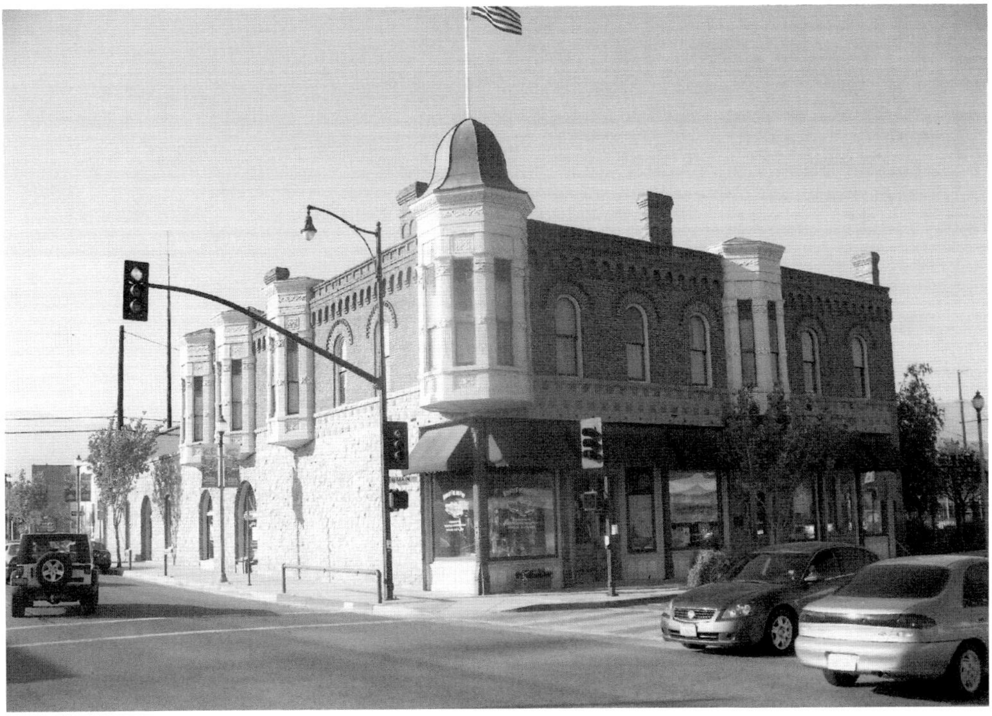

Lyman Stewart and Wallace Hardison
Lyman Stewart and partner Wallace Hardison arrived in Pico Canyon in 1883 to try their luck drilling oil. Due to Stewart's aversion to profanity, their drilling site was called Christian Hill. They drilled five wells before moving on to Santa Paula where in 1890 they started a little company called Union Oil. This photograph from 2009 shows the company's founding site in Santa Paula. (Courtesy Konrad Summers.)

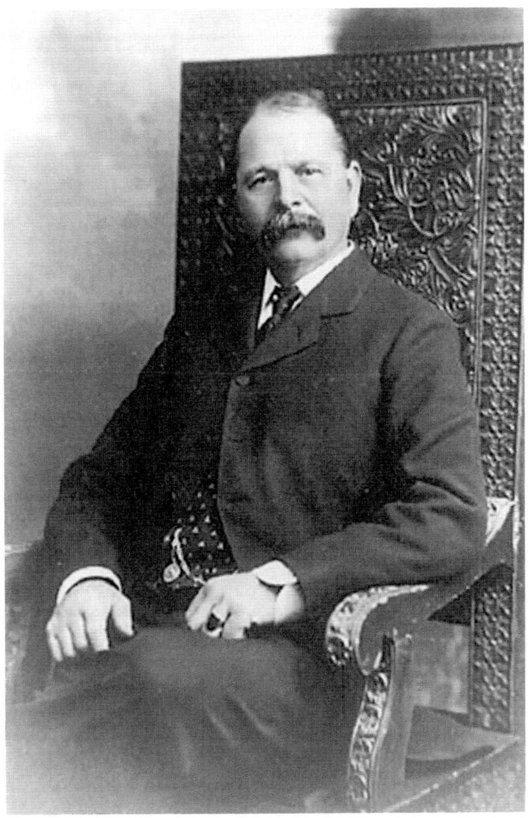

Ed Pardee
Ed Pardee didn't know what he wanted to be when he grew up. In 1883, he worked the oil fields in Pico Canyon before moving to Newhall where he opened a livery stable. Bored with horses, Pardee got himself elected constable and purchased the Good Templars Hall built by Henry Clay Needham, which he made into a home. It later became a dressing room for Tom Mix. The historic house now sits at Heritage Junction.

Henry Clay Needham

In 1888, Newhall was a two-block-long Wild West town with more saloons than churches. In rode Henry Clay Needham, pictured below, a rabid prohibitionist, who came to town with the unlikely goal of setting up an alcohol-free colony in the Santa Clarita Valley. Needham was born in Kentucky in 1851 and migrated to Kansas, where he developed an intense interest in the Prohibition movement and was responsible for drafting "dry laws" that were adopted by the Kansas legislature. Needham became friends with former Kansas governor John St. John, who, along with two investors, purchased 10,000 acres adjacent to the young town of Newhall to establish a dry colony. They sent Needham out to California in 1888 to supervise the new community, which was known as the St. John Subdivision and extended from the present-day intersection of Lyons Avenue and Main Street up to Soledad Canyon. As further enticement to potential settlers, they wrote a provision into the deeds stating that the property was subject to foreclosure if any alcohol was found on the premises. The investors found few suitors interested in joining the new colony and Needham was forced to give up his grand scheme, but he never gave up his prohibitionist dreams. In 1931, he went to the Prohibitionist National Convention in Cincinnati as a possible nominee for president. Hopes for the White House faded when he developed phlebitis and was unable to accept the nomination. Called "Daddy Mo" by his family, Henry Clay Needham died in 1936 at the age of 84. An unreconstructed prohibitionist to the end, his obituary on the front page of the *Los Angeles Times* read, "Uncompromising in his views, he insisted on complete abstinence and would not join the light wines and beer movement."

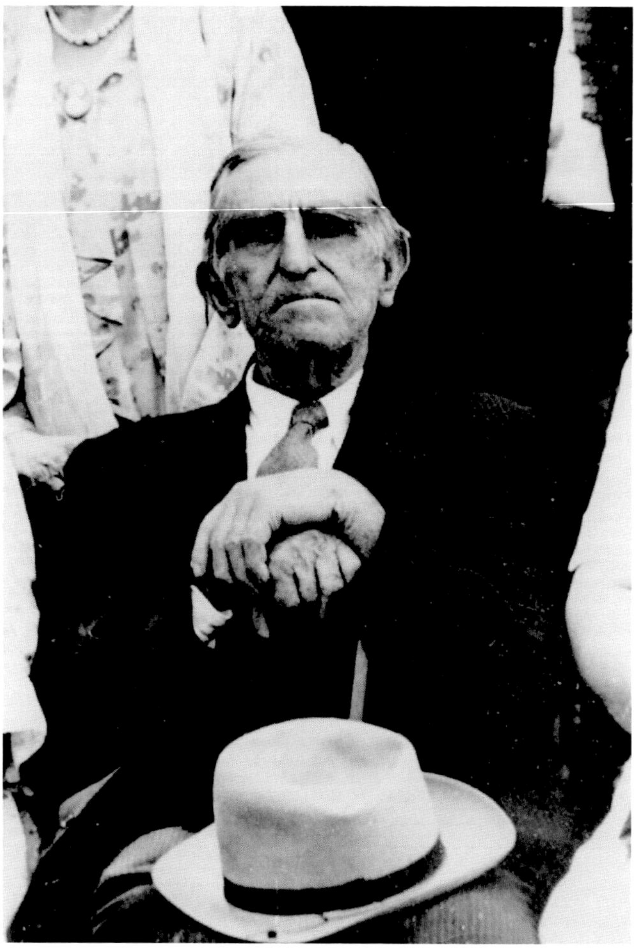

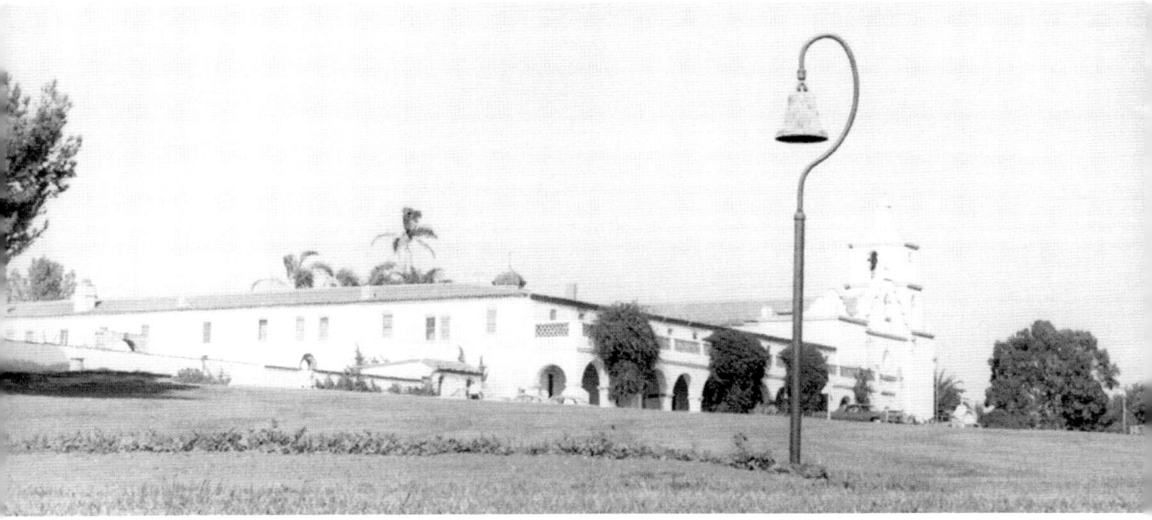

Reginaldo Del Valle
Reginaldo Del Valle followed in the political footsteps of his father, Ygnacio, becoming one of the youngest men ever elected to the California state senate. Del Valle was a great promoter of California history and helped restore California's missions. He was also instrumental in placing the distinctive "question mark" bells along the route of the historic El Camino Real. Pictured is one of the bells in front of the Mission San Luis Rey in the 1960s. (Courtesy Eloise Perkins.)

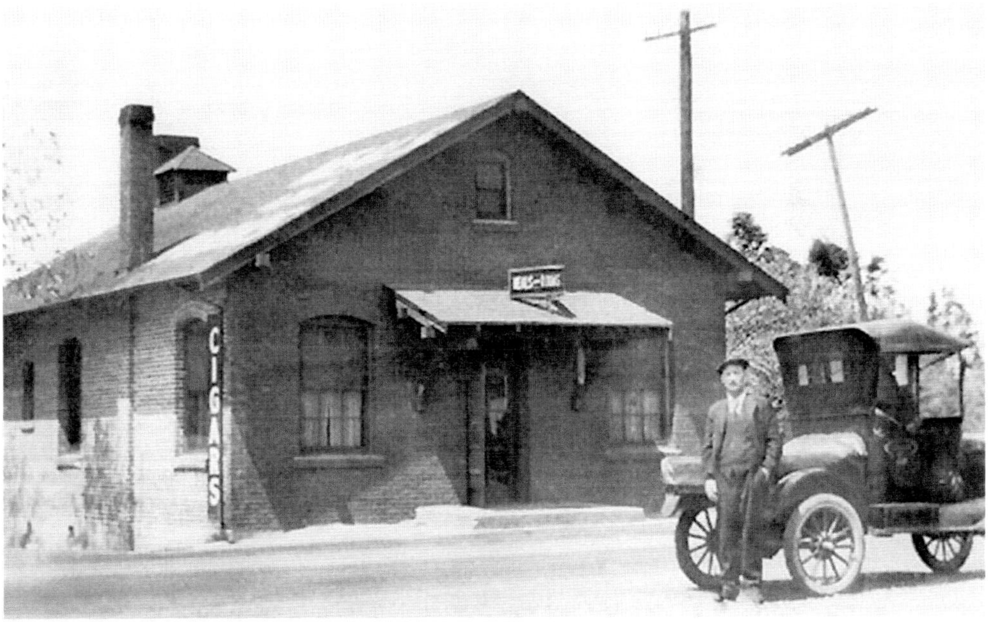

Richard and Martin Wood
In 1898, Richard Wood purchased Joseph Tolfree's Saugus Eating House, located at the north end of the Saugus Train Station. The following year, Wood's brother Martin took over management of the restaurant and renamed it the Saugus Café. In 1905, Martin moved the café across the street to its present location on Railroad Avenue. He is pictured here in front of the café in 1914.

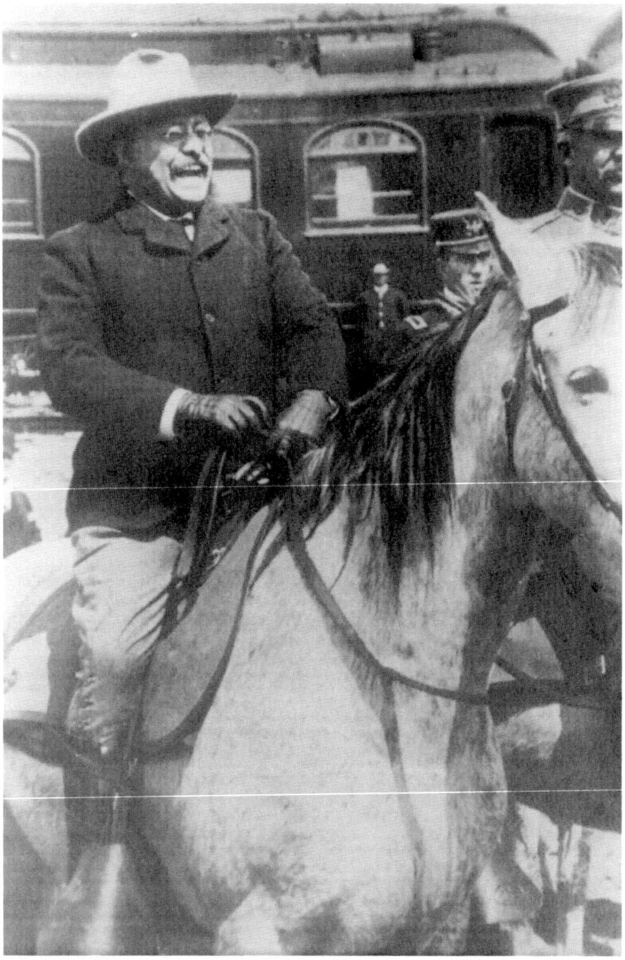

Theodore Roosevelt
Thirty-one-year-old Rudolph Nickel, the "Father of Acton," arrived in the small village in the far reaches of Soledad Canyon in October 1887. Nickel established a general store that same year and moved the post office there from the nearby town of Ravenna. A few years later, he started one of the earliest newspapers in the Santa Clarita Valley, called the *Acton Rooster.* In 1890, Nickel built the Acton Hotel, a two-story Victorian-style structure. In 1903, Henry Gage, California's governor and an owner of several gold mines in the area, hosted his pal Pres. Theodore Roosevelt at the hotel. Roosevelt is pictured (left) in Acton in 1903. Gage is pictured below, in an undated photograph, center, riding a horse.

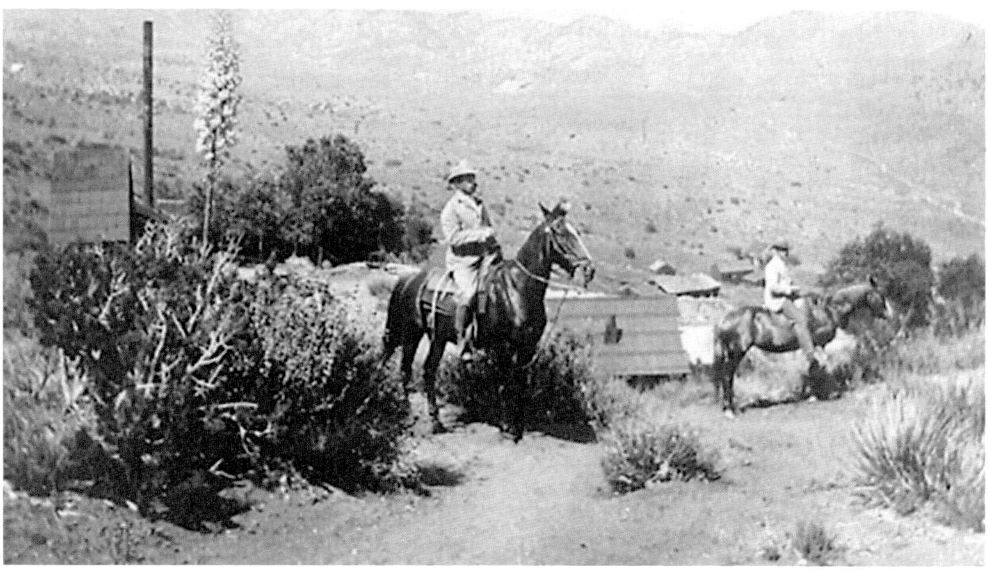

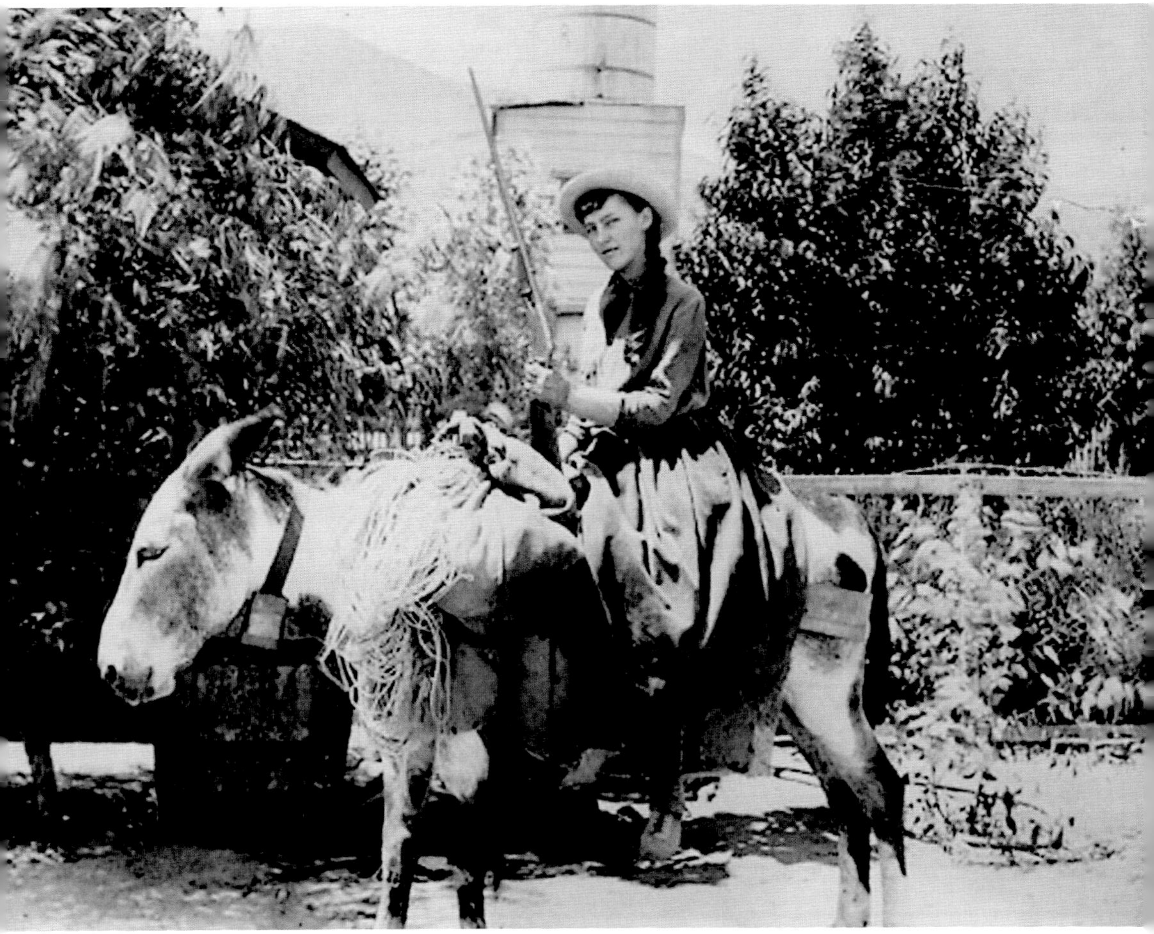

Lou Henry Hoover

Over the years, the Santa Clarita Valley has welcomed at least two US chief executives. Benjamin Harrison passed through the Saugus Train Station in 1891 on a nationwide whistle stop campaign (unfortunately for him, he lost the election to Grover Cleveland), and Theodore Roosevelt visited his friend California governor Henry T. Gage in the Acton area in 1903. A future first lady stayed in Acton for a time as well. Lou Henry, the future wife of Pres. Herbert Hoover, spent parts of the summers between 1889 and 1891 in Acton when her father brought the family along on inspection trips to a mine he owned in the area. In 1938, Mrs. Hoover wrote a letter to local historian Harry E. Heinkel reminiscing about her memories of Acton. "My father loved the mountains, and every moment that he could steal away from his indoor occupation we went exploring and camping in what would be new country to us. Thus, during those years, a number of times we used Acton as a center and made trips about in various directions. We never lived in Acton, nor did I go to school there, although I do remember the red brick schoolhouse, which stood some distance beyond the store from the railway track. Across from the railway station, or 'depot', was Mr. Nichols' store, the only one in Acton when I knew it. . . . Mr. Nichols [Rudolph Nickel] was also the postmaster, and one got one's mail there. . . . There was only one saloon in what might be called the town itself, around the neighborhood of the station, the store, and the school. . . . There would have been the houses of those section hands, for the schoolteacher, doubtless a doctor. There would probably have been a carpenter, a tinsmith, no doubt a blacksmith's shop, and just a few such people as would be absolutely necessary to carry on the life of a very tiny village . . . " The future first lady, rifle in hand, is pictured here atop a burro outside Rudolph Nickel's Acton store in August 1891.

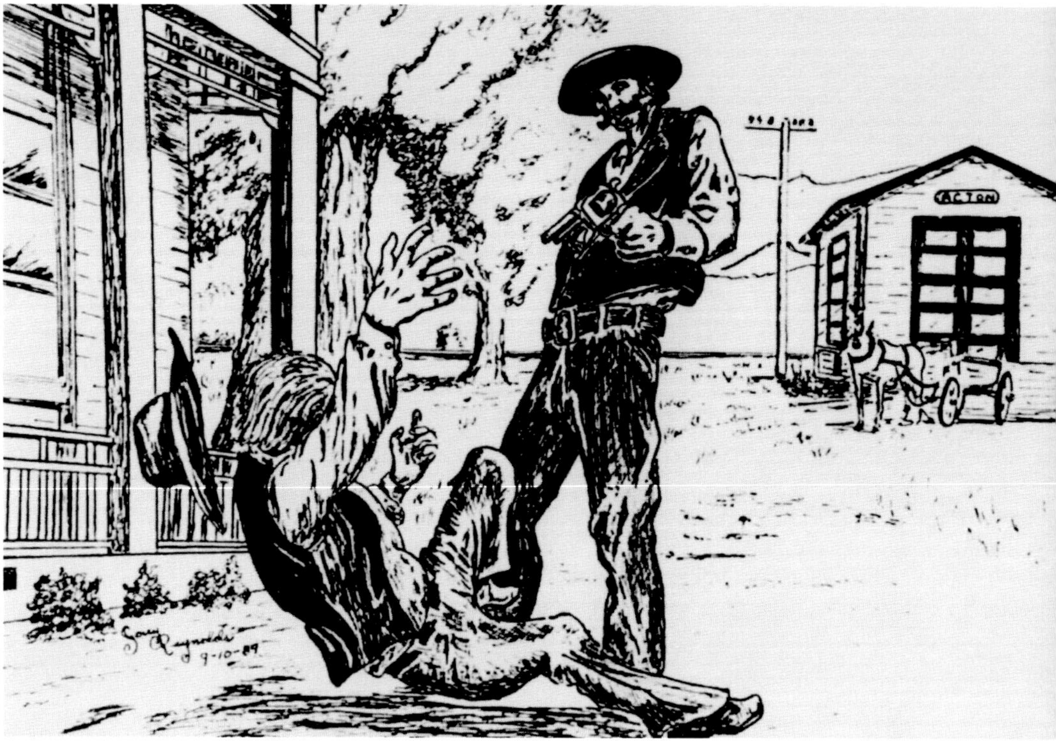

William Broome and Rosy Melrose

Acton was the site of a classic Wild West showdown-style gunfight in 1905. The shootout pitted William Broome, a New York immigrant of German descent and Acton honorary mayor, against fun-loving Kentucky-born William H. "Rosy" Melrose. The dispute centered on the fatal shooting of Broome's beloved pit bull by Melrose after the dog attacked Melrose's canine. Melrose and Broome faced off on Acton's dusty main street on February 28, 1905. Melrose, known as a quick draw and accurate shooter, got the better of Broome, sending five bullets into his torso, killing him on the spot. A sensational series of trials followed, each ending in a hung jury. Ultimately, the charges against Melrose were dropped, but feuding over the gunfight persisted in the area for many years. Pictured above is a Jerry Reynolds drawing of the gunfight. Below is a photograph of Acton taken 16 years before the gunfight.

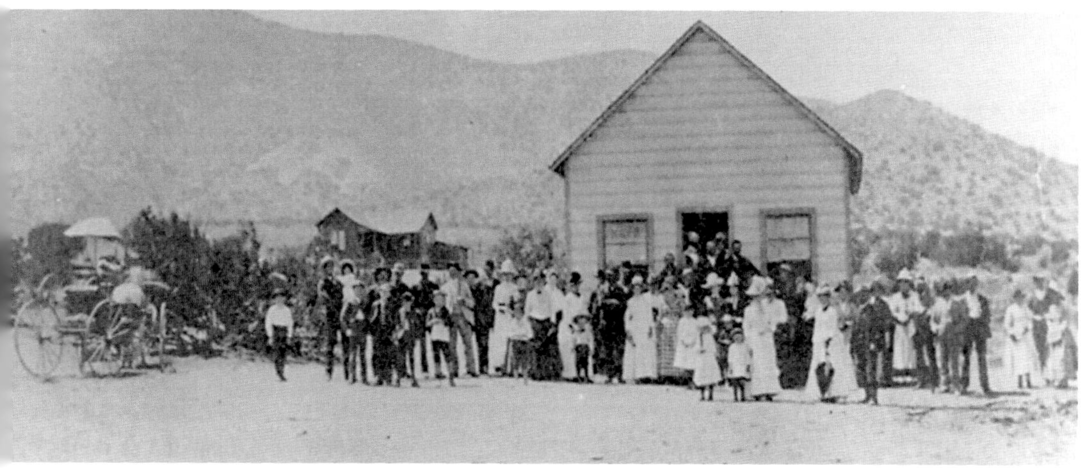

CHAPTER TWO

The Shakers

A lot of things came crashing down in the final years of the 1920s.

A fatal cocktail of hubris, poor design, and even worse materials doomed the Santa Clarita Valley's mighty St. Francis Dam in March 1928. A short time later, Wall Street collapsed, while back in Saugus, an ex-con derailed the West Coast Limited, forfeiting a lifetime of freedom in exchange for a few hundred dollars of ill-gotten gain.

The country was still legally "dry" during these years, keeping bootleggers like Mattie Fox in the black. Still rural and rustic, many in the valley loved the rodeo, while African-Americans made their way to Val Verde—the "Black Palm Springs"—for a little R&R.

The valley remained a cow town until it went from rodeos to condos after the new planned community of Valencia was brought to life.

New highways made getting here easier. This was not always such a great thing, as witnessed by the "Newhall Incident" in 1970, when four young California Highway Patrol officers were gunned down by two criminals who had just driven into town. A true hero emerged that day when a civilian named Gary Kness risked his own life attempting to save the men.

Desiring greater control over their political destiny than was provided by the county of Los Angeles, four towns formed the city of Santa Clarita in 1987. It was the first city in California history to incorporate with an initial population north of 100,000.

Today, the Santa Clarita Valley is enriched by several well-known artists, musicians, activists, and leaders in both government and the private sector.

But the area's true legendary locals rarely have household names. They are the teachers imparting knowledge and inspiration, the officers policing the neighborhoods, the emergency workers rushing to the scene of an accident, and the bus drivers helping the elderly aboard. They are the regular folks who give back to the community daily in a thousand ways that go unseen.

While they may not be recognized with a caption and picture in the following pages, their contributions are deeply appreciated by the fortunate citizenry of the Santa Clarita Valley.

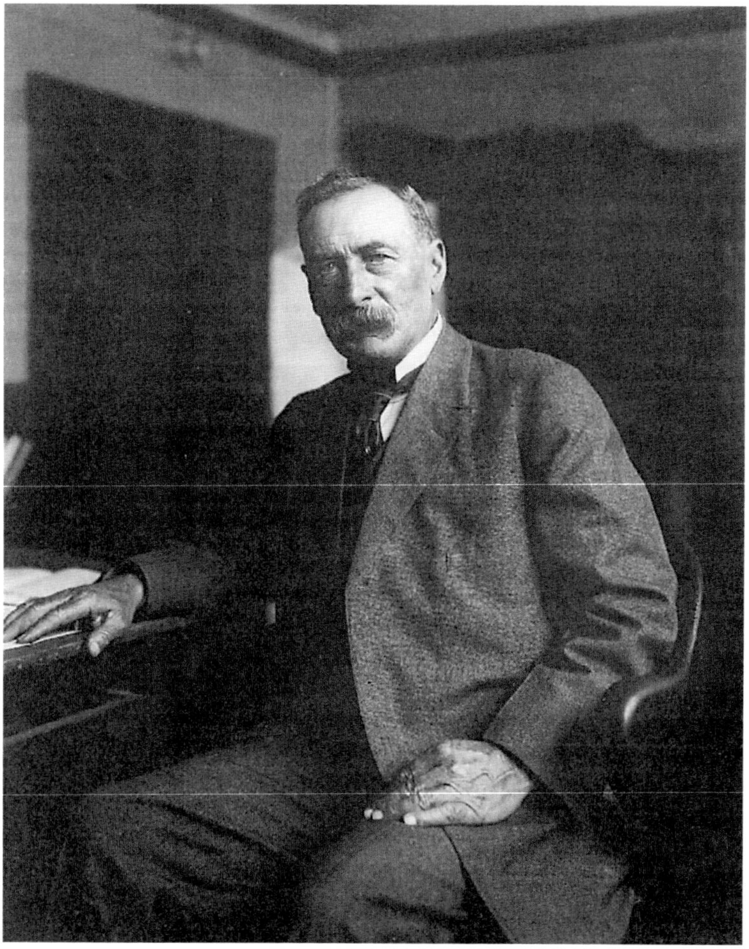

William Mulholland (The Rise)

On the triumphant day of November 5, 1913, forty thousand Los Angelenos gathered in Sylmar to witness the flowing of the first waters through William Mulholland's wondrous Los Angeles Aqueduct, ending its journey from Eastern California's Owens Valley. A hero to the citizens of the city of Los Angeles, Mulholland presided over the ceremony and instructed the water gate to be opened with the words, "There it is, take it." In the early days of the pueblo of Los Angeles, the city water supply was obtained from the Los Angeles River. By the turn of the 20th century, the population had grown to more than 100,000. It was obvious that if the city was to grow further, it would need another source of water. In 1902, the Bureau of Water Works and Supply was formed with Mulholland serving as superintendent. He traveled with his friend, the former Los Angeles mayor Fred Eaton, on a buckboard through Newhall and Saugus in 1904 on their way to explore the Owens Valley east of the Sierra Nevada Range. Eaton wanted to convince Mulholland that the Owens River might in some way be diverted to Los Angeles to become the extra water source that the growing city desperately needed. It was on this trip that the two men hatched the idea of building an aqueduct between the Owens and San Fernando Valleys. Los Angeles voters later approved bond issues to finance the aqueduct, with Mulholland designing and supervising its construction. What seemed like an impossible feat was accomplished between 1908 and 1913, as the 233-mile-long aqueduct was built on time and on budget, with the water flowing solely by gravity without the need for any pumping stations. With the opening of the aqueduct in 1913, Mulholland's popularity was at its zenith. He was asked to run for mayor, and streets and neighborhoods were named after him.

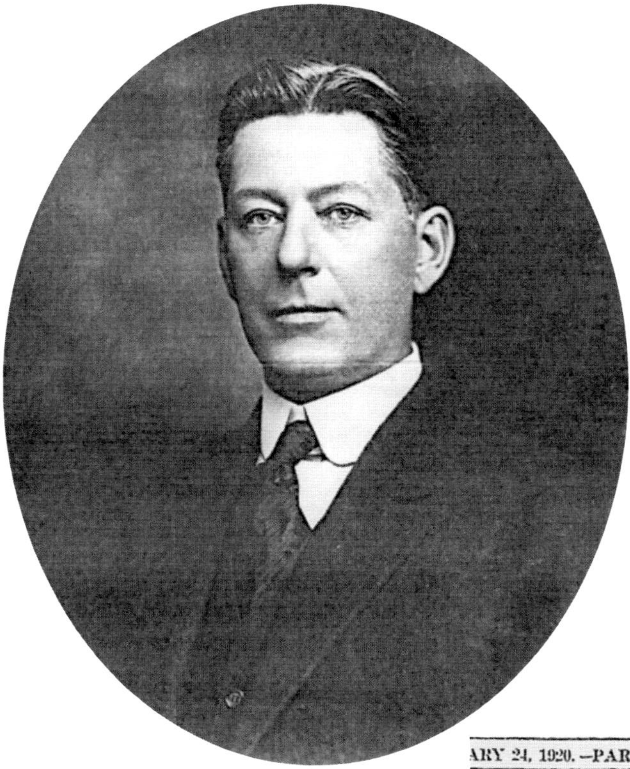

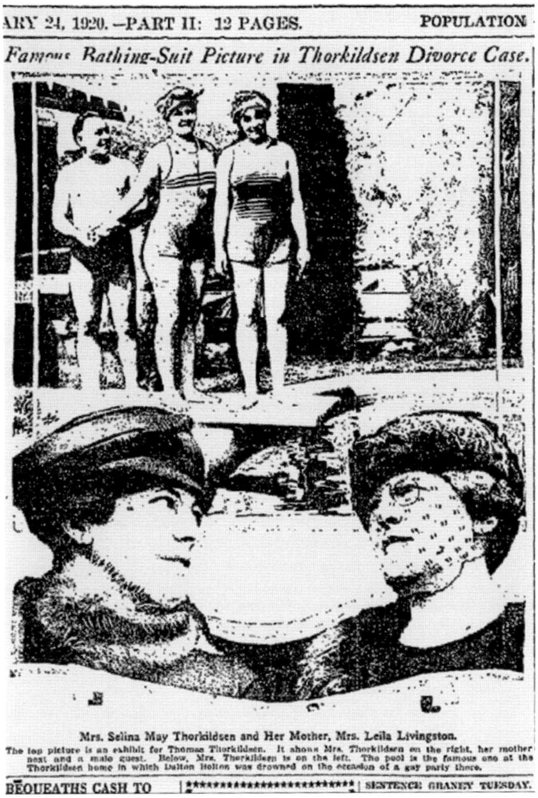

ARY 24, 1920.—PART II: 12 PAGES. POPULATION

Famous Bathing-Suit Picture in Thorkildsen Divorce Case.

Mrs. Selina May Thorkildsen and Her Mother, Mrs. Leila Livingston.

The top picture is an exhibit for Thomas Thorkildsen. It shows Mrs. Thorkildsen on the right, her mother next and a male guest. Below, Mrs. Thorkildsen is on the left. The pool is the famous one at the Thorkildsen home in which Dalton Holton was drowned on the occasion of a gay party there.

BEQUEATHS CASH TO | SENTENCE GRANEY TUESDAY.

Thomas Thorkildsen

In 1898, borax salesman Thomas Thorkildsen, pictured above, formed a partnership with Stephen Mather, which later became the Sterling Borax Company. The two men became multi-millionaires after purchasing a rich borax deposit in the SCV's Tick Canyon. Their mine closed in 1921, but Thorkildsen continued throwing wild parties at his Hollywood mansion, which he often hosted in the nude. An intoxicated Hollywood starlet drowned at one of these parties and went undiscovered until the next day. (Another night, a naked man drowned after Thorkildsen caught him in bed with his wife.) Thorkildsen died penniless after partying through his \$500-million fortune. The more prudent Mather went on to become first director of the National Park Service. The *Los Angeles Times* article at right, from January 24, 1920, covers Thorkildsen's sensational divorce trial. His former home is now owned by Brad Pitt and Angelina Jolie. (Top photograph courtesy Leon Worden.)

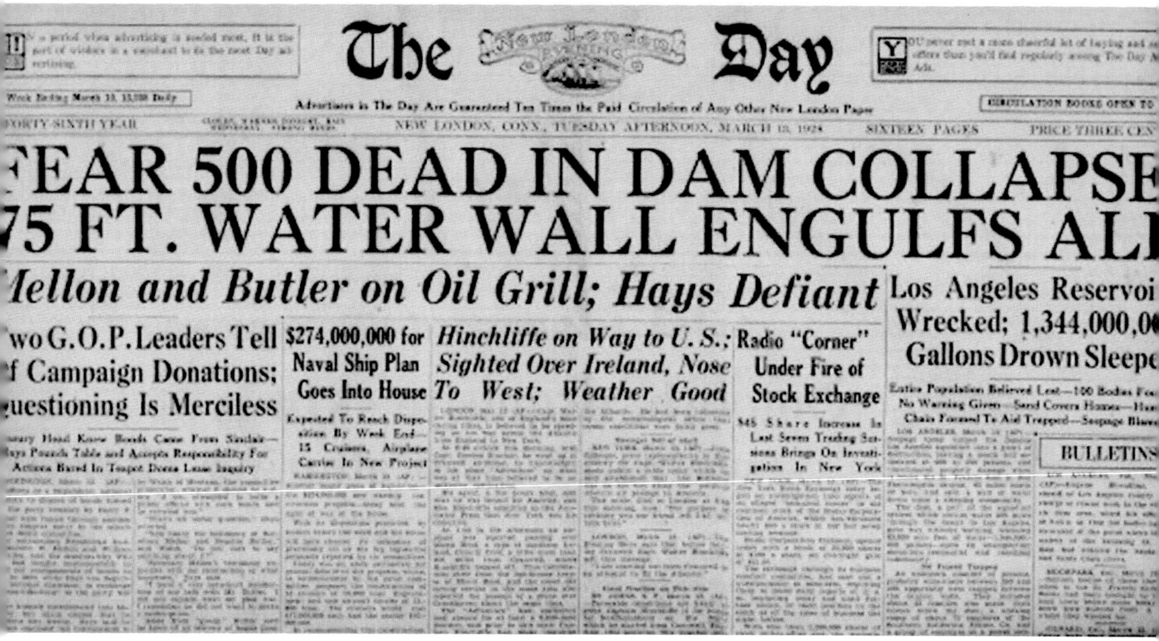

The New London Evening Day

Advertisers in The Day Are Guaranteed Ten Times the Paid Circulation of Any Other New London Paper

FORTY-SIXTH YEAR — NEW LONDON, CONN., TUESDAY AFTERNOON, MARCH 13, 1928 — SIXTEEN PAGES — PRICE THREE CENTS

FEAR 500 DEAD IN DAM COLLAPSE
75 FT. WATER WALL ENGULFS ALL

Mellon and Butler on Oil Grill; Hays Defiant

Two G.O.P. Leaders Tell of Campaign Donations; Questioning Is Merciless

$274,000,000 for Naval Ship Plan Goes Into House

Hinchliffe on Way to U. S.: Sighted Over Ireland, Nose To West; Weather Good

Radio "Corner" Under Fire of Stock Exchange

Los Angeles Reservoir Wrecked; 1,344,000,000 Gallons Drown Sleepers

BULLETINS

William Mulholland (The Fall)

While revered in Los Angeles, William Mulholland was reviled by the people of the Owens Valley who felt Los Angeles had stolen their water without adequate compensation. Beginning in 1924, Owens Valley locals began attacking the aqueduct in what would become known as the Owens Valley Water Wars. This conflict, and other factors, such as the San Andreas Fault, which the aqueduct crosses just north of the SCV, led Mulholland to create a series of reservoirs to provide Los Angeles with a water reserve in the event of a disruption. One of these reservoirs required the construction of the St. Francis Dam, which was completed in the SCV's San Francisquito Canyon in 1926. Mulholland, who was not an engineer, designed the dam, which turned out to be flawed in both materials and location. At midday on March 12, 1928, the dam keeper noticed mud coming out of a new leak. Mulholland and his assistant personally examined the leak and judged that it presented no danger. Just before midnight, a few hours after Mulholland's inspection, the dam ruptured, sending a thundering 180-foot wall of water crashing through San Francisquito Canyon into the Santa Clara River Valley, scouring everything in its path. Twelve billion gallons emptied out of the new reservoir over the next few hours, severely damaging the towns of Saugus, Castaic Junction, Fillmore, Bardsdale, Piru, and Santa Paula before emptying into the Pacific Ocean 54 miles from the dam site. The disaster killed an estimated 450 to 600 people, including 42 school-aged children. Many of the victims were swept out to sea, washing ashore as far south as the coast of Mexico. Buried bodies would occasionally be discovered over the coming decades, one as recently as 1992. To Mulholland's credit, he took full responsibility for the tragedy, saying, "Don't blame anyone else, you just fasten it on me. If there was an error in human judgment, I was the human, and I won't try to fasten it on anyone else." Mulholland never recovered from the tragedy and died a broken man in 1935. Pictured here is the front page of The *New London Evening Day*, New London, Connecticut, on March 13, 1928.

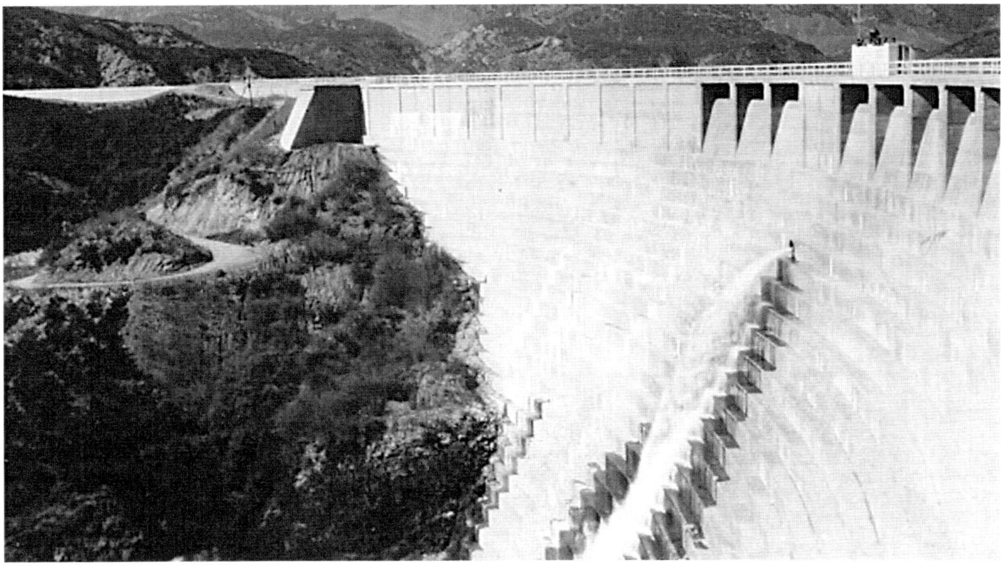

Tony Harnischfeger and Leona Johnson

On the morning of the break, dam keeper Tony Harnischfeger noticed muddy water leaking from the dam's western abutment and placed a frantic call to William Mulholland. Mulholland arrived later and concluded that the leakage appeared normal. The dam ruptured just hours after he left the site. The lifeless body of Harnischfeger's wife, Leona Johnson, was later found at the base of the dam. Harnischfeger's remains were never recovered. This postcard shows the dam shortly before the break.

Ace Hopewell

At three minutes before midnight on March 12, 1928, carpenter Ace Hopewell was riding his motorcycle a mile past the St. Francis Dam. He came to a sudden stop when he heard a landslide-like crashing sound from behind. He continued to Powerhouse No. 1, where he learned that the huge dam had ruptured. Hopewell was the last living person to see the dam before it crumbled. The photograph at right shows the wreckage of the dam.

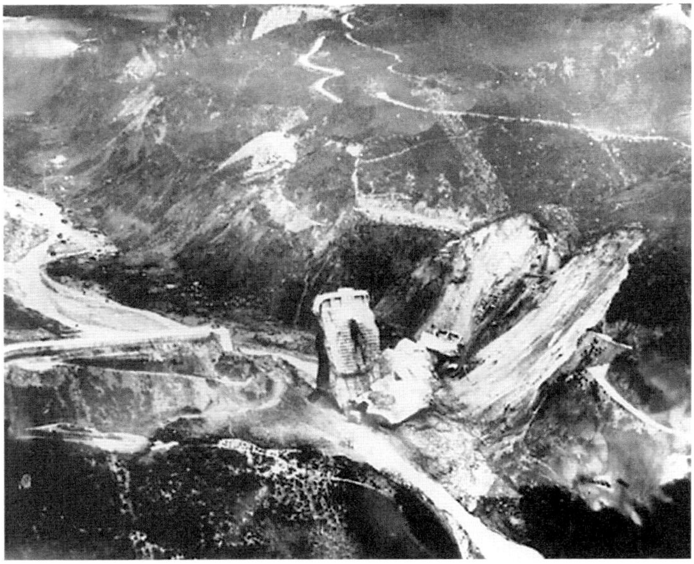

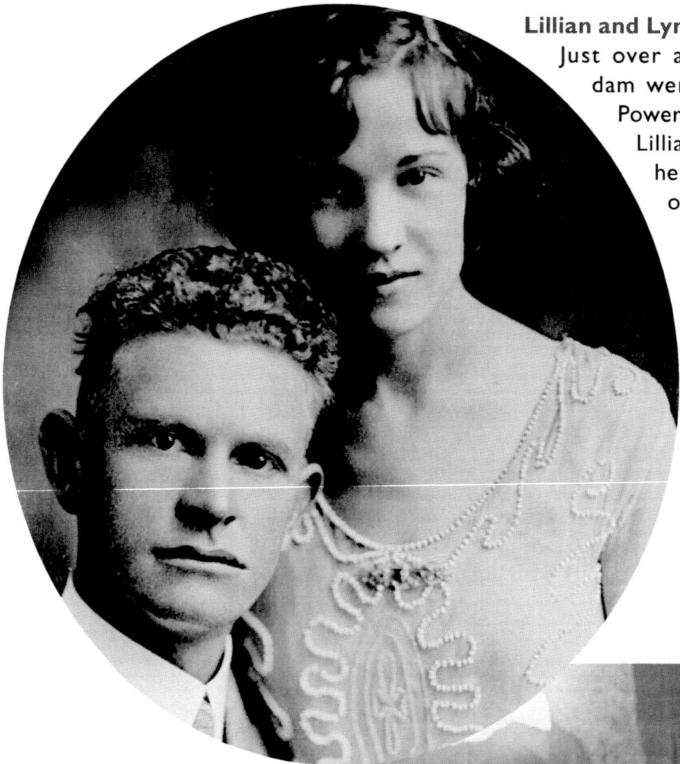

Lillian and Lyman Curtis
Just over a mile downstream from the dam were homes for the workers of Powerhouse No. 2. Around midnight, Lillian and Lyman Curtis (pictured here) were awakened by the roar of the floodwaters bearing down on them. Lillian and her son scrambled up a hillside while her husband, Lyman, went to retrieve their daughters. She never saw them again. Lillian, her son, and their dog were the family's only survivors. (Courtesy Keith Buttelman.)

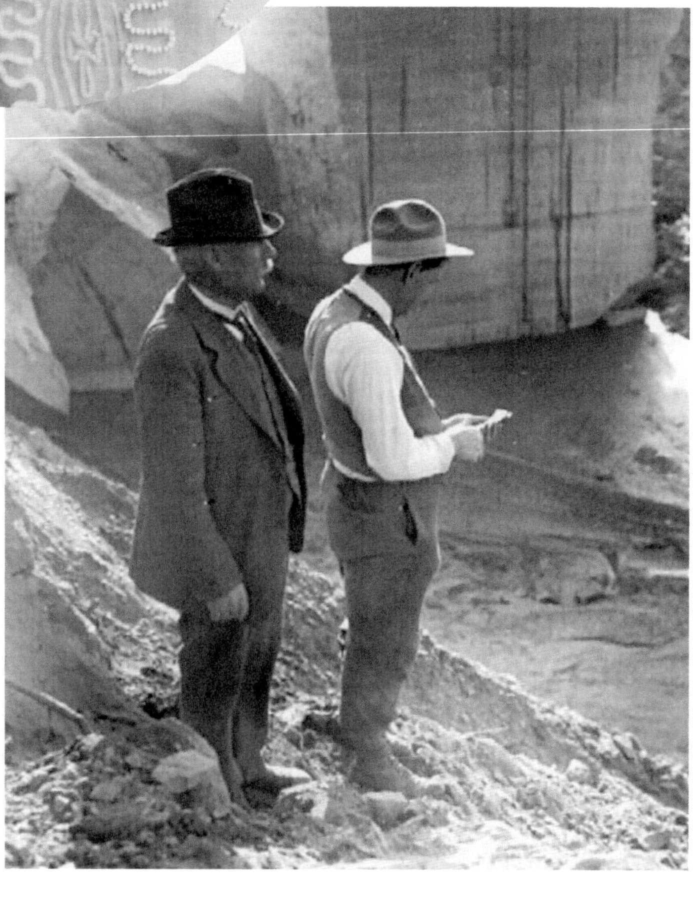

Ray Rising
Ray Rising, a utility man from Powerhouse No. 2, awoke to a 10-story wall of water. He was swept into the flood but managed to climb onto a floating rooftop, which carried him to safety. He was one of only two survivors from the powerhouse, which was swept away, leaving only the structure's slab behind. In the photograph at right, Mulholland (left) inspects the devastation with his deputy, Harvey Van Norman, on March 15, 1928.

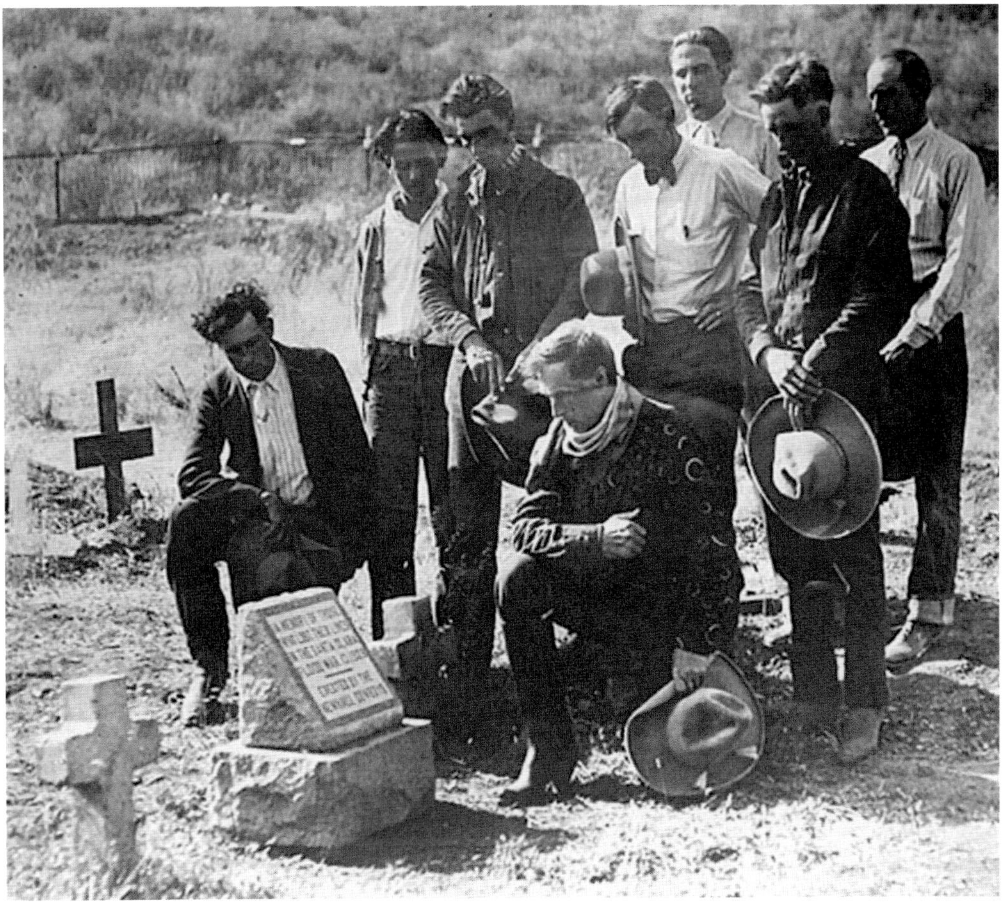

The Ruiz Family
Six miles down San Francisquito Canyon from where the St. Francis Dam once towered is a small cemetery about a half-acre square. Brush conceals many of the graves, and the burial ground is surrounded by a weathered iron fence with a gate hanging precariously off rusted hinges. It is a lonely place, but a handmade sign by the gate with "Cemetery Ruiz" spelled out in turquoise reveals that it still gets the occasional visitor. The cemetery is dominated by the large granite Ruiz family monument in the southwest corner. In a line at the front of the monument are six smaller stones for "Sister Susana B.," "Brother Raymond C.," "Brother Martin F.," "Sister Mary S.," "Mother Rosaria P.," and "Father Enrique R." Off to the right are the graves of Rosarita A. Erratchuo, who was the eldest daughter of Enrique and Rosaria, and her infant son Roland. Each of the monuments lists the date that all eight Ruiz family members died: March 13, 1928. The Ruizes and Erratchuoes were among the first of the estimated 600 victims of the St. Francis Dam disaster who were crushed under the weight of 12 billion gallons of water that flushed through the canyon that night. Nearby is a small weatherworn memorial that reads, "In memory of those who lost their lives in the Santa Clara flood Mar. 13, 1928 / Erected by the Newhall Cowboys." This stone was placed here by some real-life cowboys who worked the ranches in the area, and by William S. Hart, a man who played a cowboy on screen. Hart lived in nearby Newhall and was deeply troubled by the destruction that took place near his home. He took on the responsibility of burying a young boy whose body lay unclaimed. Hart intended to inter the child in the cemetery and bought a tiny cowboy outfit for the boy's burial. But shortly before his funeral he was identified and buried in Chatsworth beside his mother, who also perished in the flood. William S. Hart (center, kneeling), surrounded by the other "Newhall Cowboys," is pictured at the monument's dedication on March 25, 1928.

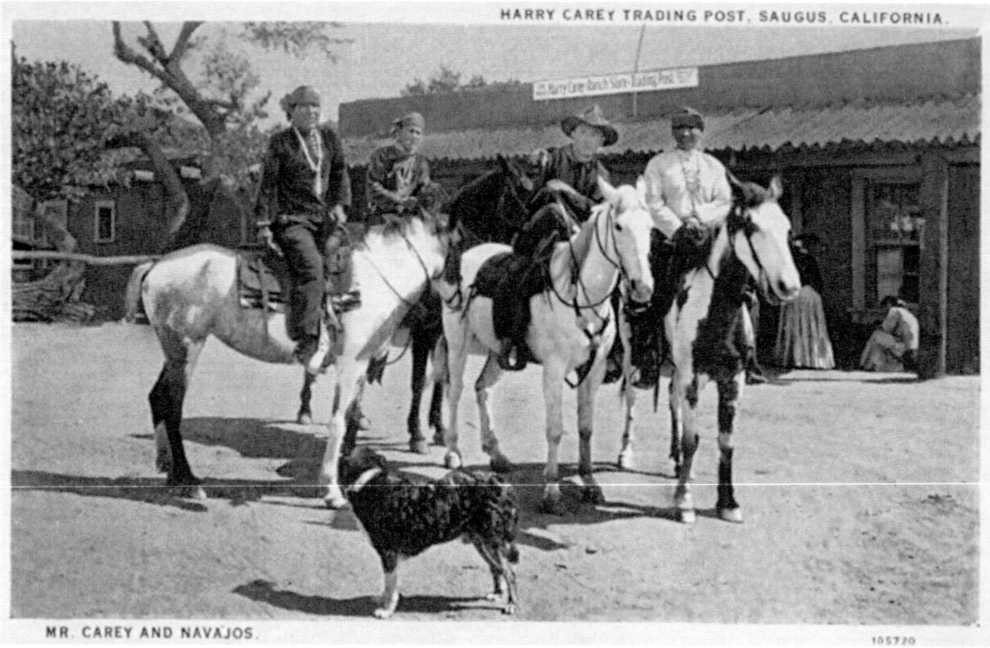

Harry Carey

Near the entrance to San Francisquito Canyon was the ranch of movie star Harry Carey. The flood from the St. Francis Dam rupture destroyed a good part of his property, including a Navajo Trading Post that had been a popular tourist attraction. Legend has it that the Navajos who ran the trading post called Carey, while he was on business in New York, to tell him about their medicine man's premonition of an impending rupture just days before the break. But according to a recent interview with Carey's son, Harry Carey Jr., the Navajos actually told Carey one month before the disaster after the medicine man had gone hunting near the dam and noticed a big crack in its face. Above is a postcard from the late 1920s. Below is a modern-day photograph of the ranch house.

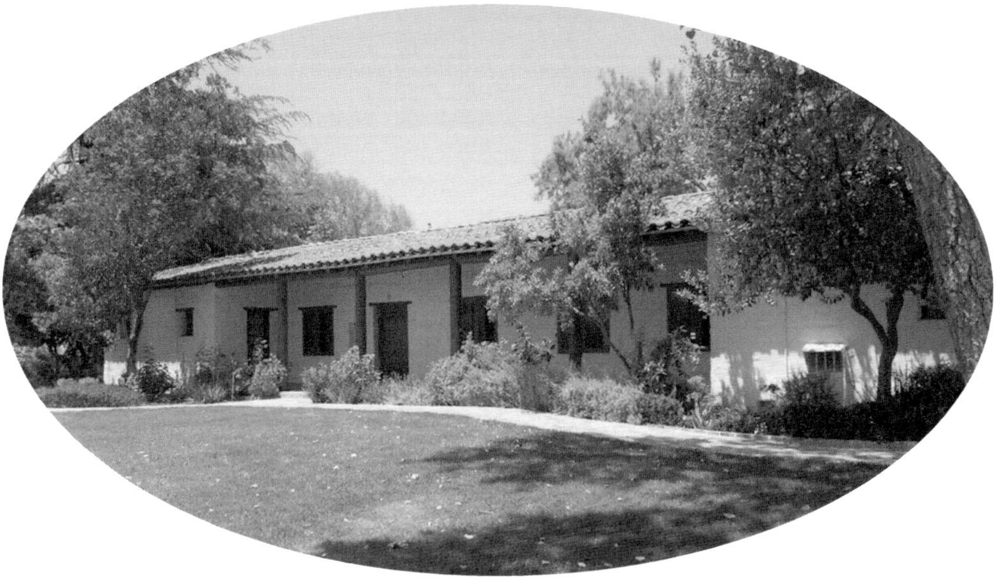

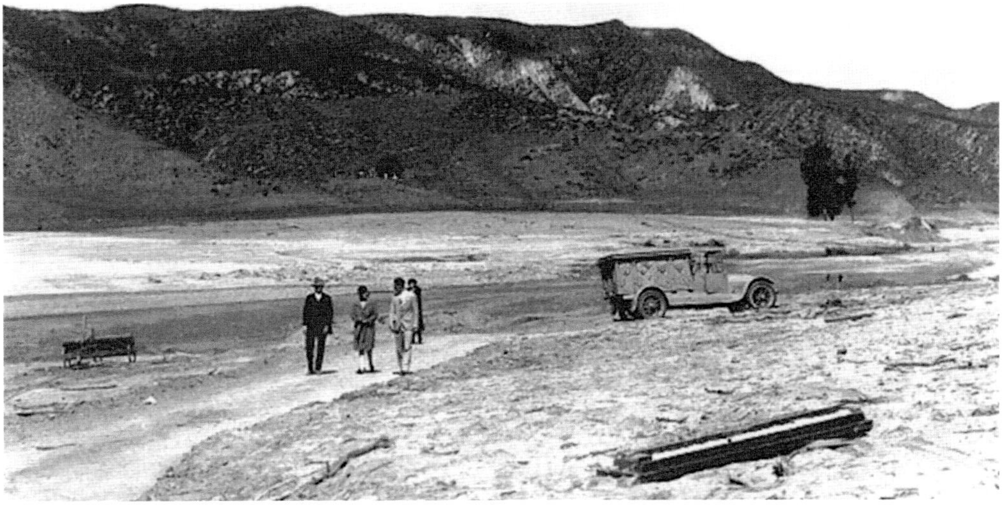

Raymond Starbard

Raymond Starbard was nearly washed away by the torrent near Castaic Junction. An Edison patrolman, Starbard hitched a ride to Saugus and made a call to the sheriff, becoming the first person to sound the alarm. Starbard lived in a home provided by his employer. It survived the flood and can be seen today at Heritage Junction in Newhall. The photograph above shows four people surveying the damage left behind by the flood, including an orphaned piano keyboard.

Rev. Wolcott H. Evans

Lovingly nicknamed the "pastor of the disaster," Rev. Wolcott H. Evans was one of the first men to arrive at the dam site and spent countless hours comforting those in need. Over the following days, he conducted numerous services for the dead. Below is the *Los Angeles Times'* first report of the disaster, dated March 14, 1928. (Courtesy *Los Angeles Times.)*

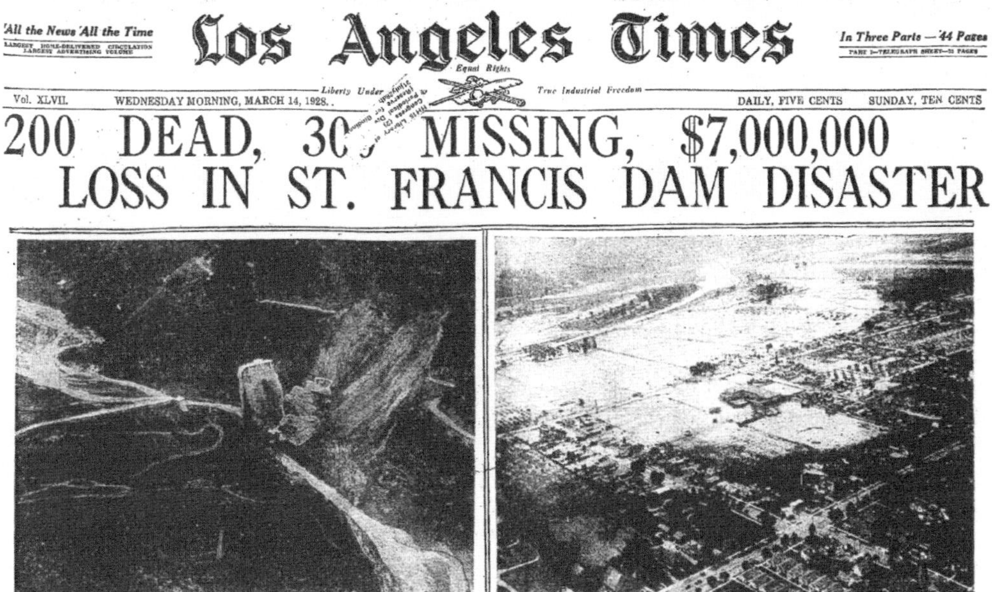

'All the News 'All the Time

Los Angeles Times

In Three Parts — 44 Pages

Liberty Under Equal Rights True Industrial Freedom

Vol. XLVII. WEDNESDAY MORNING, MARCH 14, 1928. DAILY, FIVE CENTS SUNDAY, TEN CENTS

200 DEAD, 30[illegible] MISSING, $7,000,000 LOSS IN ST. FRANCIS DAM DISASTER

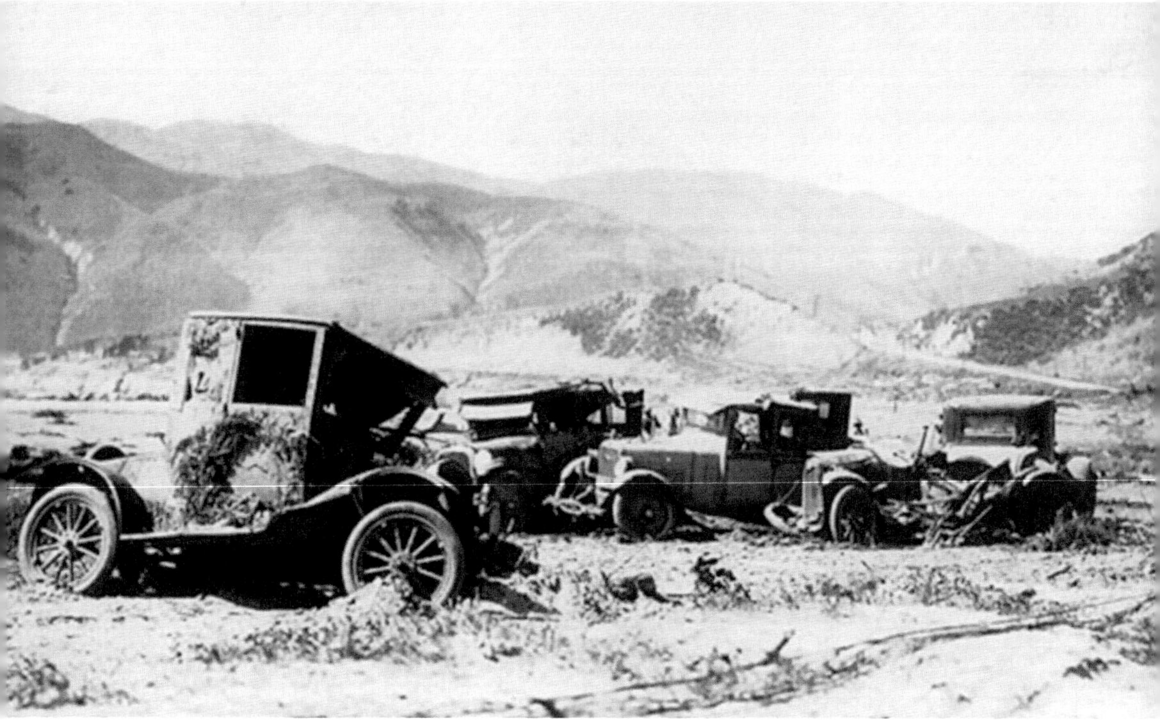

Ed Locke

Just past the Ventura County line was a railroad siding called Kemp, where a group of 150 workers for the Edison Company were fast asleep in a tent camp. Night watchman Ed Locke watched in horror as the huge flood approached. He ran through the encampment, waking up as many men as possible. Locke saved many lives but lost his own, perishing that night along with 84 of the workers as the flood hit a geologic outcropping called Blue Cut, which created a whirlpool effect that uprooted the tents. Most of the survivors had their tents zipped up, which allowed them to float on top of the swirling waters. These two photographs show wreckage left behind in the disaster's wake.

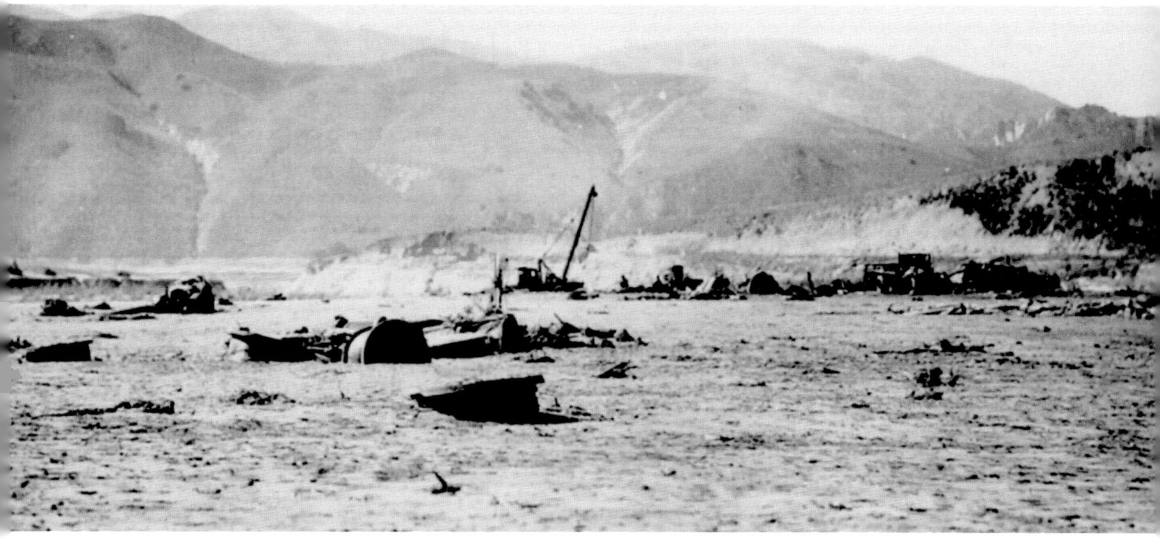

St. Francis Dam Survivors

When the St. Francis Dam ruptured, Santa Paula was one of several hamlets in its path. In 2008, on the 80th anniversary of the dam disaster, some survivors, including three members of the Grainger family, met in Santa Paula to talk about their memories from that night. "The water came through and was about 20 feet deep," recalled Donald Grainger, 85. "It knocked the house off the foundation and washed it about two blocks down the street." Peggy Grainger, 82, Donald's sister-in-law, remembered a similar experience: "My house was found in Saticoy wrapped around a walnut tree." The Graingers were among the fortunate residents of Santa Paula who received adequate warning. Many of the other residents were not so lucky. Ninety-one-year-old Stanley Griffiths remembered seeing bodies covered in mud being hosed off outside the mortuary. Donald Grainger recalled seeing a flatbed truck go by with bodies stacked in the back. The official death toll from the disaster was 450, but many believe it claimed dozens of additional lives, mostly those of Spanish-speaking migrant workers who were camped in low-lying areas. None of the living survivors saw the water come through town because it hit Santa Paula while it was still dark, between the hours of two and three o'clock in the morning. But they did remember the sounds of that night. "The Union Oil Company had a refinery in Santa Paula that had a big steam whistle that in the case of a disaster they would toot instead of blow," said 87-year-old survivor Robert Daries. "The 'toot, toot, toot' is what woke us up." Donald Grainger remembered being on top of Seventh Street Hill with his family for about a half-hour before hearing a "terrific crash" when the flood slammed into the Willard Bridge. "It was a steel bridge, and (the water) just mangled the thing. There were pieces of it up and down the river for years." Pictured from left to right are Eva Grainger Griffiths, Robert Grainger, and Donald Grainger. Robert holds a picture of the Grainger house that was destroyed by the flood.

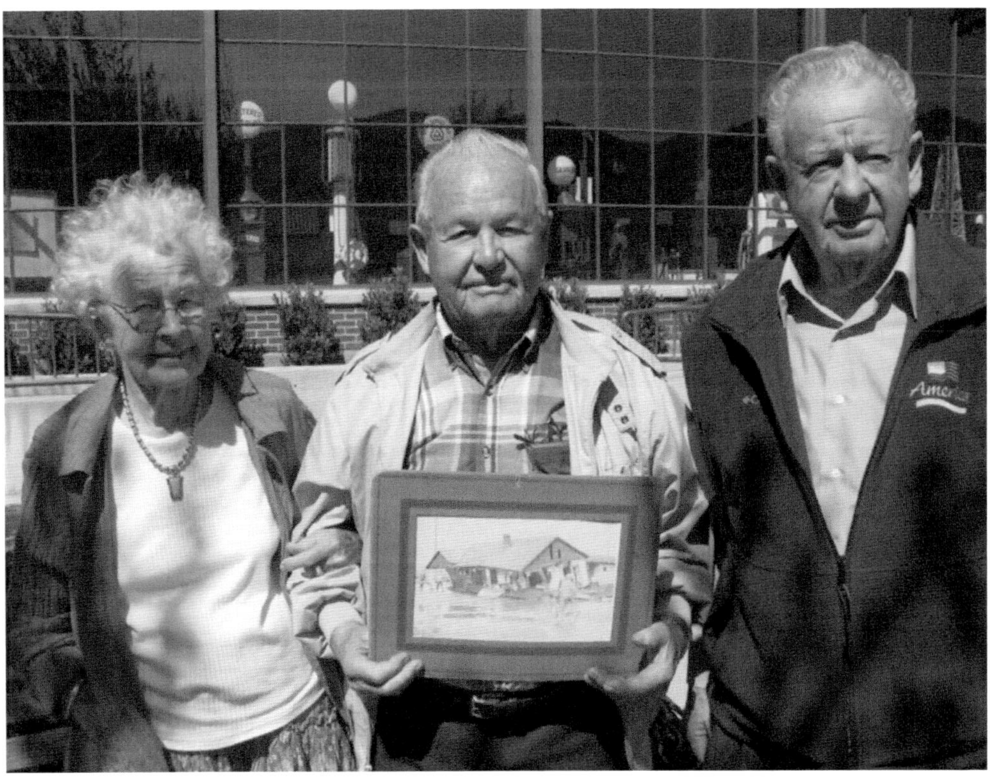

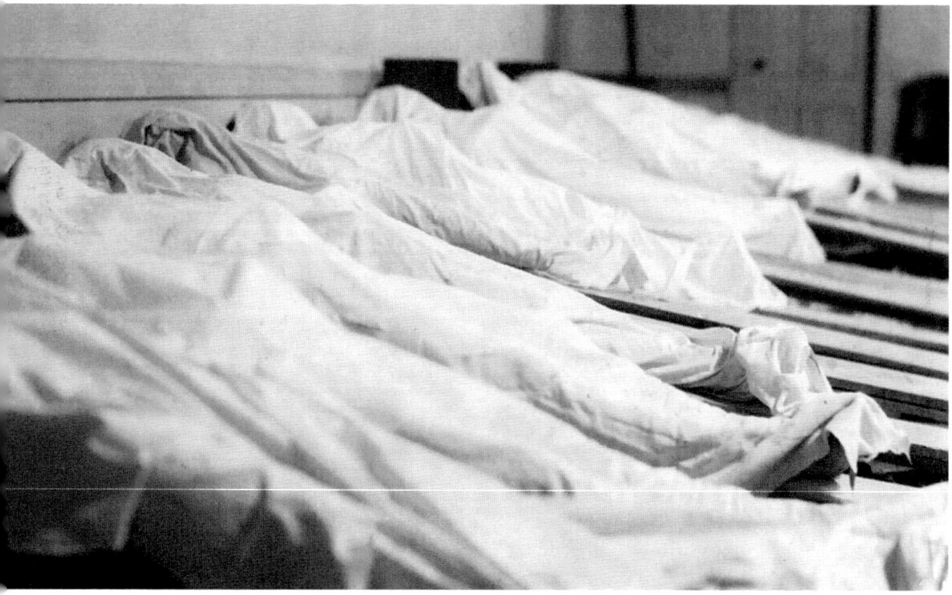

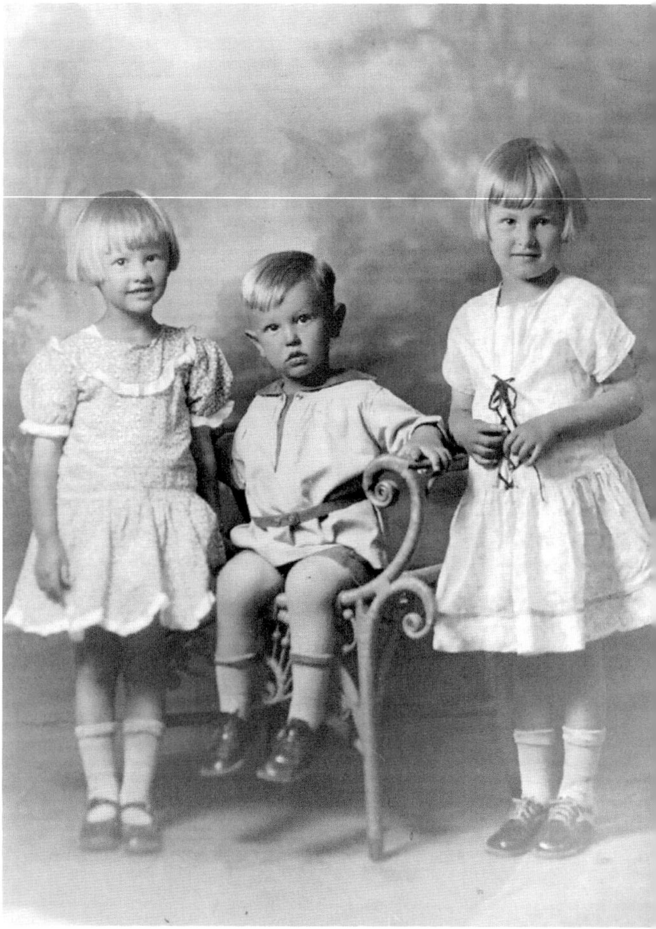

St. Francis Dam Victims
According to St. Francis Dam survivor Robert Daries, there was talk of substandard materials being used in the dam's construction long before it actually crashed down. "My uncle used to haul gravel to the dam when it was being built and he told my parents never to buy property in Santa Paula below Main Street." Eva Griffiths, another survivor, remembered that her mother heard about other problems at the dam shortly before the break. "My mother had a friend who lived up above the dam who called earlier in the week and said there was quite a crack in it," she recalled. The photograph above shows a row of dead bodies covered by sheets inside Newhall's Masonic Hall. At right is a photograph of Marjorie, Mazie, and Danny Curtis taken in 1928. Danny survived the flood, but both of his young sisters perished. (Courtesy Keith Buttleman.)

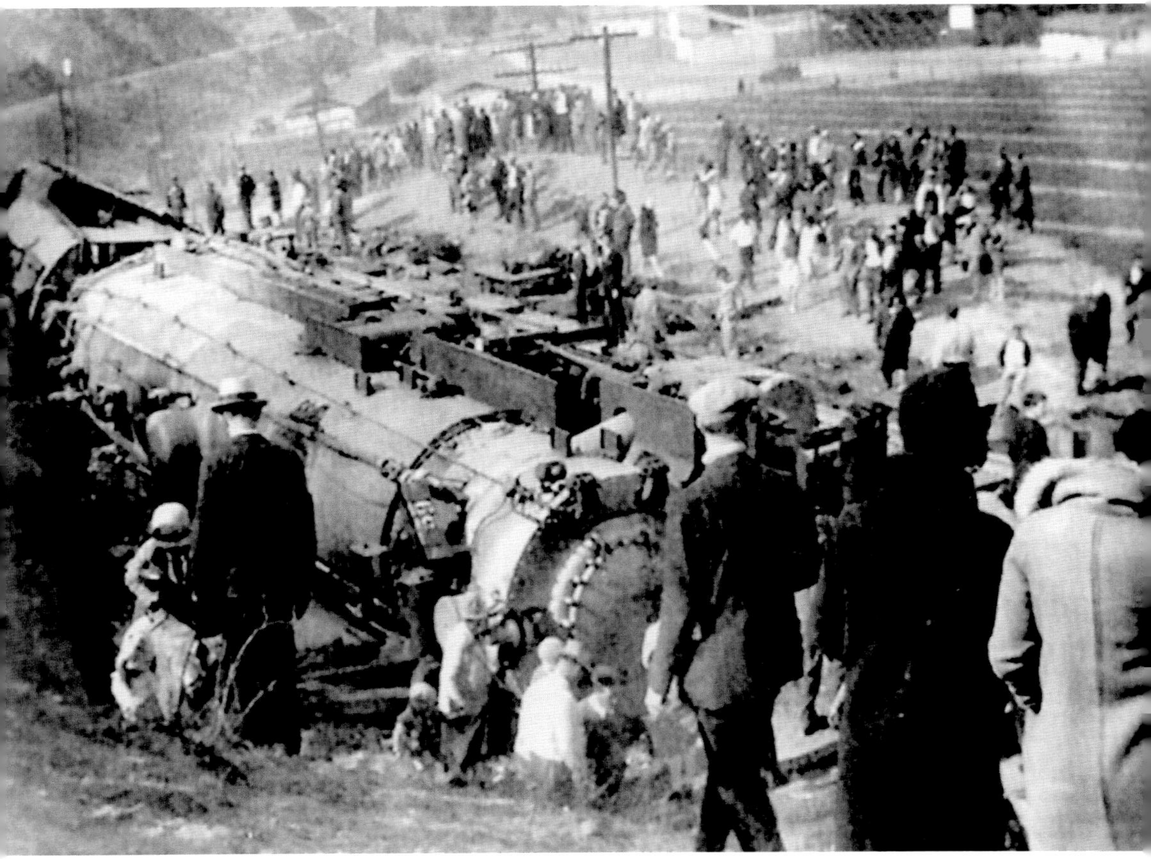

Buffalo Tom Vernon

In the early evening hours of November 10, 1929, the Southern Pacific's West Coast Limited chugged north towards the Santa Clarita Valley. In the shadows hid a 45-year-old ex-rodeo rider who called himself "Buffalo Tom" Vernon. Earlier, Vernon had stolen a claw bar and wrench and removed spikes from about 60 feet of rails. Around 7:30 p.m., the Limited rounded the bend at 25 miles per hour and derailed, miraculously injuring only the engineer. Within minutes, Tom and his pistol separated the passengers from $300 and he disappeared into the night. Vernon later claimed to have begun life as Tom Averill, the son of a Wyoming cattle-stealing couple named James Averill and Ellen "Cattle Kate" Watson, who were lynched for rustling in 1889. Vernon was only six years old at the time and was purportedly present at the hangings. He also claimed that he was left for dead and was rescued and raised by a Dakota Indian chief. He allegedly rode in Buffalo Bill's Wild West show, where he picked up the name "Buffalo Tom." Perhaps not surprisingly, he turned to a life of crime and did time in the Ohio State Penitentiary, San Quentin, and Folsom. Upon his release, Vernon drifted into the SCV and unsuccessfully sought employment with the Southern Pacific Railroad. Changing strategies, he decided to rob a Southern Pacific train instead. Vernon was eventually caught in Oklahoma and implicated in an additional train robbery in Wyoming. He confessed to the Saugus crime and was sent to Folsom to serve a life sentence. At least one eyewitness to the "Great Saugus Train Robbery" was happy to have been present during one of the Old West's final train heists. An English passenger named Irwin Bennett was quoted as saying, "It was really quite an experience. I had begun to think all these tales of your 'Wild West' were fiction, but now I can see they are based on fact." The derailed West Coast Limited lies on its side in this photograph from November 11, 1929. (Courtesy Ray Ayers.)

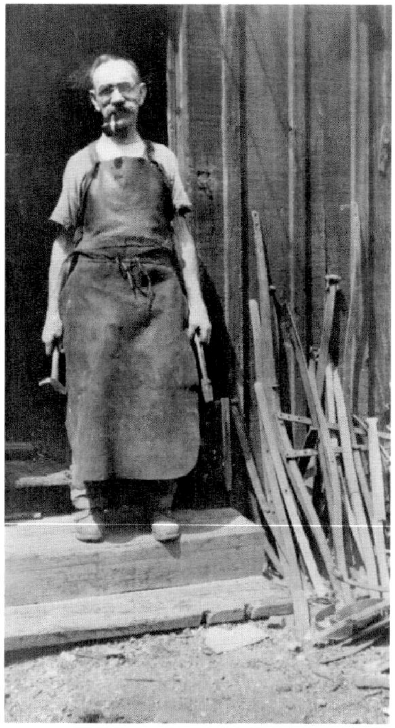

Tom Frew
In 1900, Tom Frew (pictured here, outside his blacksmith shop), who spoke with a gentle Scottish brogue, stopped in Newhall on a journey to his would-be home and was asked to stay on as town blacksmith. The Frew family became an integral part of the valley, and for the next seven decades, generations of Frew sons kept the family business alive. Tom Frew IV finally sold it in 1970.

The Walker Family
Frank Walker built the first homestead in Placerita Canyon in 1919. The Walker clan (several of whom are pictured here) eventually included 12 children. They later moved into a postcard-sized cabin in the 1930s, which can still be seen on the grounds of the Placerita Canyon Nature Center. The ranch hosted several film shoots and a portion was later sold to Walt Disney in the 1950s.

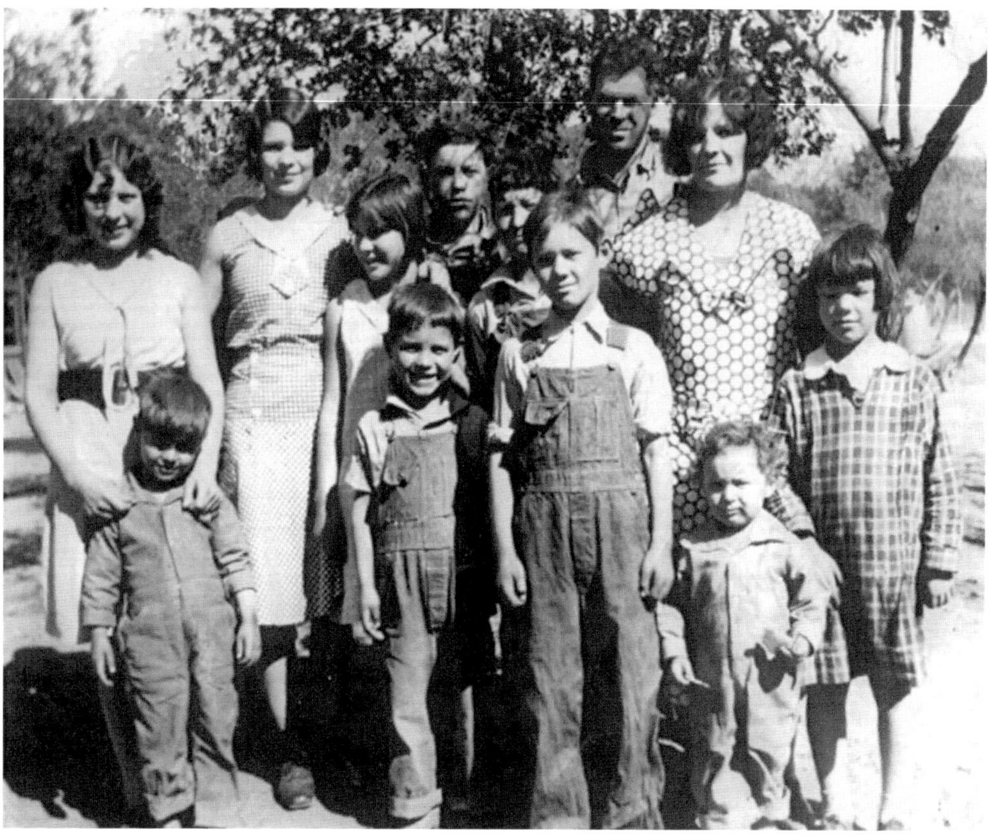

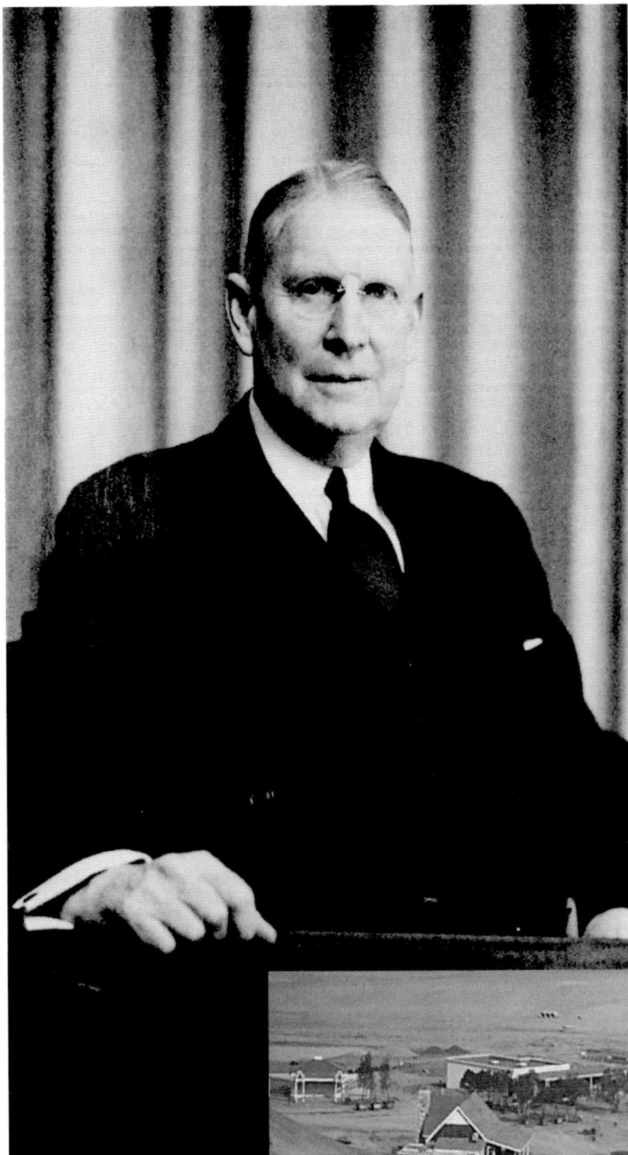

Atholl McBean

After the stock market crashed in October 1929, William "Mayo" Newhall, the last of Henry Mayo Newhall's surviving sons, found the Newhall Land and Farming Company—the enterprise created by his family—to be tottering on the brink of collapse. Mayo placed his son-in-law, Atholl McBean (pictured at left) in charge. The 41-year-old McBean was the president of San Francisco's chamber of commerce and a director of many major corporations. Against the objections of some Newhall family members, McBean suspended their dividends until the troubled company was righted again. After some skillful business maneuvers, he had the company back on solid financial ground by 1935. In the 1960s, McBean spearheaded the creation of the city of Valencia. Below is an aerial photograph of the construction of Magic Mountain in 1970. The theme park's creation was part of McBean's master plan for the new city.

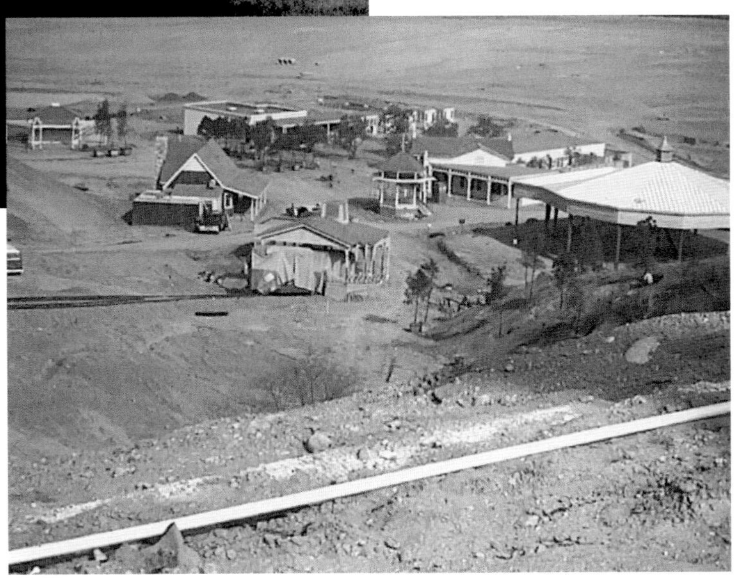

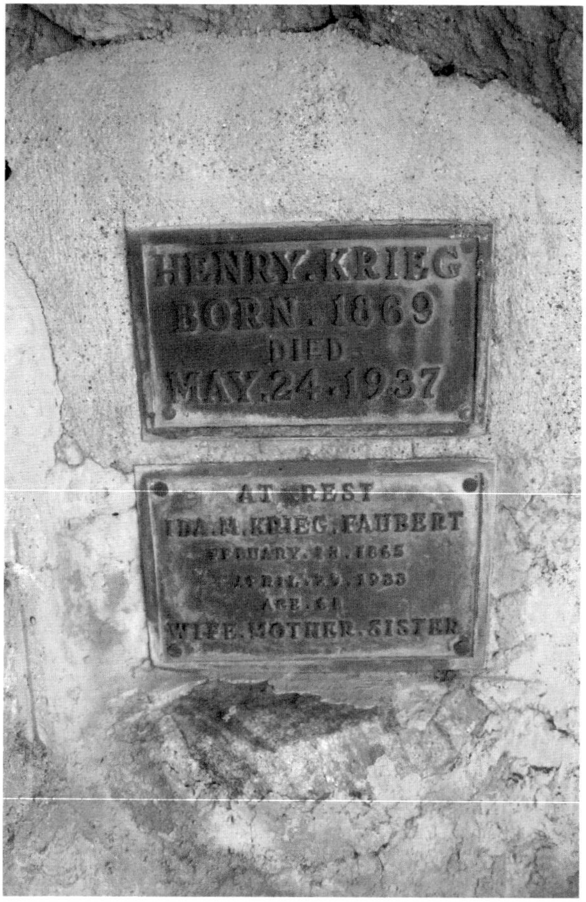

Mattie Fox and Henry Krieg
Mattie "Nellie" Fox lived at Vasquez Rocks in one of the nicer bungalows owned by Santa Clarita pioneer Henry Krieg. She operated a beer garden during Prohibition that enjoyed a steady stream of customers from all over Los Angeles. Mattie lived on the property until her death in the 1930s. Today, visitors to Vasquez Rocks can still visit her grave, located near the remains of her cabin. Krieg, who homesteaded Vasquez Rocks in 1910, supported his family by building rental cabins and charging a quarter per car to see the rocks. Krieg and some members of his family are also buried at Vasquez Rocks (right). From the scenic vantage point of their grave markers (below), it can be said they still keep watch over the property today.

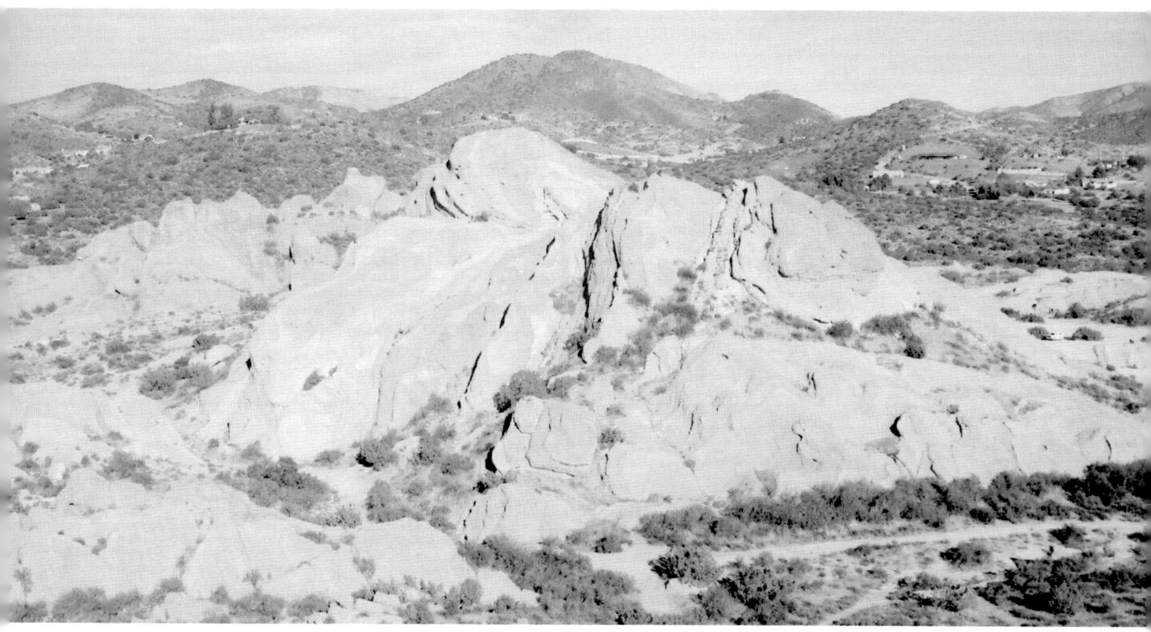

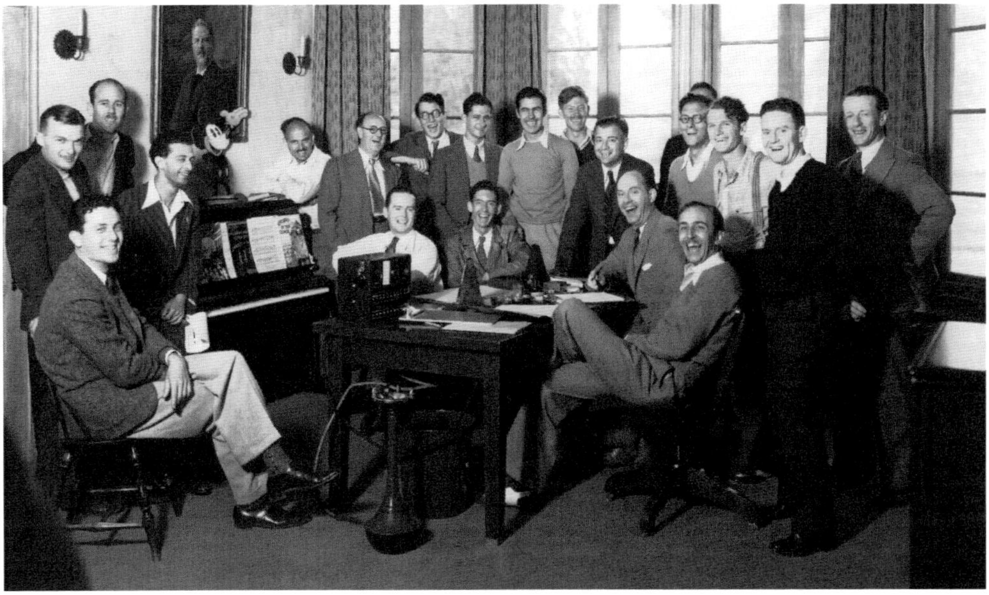

Frank Churchill
Frank Churchill, the Academy Award–winning composer of such Walt Disney classics as "Who's Afraid of the Big Bad Wolf?," "Whistle While You Work," "Heigh-Ho," and "Some Day My Prince Will Come," was plagued by depression and alcoholism. In 1942, Churchill shot himself at his home in Castaic. The photograph above from 1931 is of the key members of the Disney animation staff. Churchill is pictured standing second from the left. (Courtesy michaelbarrier.com.)

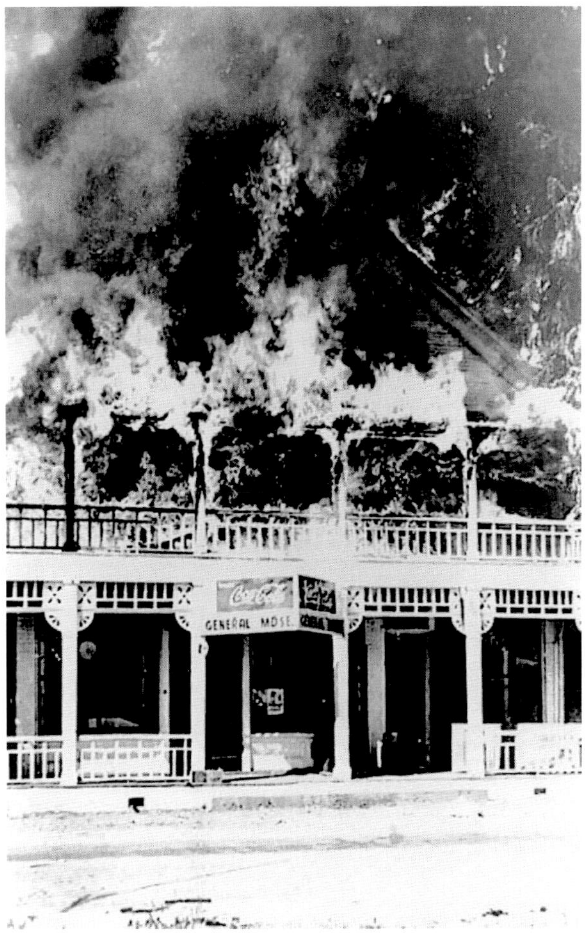

Clarence Rush
The Acton Hotel burned down on October 19, 1945. Although never proven, arson was suspected on the part of town postmaster Clarence Rush. Rush ran the hotel while owner Samuel H. Schorr served in World War II. Schorr accused Rush of stealing furnishings from the hotel during his absence. Rush was arrested and arraigned after the fire, but his case was dismissed when Schorr failed to appear in court.

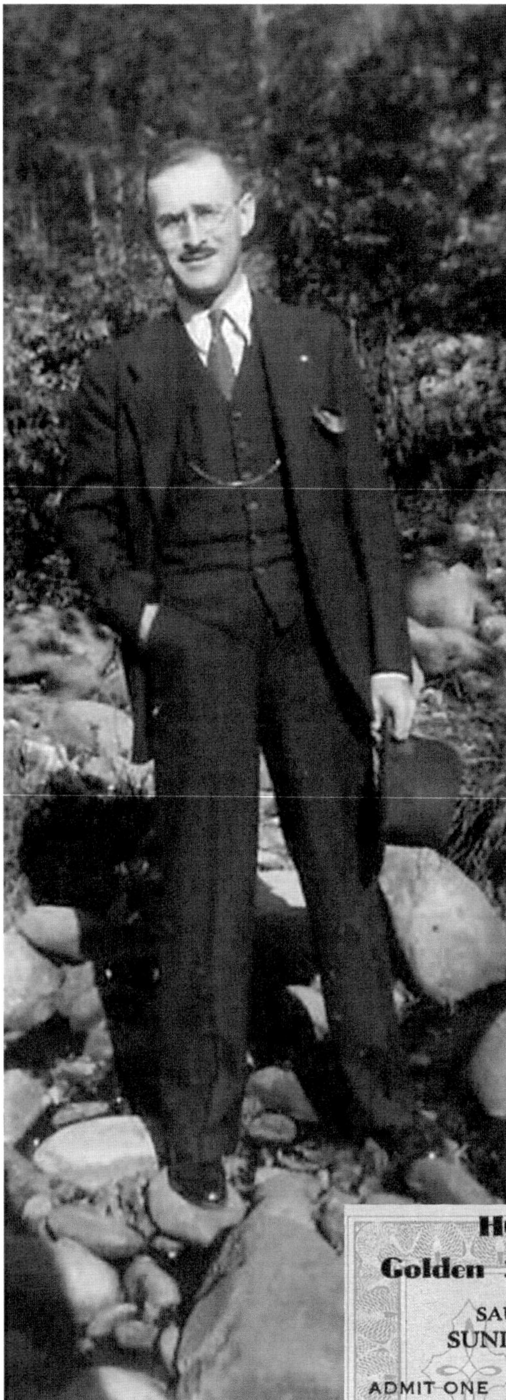

Alfred L. Clark

Canyon Country old-timers have fond memories of the Solemint Store, which was located at the corner of Soledad Canyon Road and Sierra Highway. Alfred L. Clark (pictured here in the 1930s) was the owner of this beloved establishment, which featured risqué advertisements, autographed photographs of Hollywood stars, and a maze of piled-up merchandise. Clark's slogan was, "If you can't get it anywhere else, try Solemint." (Courtesy Charlie Clark.)

Roy Baker

In 1927, Roy Baker built an 18,000-seat rodeo arena called the Baker Ranch and Stadium. Hit hard financially by the Great Depression, he was forced to sell to cowboy actor Hoot Gibson in 1930. Gibson continued to hold rodeos, regularly drawing a Hollywood crowd that included William S. Hart, Harry Carey, Tom Mix, and John Wayne. He would sometimes use the stadium as a movie set. Pictured is an entry ticket from 1931.

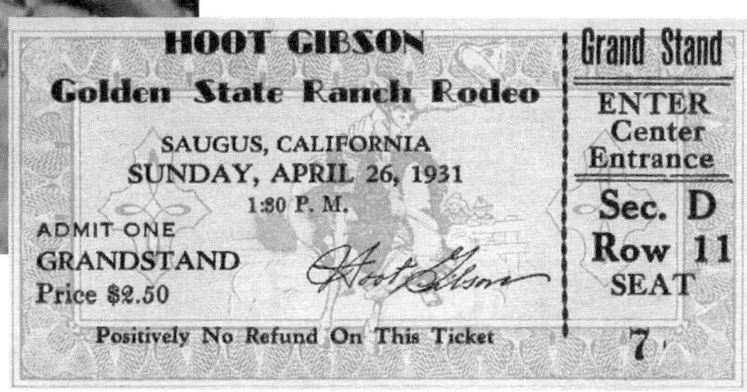

HOOT GIBSON
Golden State Ranch Rodeo
SAUGUS, CALIFORNIA
SUNDAY, APRIL 26, 1931
1:30 P. M.
ADMIT ONE
GRANDSTAND
Price $2.50
Hoot Gibson
Positively No Refund On This Ticket

Grand Stand
ENTER
Center
Entrance
Sec. D
Row 11
SEAT
7

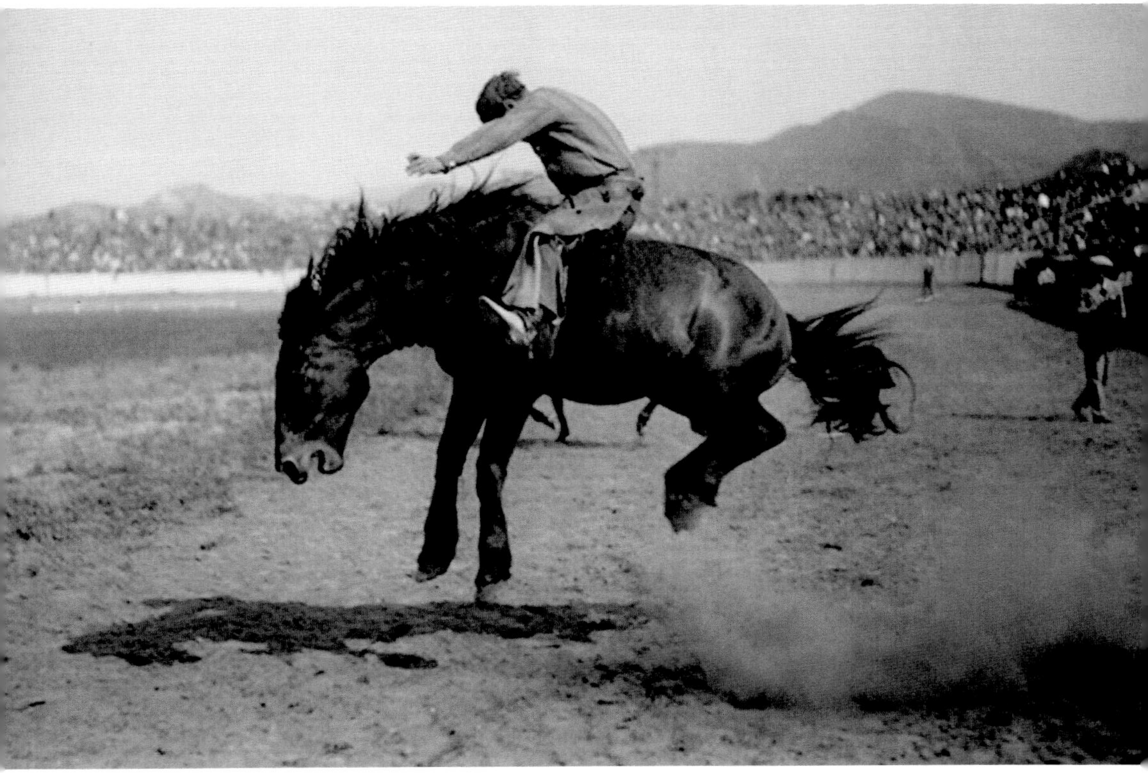

Paul Hill

Hoot Gibson sold the stadium to Paul Hill in 1934 and floods three years later filled it with debris. Hill went broke, and ownership passed to William Bonelli, who renamed it Bonelli Stadium. It later became the Saugus Speedway, an automobile race track. Today, it is the site of the Saugus Swap Meet. The photograph of the cowboy atop the bucking bronco was taken at the rodeo grounds in 1927.

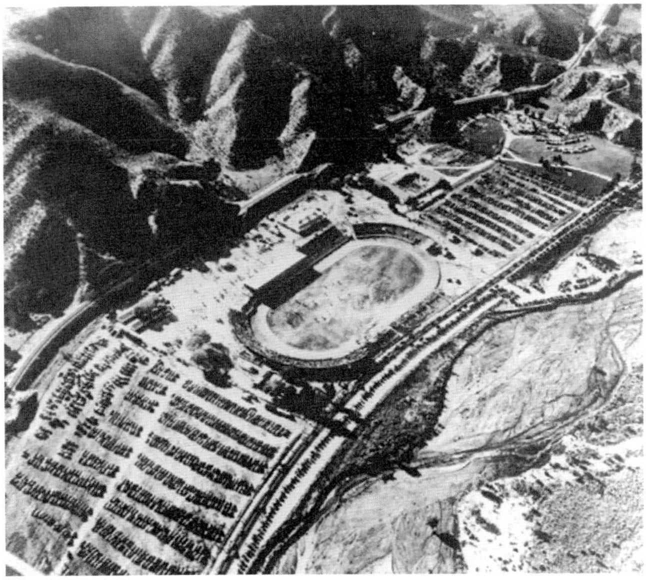

William Bonelli

Los Angeles city council member William Bonelli was once accused by the *Los Angeles Times* of taking bribes. Following an indictment, he fled to Mexico. In spite of this, Bonelli was named Outstanding Citizen of the Year by the Newhall-Saugus Chamber of Commerce in 1966. He was cleared of all charges just before his death in 1970. The aerial photograph of the Bonelli Speedway was taken in the 1950s.

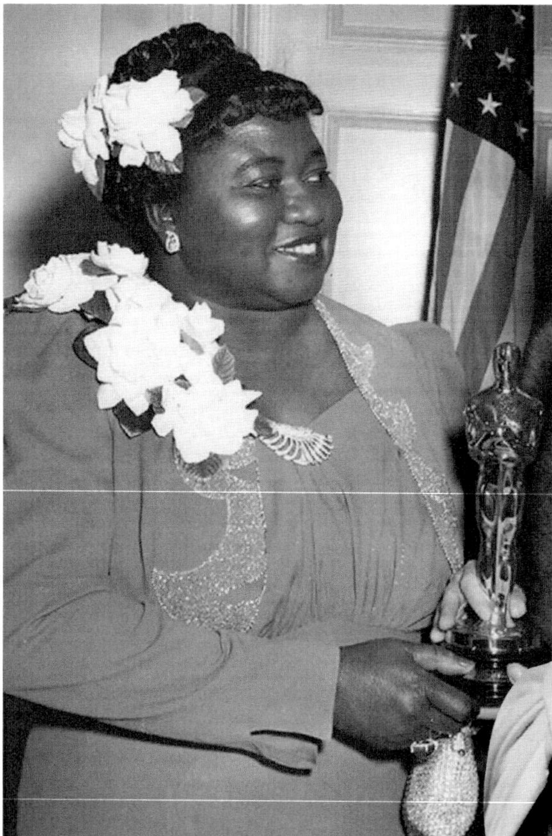

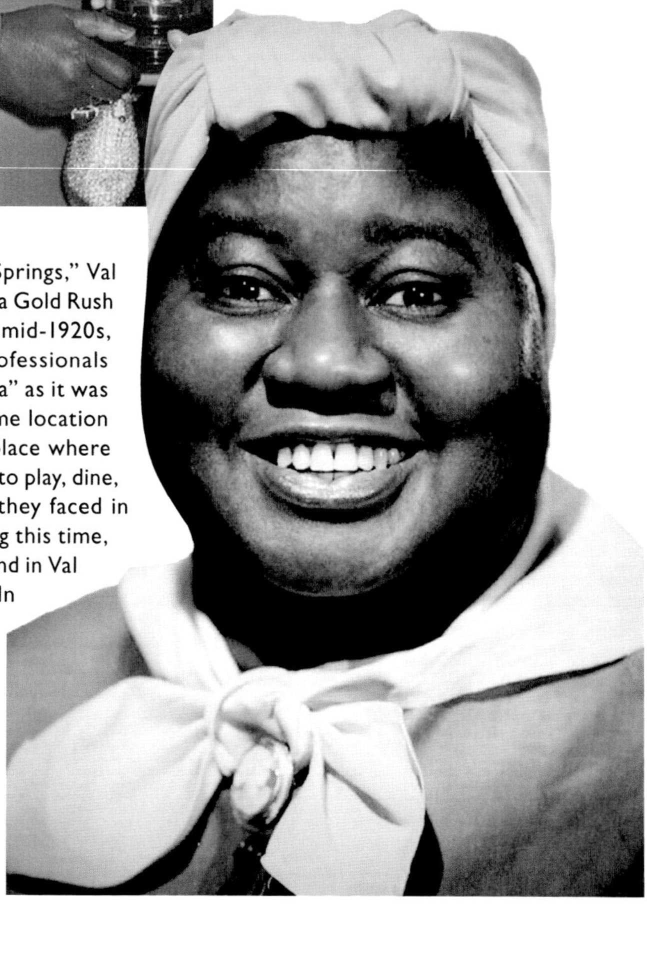

Hattie McDaniel
Once known as the "Black Palm Springs," Val Verde was originally established as a Gold Rush boom town in the 1800s. In the mid-1920s, a group of African-American professionals decided that Val Verde, or "Eureka" as it was known for a time, would be a prime location for a black resort community, a place where families could come for a weekend to play, dine, and find relief from restrictions they faced in other areas of Los Angeles. During this time, many black professionals bought land in Val Verde and built summer homes. In 1939, a community pool was built, and actress Hattie McDaniel, who was filming *Gone with the Wind* at the time, was on hand for the dedication festivities. McDaniel is pictured at right in a publicity shot from 1939, and above, holding the Oscar she won the following year.

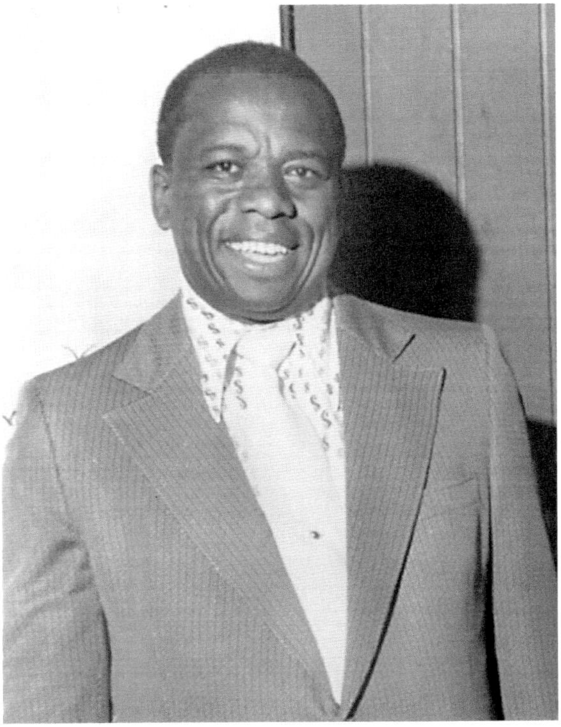

Samuel Dixon and Miriam Canty
Rev. Samuel Dixon (pictured here in 1973) and Miriam Canty worked together to establish the first Samuel Dixon Family Health Center. It opened in the annex of Dixon's church in Val Verde in 1980. With the support of the Henry Mayo Newhall and Santa Monica Hospitals, the center now has three Santa Clarita locations with the goal of providing quality, low-cost medical care to uninsured Santa Clarita families.

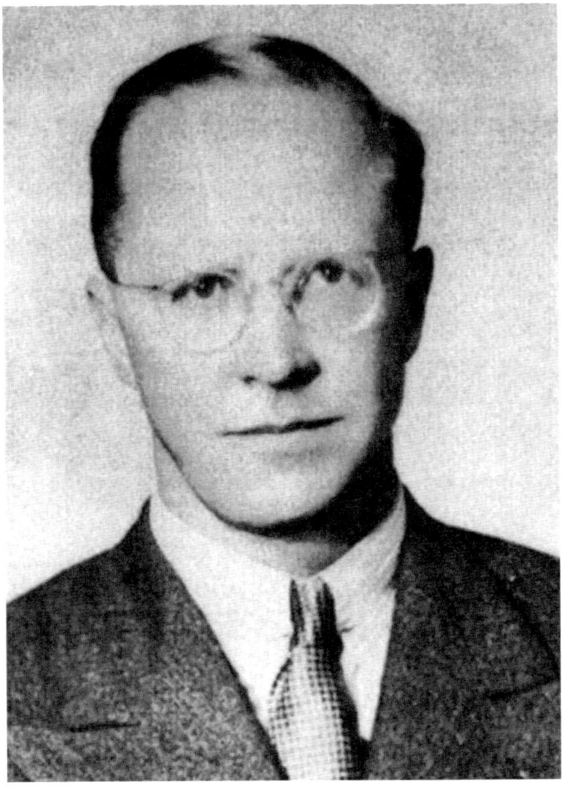

August Rubel
Swiss native August Rubel (pictured here) purchased Rancho Camulos in 1924. Rubel did much to protect its Mission architecture and to preserve the history of the Del Valle family and the *Ramona* phenomenon (see page 30). Rubel served his country in both World War I and II. He was killed in Tunisia in 1943 while driving an ambulance that hit a German mine.

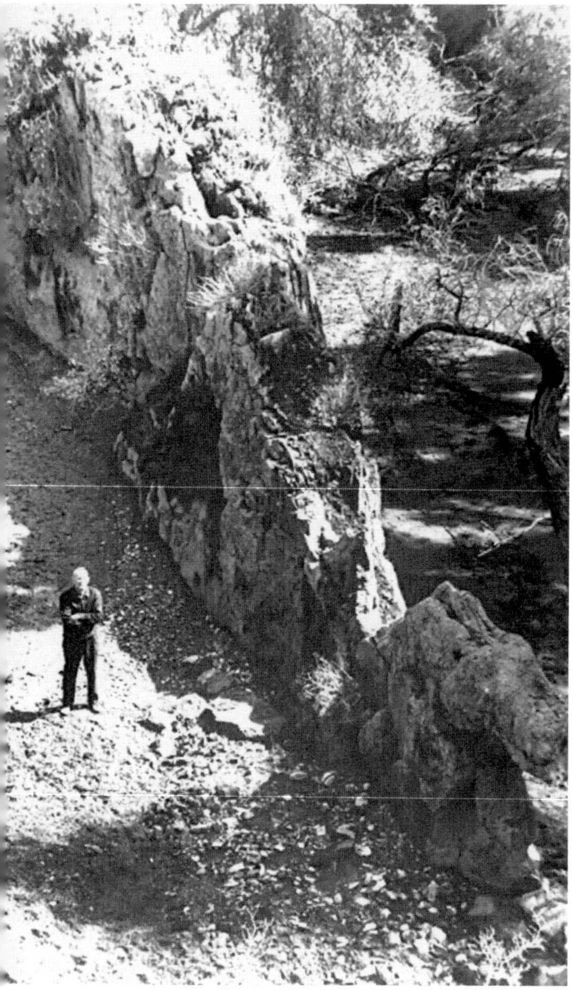

A.B. Perkins

Arthur B. Perkins, seen here hiking the old wagon road at the bottom of Elsmere Canyon in 1963, managed the local water company, served as justice of the peace, and organized Newhall's early Fourth of July parades. In retirement, he passionately collected photographs and historical documents related to the SCV's early years. If not for him, much of the history of the Santa Clarita Valley would have been lost forever. (Courtesy Ted Lamkin.)

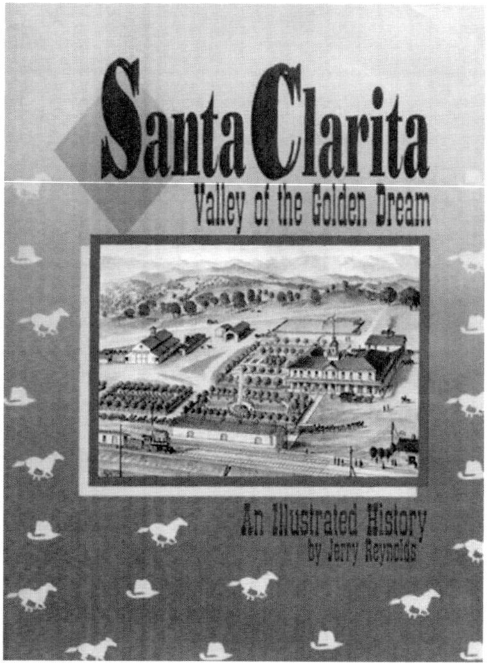

Jerry Reynolds

Jerry Reynolds worked as a private investigator and tour guide at Hearst Castle before moving to Newhall in 1971. Reynolds became one of the valley's premier local historians, helping to organize the Santa Clarita Valley Historical Society. Pictured is the cover of *Santa Clarita: Valley of the Golden Dream*, which Reynolds wrote in 1992.

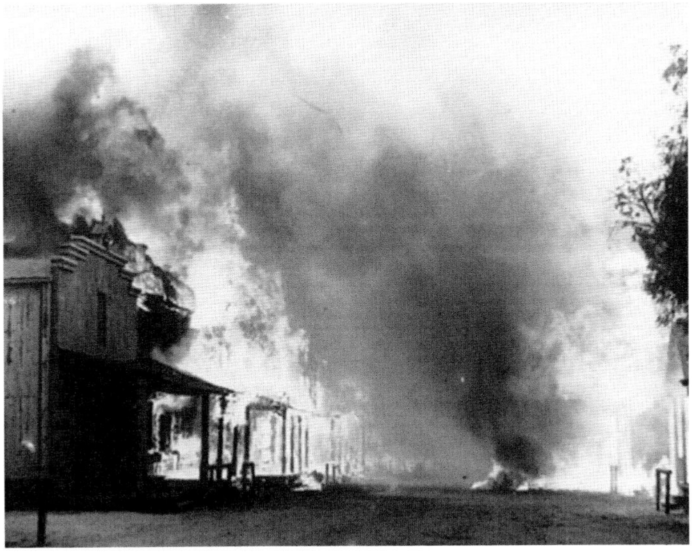

Fred Trueblood
Fred Trueblood ran *The Newhall Signal* for two decades. He did not just report the news, he occasionally created it. In 1955, Trueblood heard cries for help coming from a boy who had wandered onto the grounds of Melody Ranch and fallen into a pool of water. He rescued the boy and in the process added "local hero" to his resume. Trueblood snapped this photograph of Melody Ranch burning in 1962.

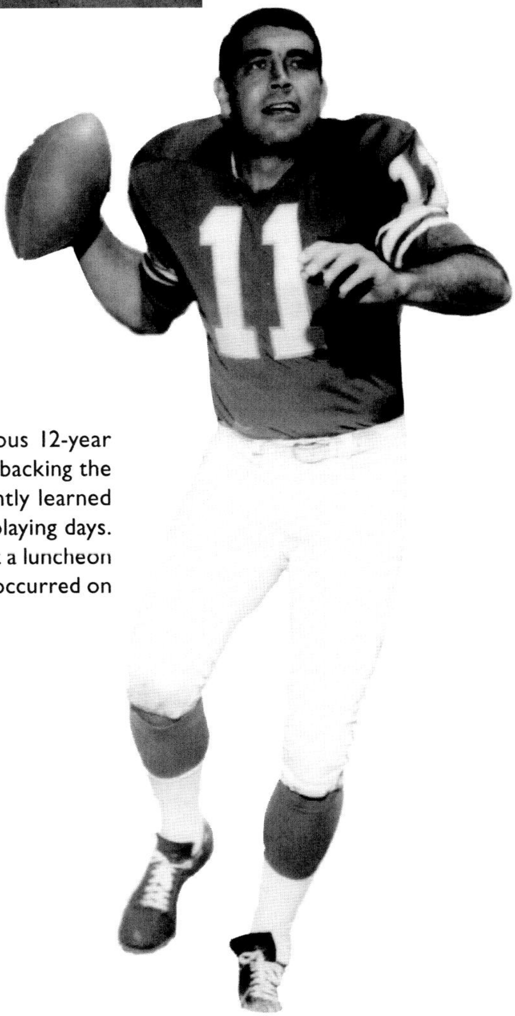

Joe Kapp
Hart High School alum Joe Kapp had an illustrious 12-year career in the NFL and CFL in the 1960s, quarterbacking the Minnesota Vikings to Super Bowl IV. He apparently learned to hold a grudge as well as a football during his playing days. In 2011, the 74-year-old Kapp got into a fistfight at a luncheon with another former player over an incident that occurred on the field in 1963!

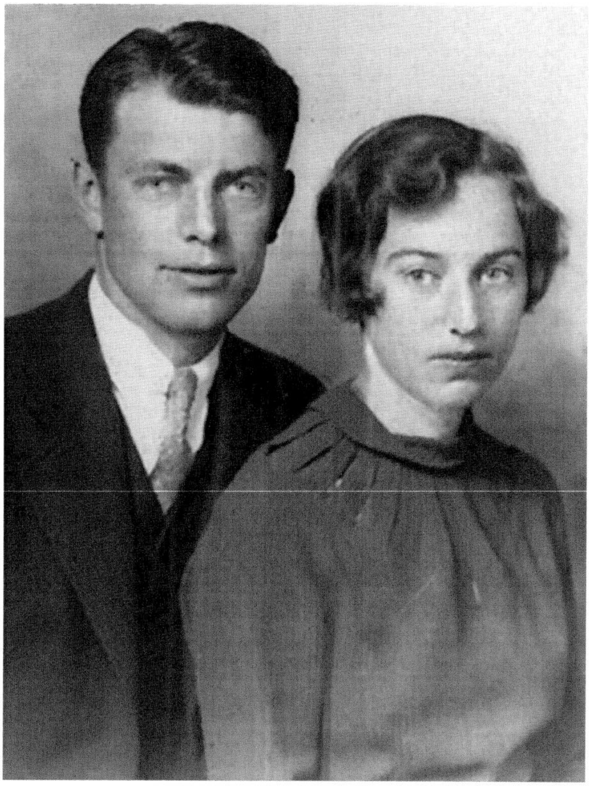

Scott Newhall

Forever the scrapper, Scott Newhall (pictured with wife, Ruth) took on lots of foes during his newspaper career (including a horse, which cost him a leg). Newhall started as a photographer for the *San Francisco Chronicle* in 1934, despite having no idea how to develop a picture. As editor, he launched the career of advice columnist Popo Phillips (better known as Abigail Van Buren, or *Dear Abby*), and in 1963 purchased the *Newhall Signal.* Newhall not only shares a name with one of the valley's towns, but provided the name for another. When asked to recommend a moniker for the valley's new planned community, Scott suggested the name Valencia. The bottom photograph from the *Chronicle* in the 1940s shows Ruth and Scott at the far right. Noted columnist Herb Caen is one of the two men on the left.

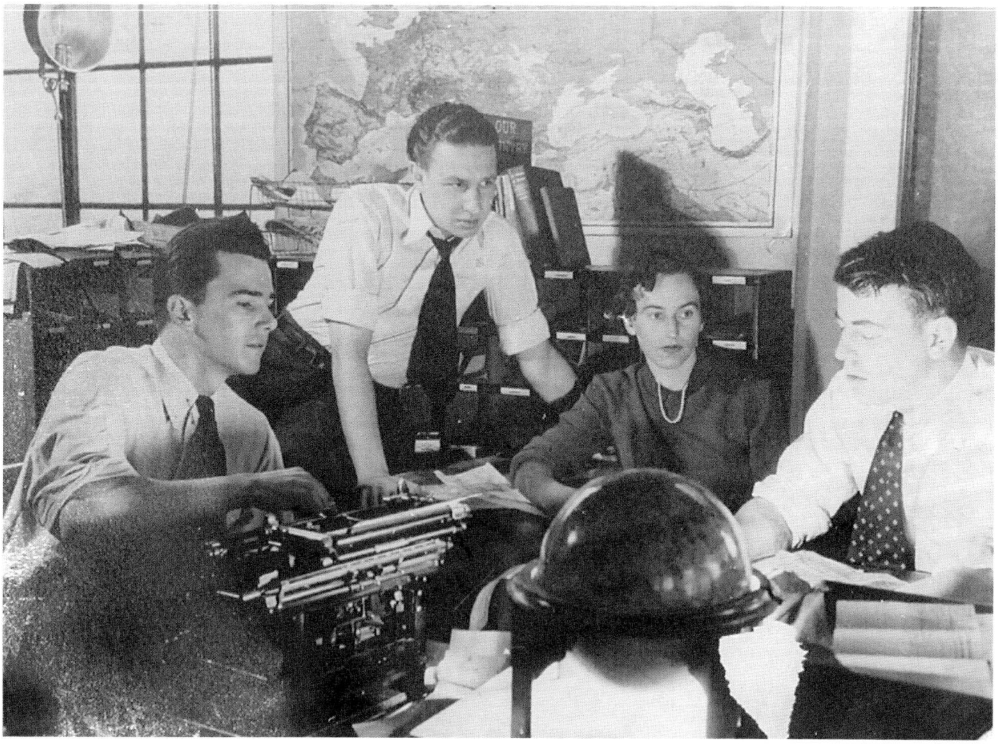

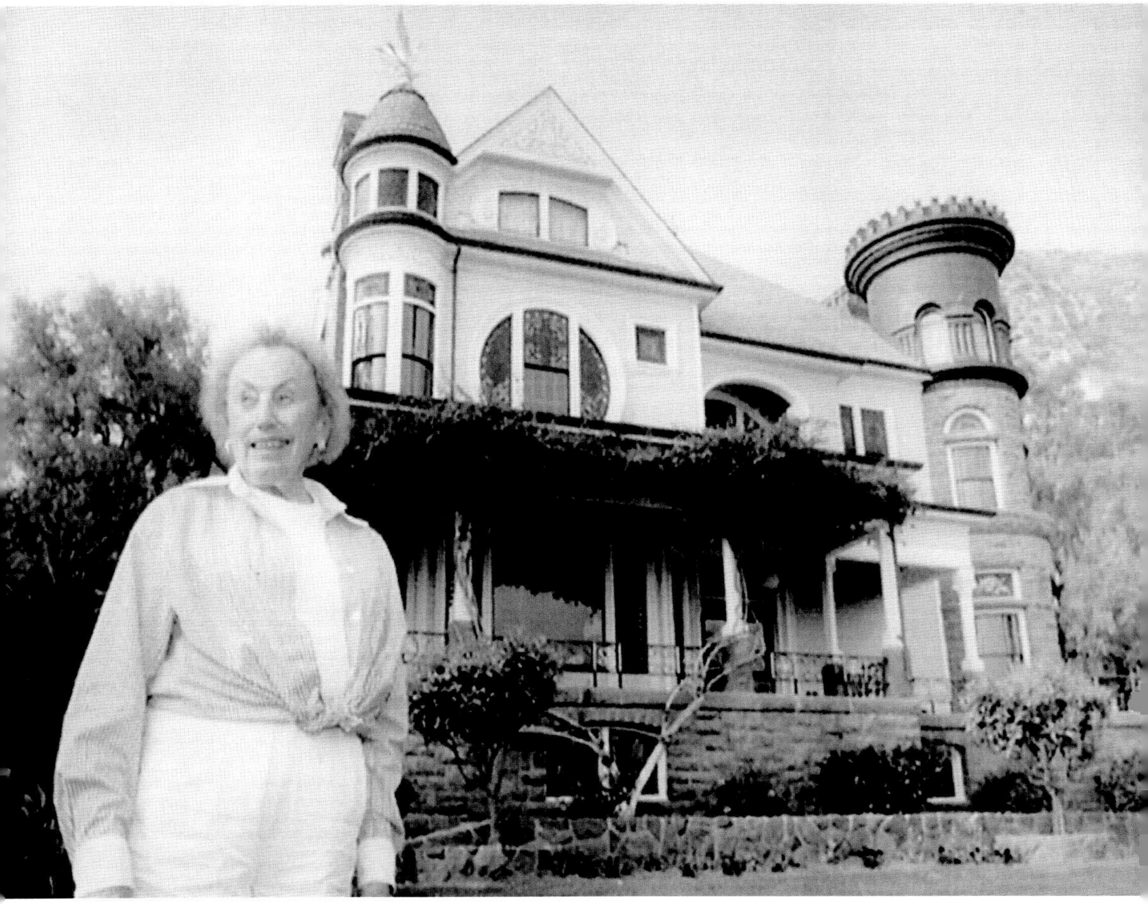

Ruth Newhall

As editor for *The Newhall Signal*, Ruth Newhall was known for her wit and stoic demeanor. She created a "Demon Rum" section to publish names of drunk drivers and featured a column called "The Gossip of Mimi" in which she lampooned the prominent people of the valley. In 1980, Ruth spearheaded the move of the Saugus Train Station from its former location to Heritage Junction, three miles to the south. To save the historic structure, the Santa Clarita Valley Historical Society needed $50,000. Ruth measured the length and calculated that each foot would cost $3. To mark the progress of the campaign, Ruth used her own car, a beaten-up 1968 Ford Ranchero, which she parked along the route with a sandwich-board sign in the back that read, "Our station has reached this point. Your $3 moves it one foot." Each night she would count the donations sent in, then convert the money to feet and inches. Her husband, Scott Newhall, would drive her to the car, where she would pace off the distance, and move the Ranchero the exact distance farther south down Railroad Avenue, and leave it parked there for the next 24 hours. Passersby were fascinated to see the Ranchero slowly inch its way south. Even schoolchildren chipped in and would come running out to pose by the car, proud of how far they helped move the station. At one point a $100 donation check bounced, and Ruth wrote in her "Mimi" column that the car was being moved back 33 feet because of the loss of funds. But this story got so much sympathy that even more donations poured in (and the check ultimately cleared). Finally in mid-June, the Ranchero arrived at its destination in Hart Park. In the early morning hours of June 24, 1980, the money Ruth Newhall and her old Ranchero helped raise—foot-by-foot—was joyfully spent moving the historic structure to its new home at Heritage Junction in Newhall, where it can be seen today. In this photograph from *The Newhall Signal*, Ruth stands in front of her Victorian Piru mansion in March 1993.

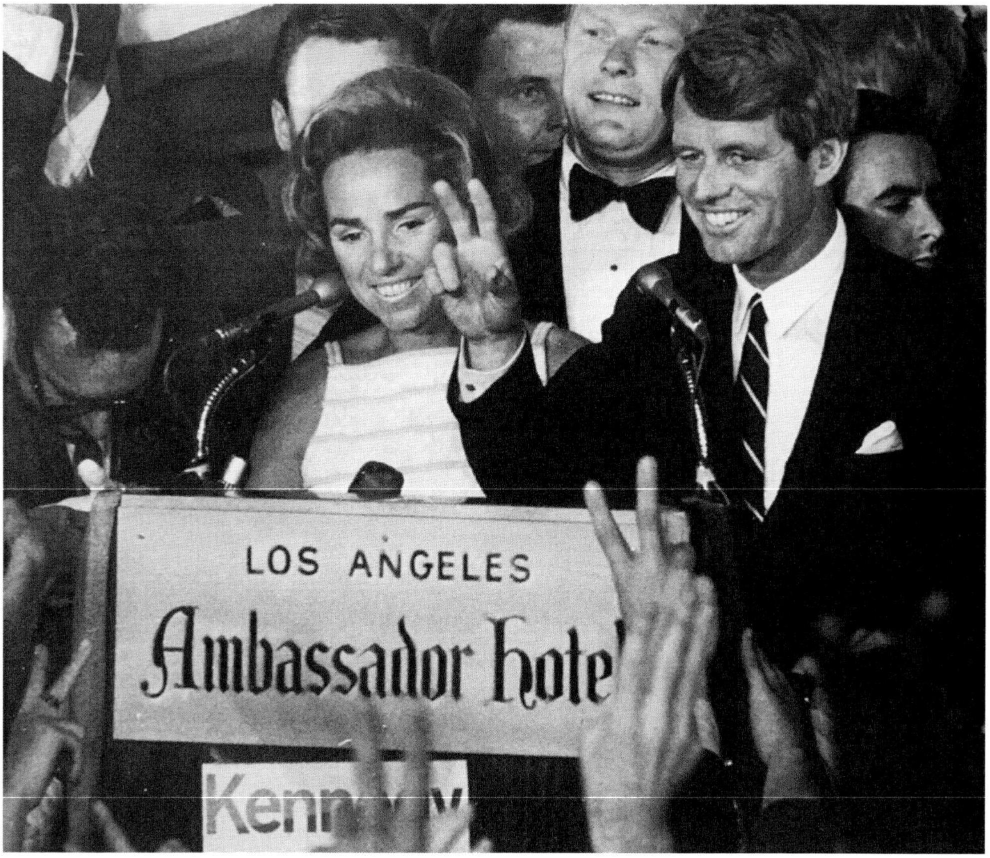

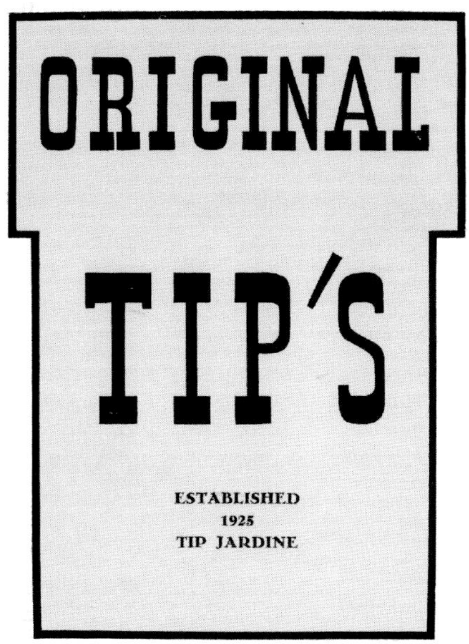

Art and Betty Evans

When Sirhan Sirhan shot Robert F. Kennedy at the Ambassador Hotel, Sand Canyon resident Betty Evans was standing nearby and miraculously survived a shot to the head. Betty's husband, Art Evans, was the editor of *The Sentinel*. Like his village-naming rival Scott Newhall at *The Newhall Signal*, Evans provided Canyon Country with its name. This photograph of RFK was taken just minutes before he was gunned down in June 1968.

Bobby Batugo

Tip Jardine opened his first restaurant in the SCV in 1948. In time, a trio of popular Tip's eateries dotted Highway 99 in the valley. One of the draws was acclaimed "mixologist" Bobby Batugo, who arrived from the Philippines at age 20 and began tending bar during Prohibition in speakeasies. Moving to the valley, the gregarious Batugo was proclaimed the world's greatest bartender after winning several international competitions. Pictured is a Tip's menu from 1956.

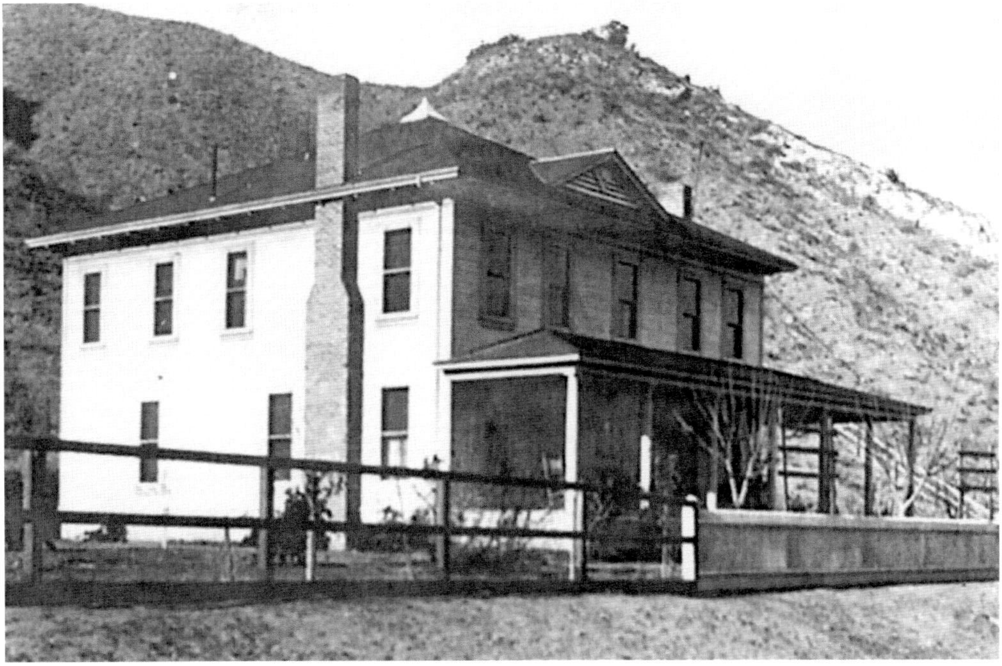

Carol and Frenchy Lagasse

In 1966, Carol and Frenchy Lagasse and their three daughters—Nanette, Laurette, and Suzette—were living in Saugus when they learned that Chevron, Frenchy's employer, was planning to tear down the "Big House" at the ghost town of Mentryville. Rather than see a house they loved fall to the wrecker's ball, they decided to move in and save the former home of renowned oilman Alexander Mentry, which had become the domicile of birds and honeybees. The Lagasses transformed the Big House into an antique-filled showcase and rebuilt the Felton School and other buildings. They remained in Mentryville until the 1994 Northridge earthquake rendered the Big House uninhabitable. The Lagasses moved on, but thanks to their love of an old house, visitors are still enjoying Mentryville today. The undated top photograph is of the Big House. The bottom photograph is of Mentryville around 1900.

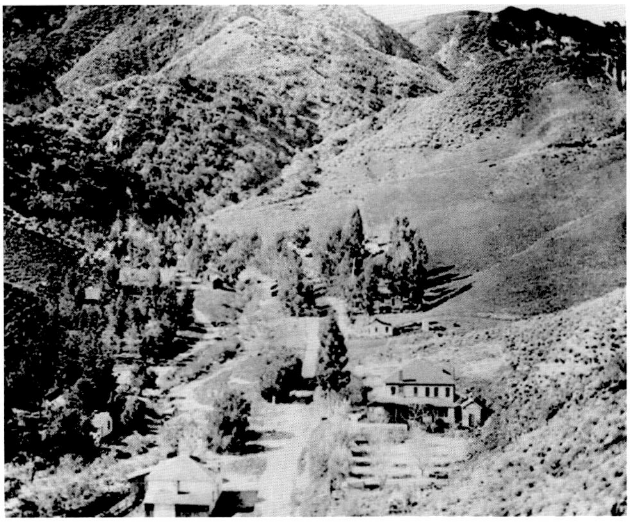

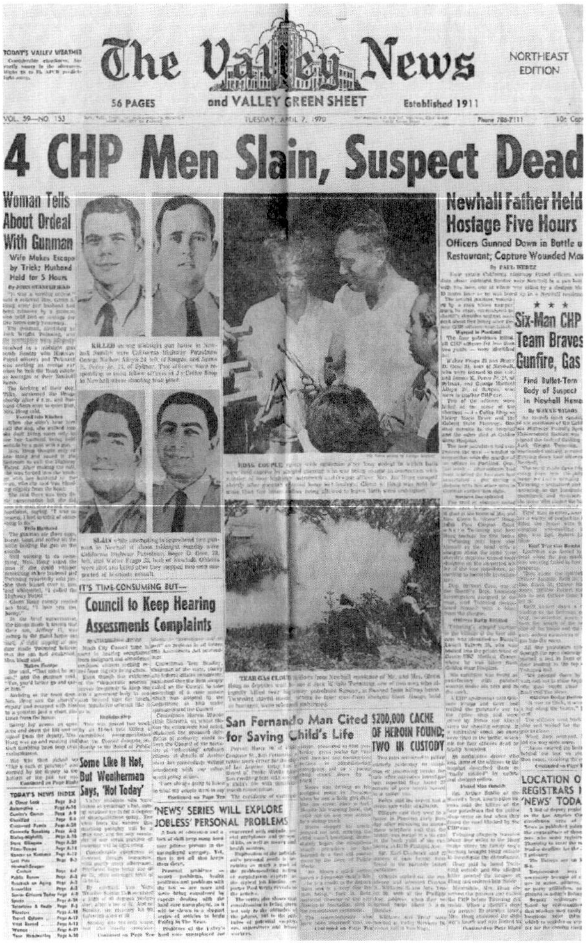

The Valley News and VALLEY GREEN SHEET

NORTHEAST EDITION

56 PAGES

Established 1911

4 CHP Men Slain, Suspect Dead

Woman Tells About Ordeal With Gunman

Newhall Father Held Hostage Five Hours

Six-Man CHP Team Braves Gunfire, Gas

IT'S TIME-CONSUMING BUT—

Council to Keep Hearing Assessments Complaints

Some Like It Hot, But Weatherman Says, 'Not Today'

San Fernando Man Cited for Saving Child's Life

$200,000 CACHE OF HEROIN FOUND; TWO IN CUSTODY

'NEWS' SERIES WILL EXPLORE JOBLESS' PERSONAL PROBLEMS

George Alleyn, Walt Frago, Roger Gore, Skip Pence

One of the Santa Clarita Valley's most horrific events happened on the evening of April 5, 1970. That night, four California Highway Patrol officers named George Alleyn, Walt Frago, Roger Gore, and James "Skip" Pence were brutally gunned down by two career criminals in the parking lot of a service station in what is now Valencia. The two killers, Jack Twinning and Bobby Davis, were ex-cons who had recently arrived in California with plans to rob an armored truck. In search of explosives for the heist, they drove to a construction site in the SCV alongside Highway 99. Road rage ensued after Davis nearly sideswiped a car while making a U-turn, threatening the other car's occupants with a revolver. The driver pulled over and reported the incident to police, who quickly located the vehicle traveling southbound towards Newhall. Officers Gore and Frago followed the suspects as they pulled into a gas station. While Gore patted down Davis, Frago covered him with a shotgun. Twinning suddenly jumped out of the car and fatally shot Frago. Startled by the shots, Gore was distracted just long enough for Davis to pull a gun and shoot him. At that moment, officers Pence and Alleyn arrived to find their two comrades lying on the pavement. A gun battle ensued, and both Pence and Alleyn were killed. Davis and Twinning took off on foot in opposite directions. Twinning barricaded himself inside a home, where he shot himself to death after the house was surrounded by police. Davis was apprehended, convicted, and given the death penalty. His sentence was later commuted to life in prison where Davis remained until committing suicide in August 2009. April 5, 1970, was the single bloodiest day in the history of the California Highway Patrol, but officers Gore, Frago, Pence, and Alleyn did not die in vain. As a direct result of their sacrifice, police safety procedures were updated, saving countless lives across the country. The photograph is from the front page of *The Valley News and Valley Green Sheet,* dated April 7, 1970.

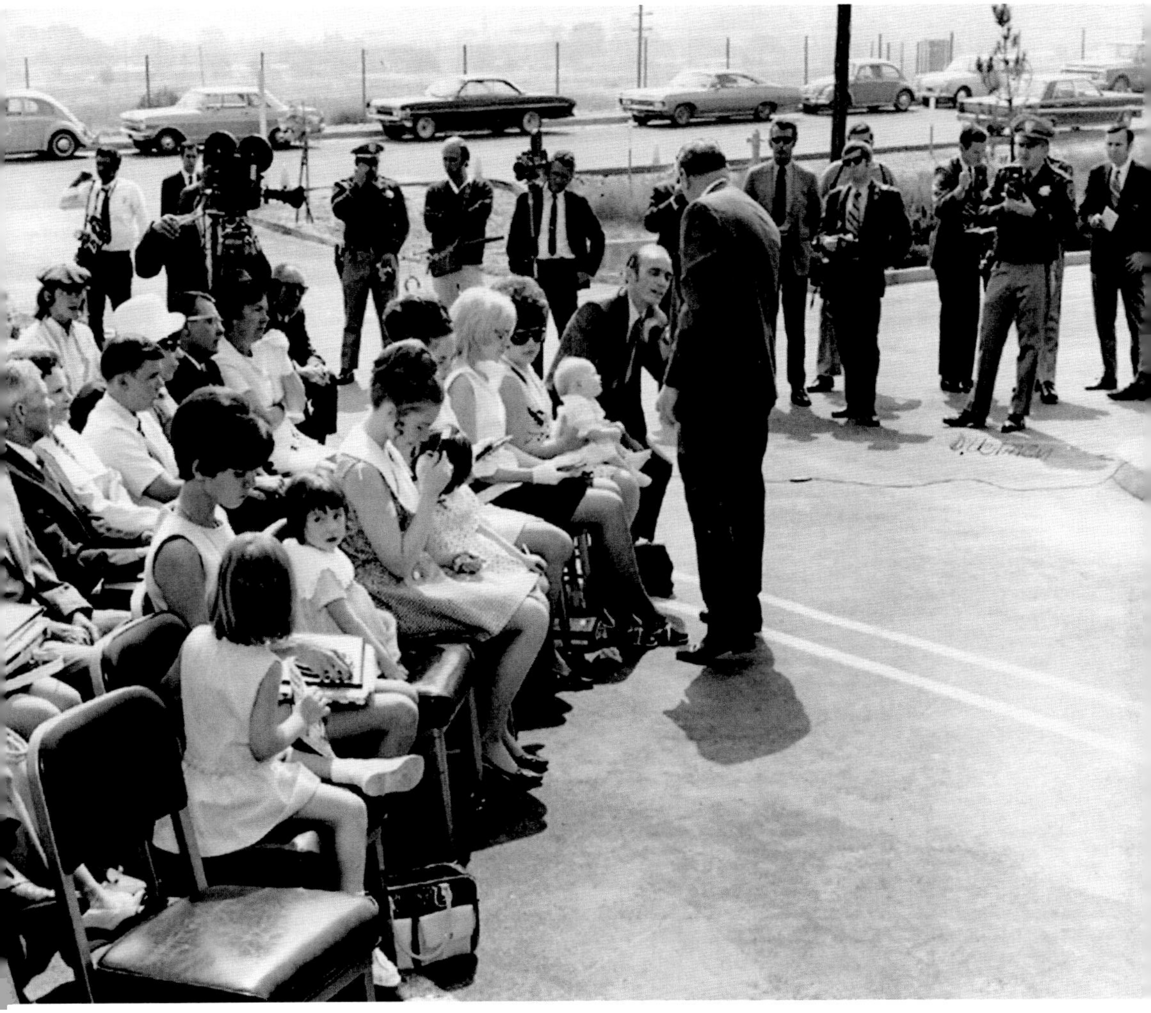

Gary Kness

Great tragedy is often coupled with great heroism, and the "Newhall Incident" is no exception. Gary Dean Kness was driving by J's Coffee Shop on his way to work on the evening of April 5, 1970, when he witnessed a gun battle taking place at the Standard gas station next door. At first, he thought filmmakers from Hollywood were making a movie, but when he saw one of the wounded officers fall to the ground, he realized this was the real thing. Kness ran to the officer's side in an attempt to pull him out of the line of fire and saw one of the killers approaching with a sawed-off shotgun. An ex-Marine, Kness instinctively picked up the downed officer's shotgun and fired at the man, but the weapon was empty. He then picked up a revolver and squeezed off a single shot, wounding the gunman. Seeing he could provide no further aid, he dashed into a ditch where he remained until backup officers arrived. Two months after the shooting, Kness was honored for his heroic efforts at a memorial wall dedication ceremony (pictured here), which took place at the Highway Patrol office on the Old Road. He was again honored in April 2008 when a portion of Interstate 5 was named for the four downed officers. A year later, he was similarly recognized at William S. Hart Park at an event sponsored by the Santa Clarita Valley Historical Society. The Newhall Incident was the worst massacre of police officers in the 80-year history of the California Highway Patrol. Rather than remain simply a tragic tale from the past, it has helped improve police procedures nationwide. It also created a true American hero.

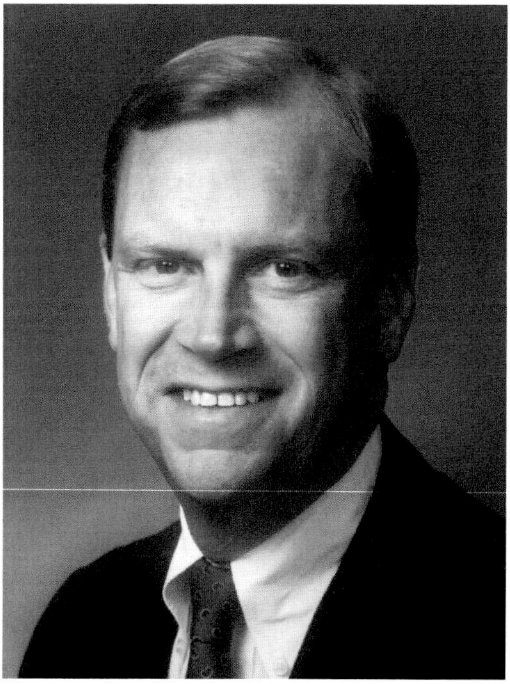

Tom Lee

As Newhall Land chief executive officer, Tom Lee insisted that every executive be involved with the community. Lee set a fine example by helping establish the local YMCA and chairing campaigns for the SCV United Way and the Child & Family Center. A board member of the SCV Boys and Girls Club, he was their Man of the Year in 1974 and later the SCV Man of the Year in 2000. (Courtesy Leon Worden.)

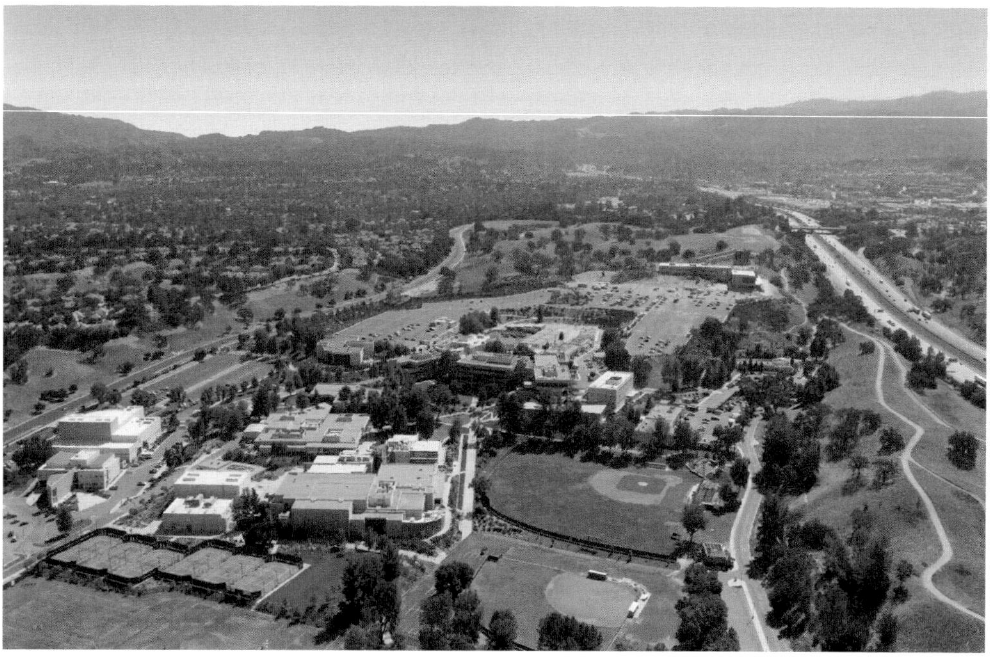

Robert C. Rockwell

As the first president of College of the Canyons, Robert C. Rockwell helped transform it from a small night school with 700 students to the sprawling 24,000-student campus that exists today. Rockwell hired the first instructors, developed new curriculums, and directed construction of the first permanent buildings on campus. He envisioned a broad range of programs encompassing academics, sports, the arts, and vocational opportunities. Above is a recent aerial photograph of the College of the Canyons.

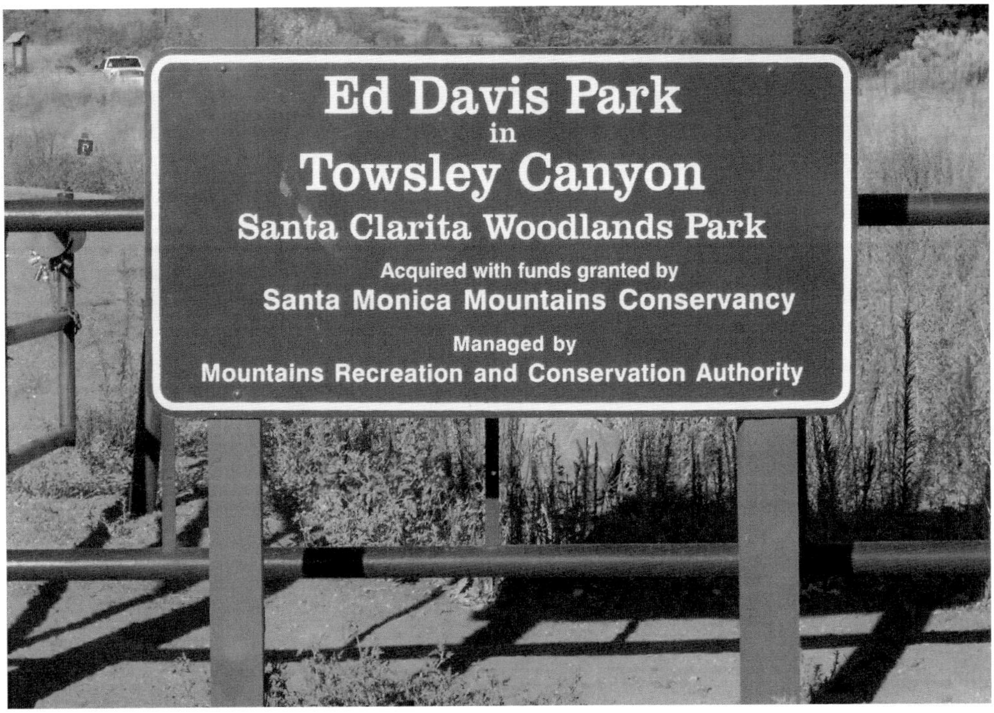

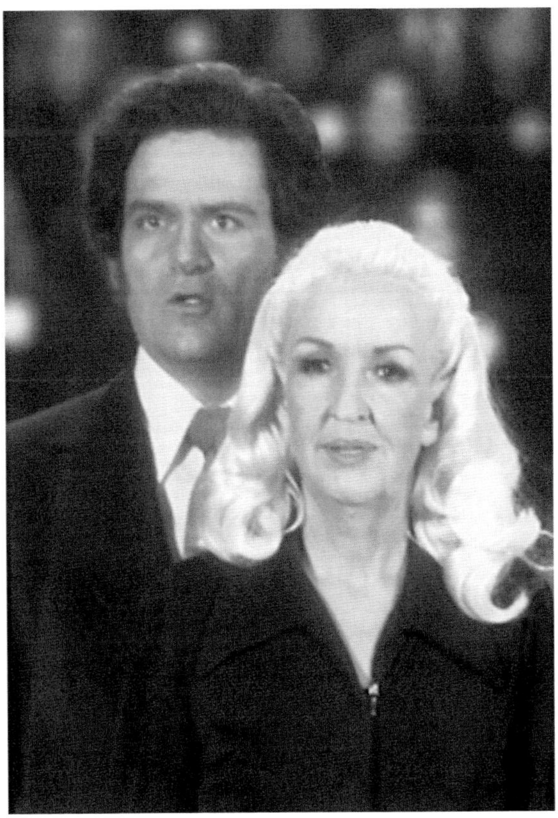

Ed Davis
Ed Davis Park in Towsley Canyon is named for the former California state senator who was responsible for the protection of the 3,000-acre Santa Clarita Woodlands State Park. During his controversial stint as Los Angeles police chief, Davis's LAPD arrested Charles Manson and shot it out with the Symbionese Liberation Army. Chief Davis once made headlines by advocating the reinstatement of the death penalty for airline hijackers.

Tony Alamo
The Santa Clarita Valley is not without its share of notorious characters. Bernie Lazar "Tony Alamo" Hoffman, the charismatic leader of Tony Alamo Christian Ministries, has long been a controversial figure. Alamo, pictured here in 1982 with his second wife, Susan, established a religious compound on Sierra Highway in 1967. Despite being incarcerated on a 175-year sentence for child molestation, Alamo still has many loyal followers.

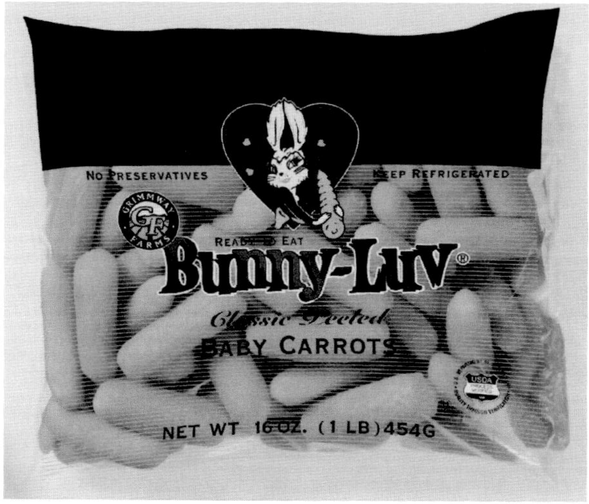

Mike and Sue Yurosek

Everybody loves a baby. Mike Yurosek invented the mini carrot in the mid-1980s because he was tired of seeing tons of imperfect carrots thrown away at his packing plant. Instead, the Santa Clarita Valley farmer cut the discards into two-inch pieces, simultaneously reducing waste and enjoying huge success marketing them as "baby" carrots. Mike's wife, Sue, came up with the logo, and today Bunny-Luv carrots (pictured above) are found in supermarkets across the country. Mike passed away in 2005, but Sue remains a passionate supporter of local history as a member of the board of directors of the SCV Historical Society. She supports historic building restoration through the local Questers group. One of the buildings the group restored was the Kingsburry House (below) at Heritage Junction.

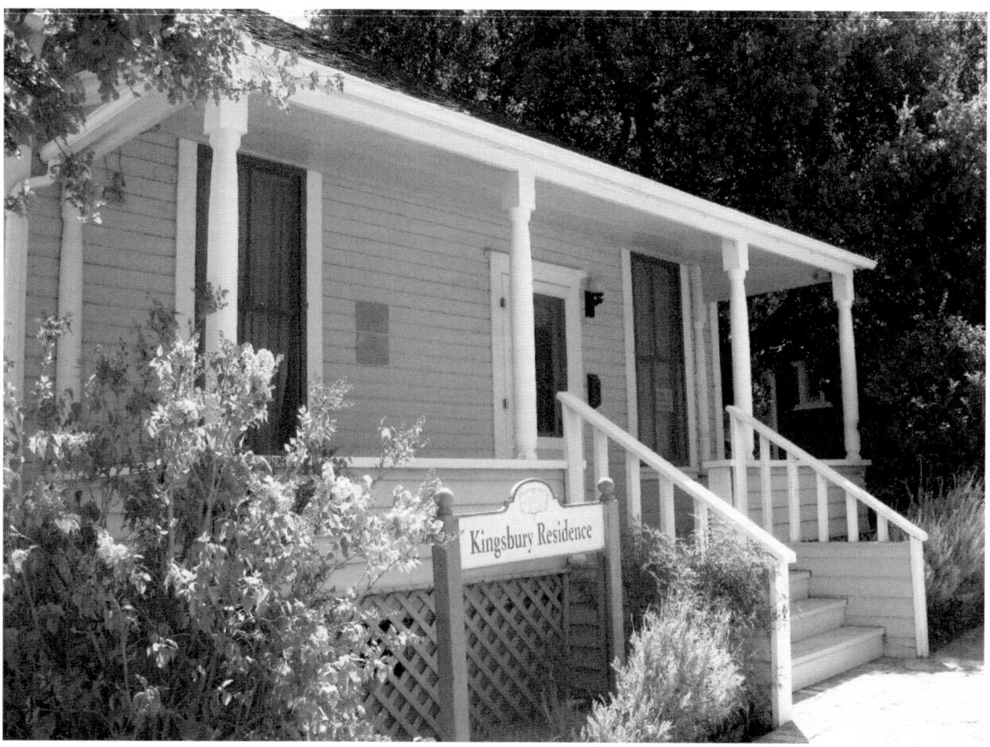

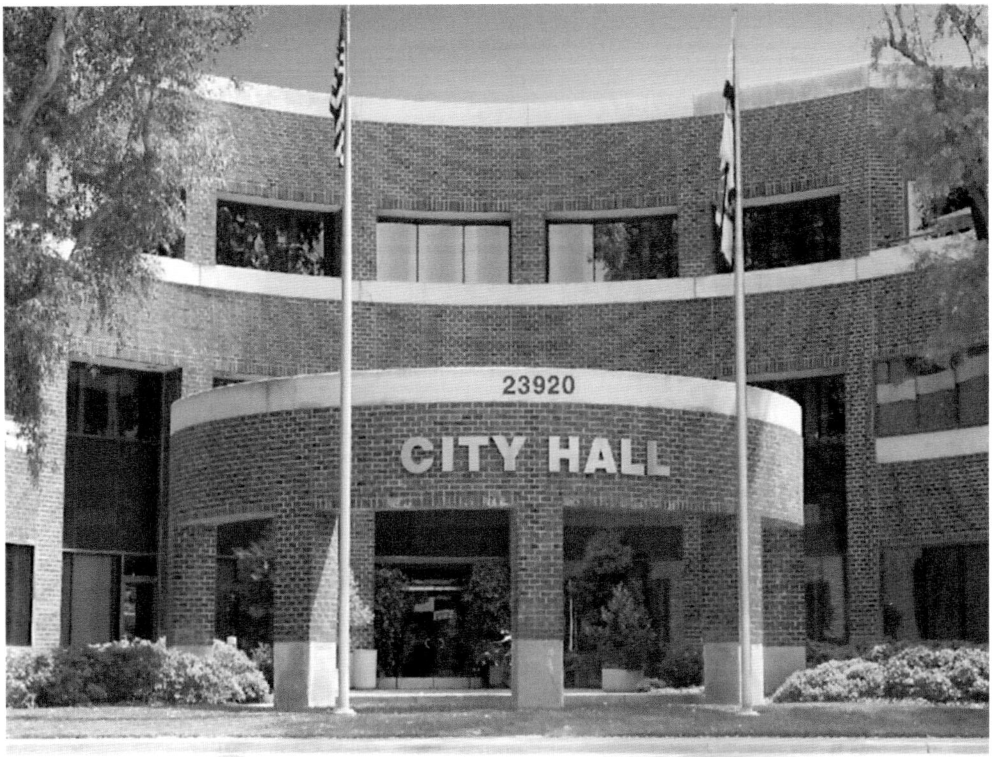

Santa Clarita City Founders
After a difficult labor, the city of Santa Clarita was born on November 3, 1987, when voters approved the creation of a new city comprising the towns of Newhall, Saugus, Valencia, and Canyon Country. When measures to form a new county failed, a city formation committee was assembled, consisting of Louis Garasi, Connie Worden, JoAnne Darcy, Jan Heidt, Jill Klajic, and Carl Boyer. Because of their efforts, Santa Clarita became the first city in California history to incorporate with an initial population greater than 100,000. The first city council consisted of future congressman Howard P. "Buck" McKeon, Jan Heidt, JoAnne Darcy, Dennis Koontz, and Carl Boyer.

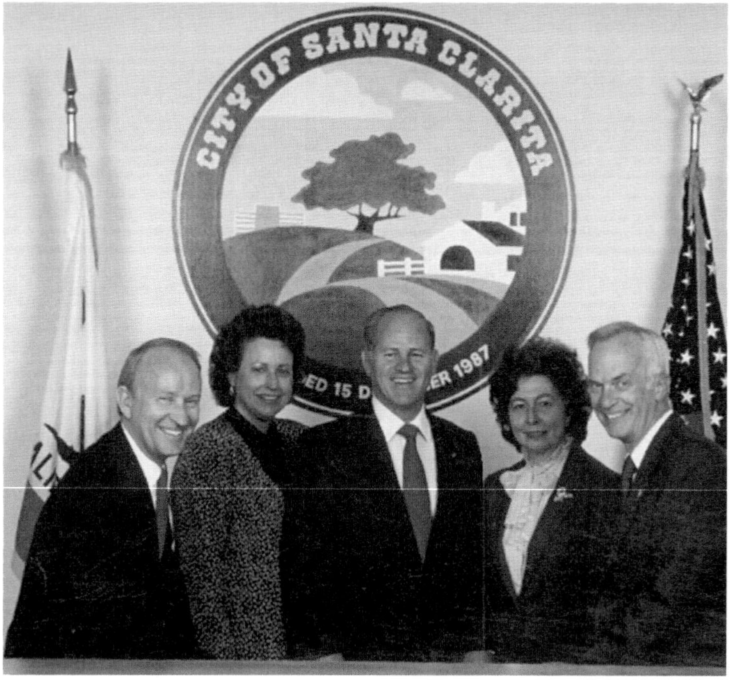

JoAnn Darcy
When an Acton gas station owner refused to sell fuel to a biker gang in 1972, they retaliated in a wild crime spree inside JoAnn Darcy's '49er Saloon. Business died after that, but Darcy went on to become one of the charter members of the Santa Clarita City Council (pictured here). From left to right are Howard P. "Buck" McKeon, Jan Heidt, Dennis Koontz, JoAnne Darcy, and Carl Boyer in 1987.

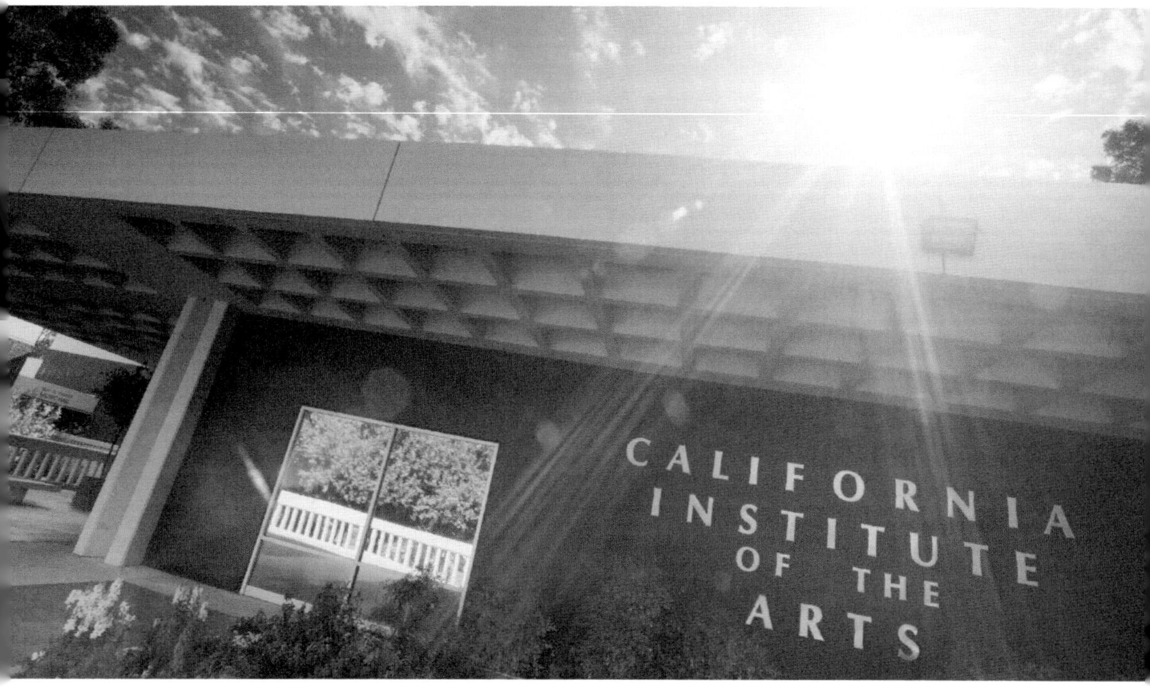

John Fuller
John Fuller pieced the shattered CalArts campus back together after the devastating 1994 Northridge earthquake. Prior to his work there, Fuller was chairman of the board at Henry Mayo Newhall Memorial Hospital, where he directed volunteer activities. In retirement, the 1979 SCV Man of the Year continues to work with the YMCA and SCV Rotary Club. (Courtesy Valencia.com.)

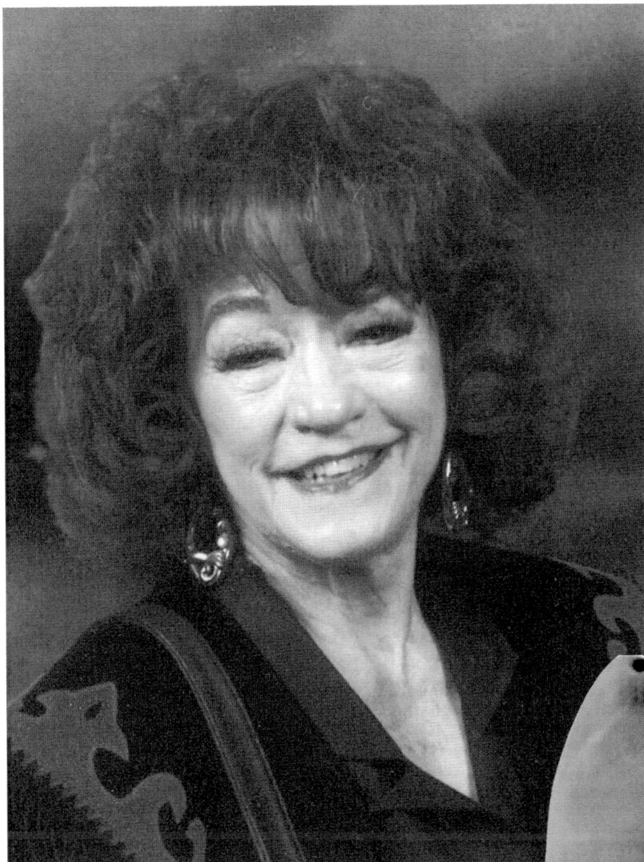

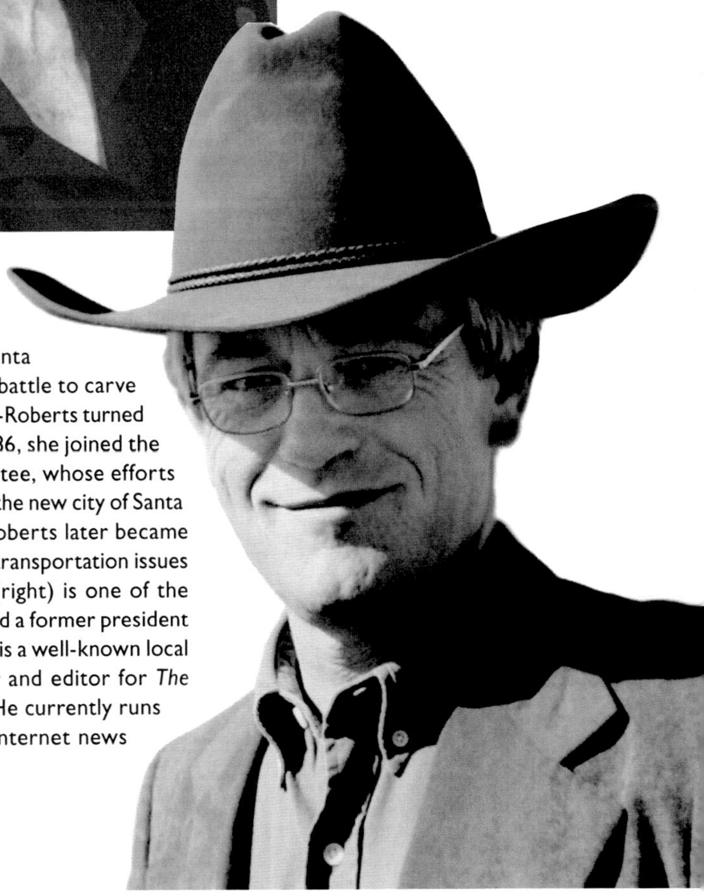

Connie Worden-Roberts and Leon Worden
Connie Worden-Roberts (above) was a "founding mother" of the city of Santa Clarita. After fighting an unsuccessful battle to carve out a new county in the region, Worden-Roberts turned her sights to creating a new city. In 1986, she joined the Santa Clarita City Formation Committee, whose efforts bore fruit on November 3, 1987, when the new city of Santa Clarita was incorporated. Worden-Roberts later became the city's "road warrior," helping solve transportation issues in the SCV. Her son Leon Worden (right) is one of the premier local historians of the valley and a former president of the SCV Historical Society. Worden is a well-known local media personality and former writer and editor for *The Santa Clarita Valley Signal* newspaper. He currently runs local television station SCVTV and internet news and information outlet SCVTV.com.

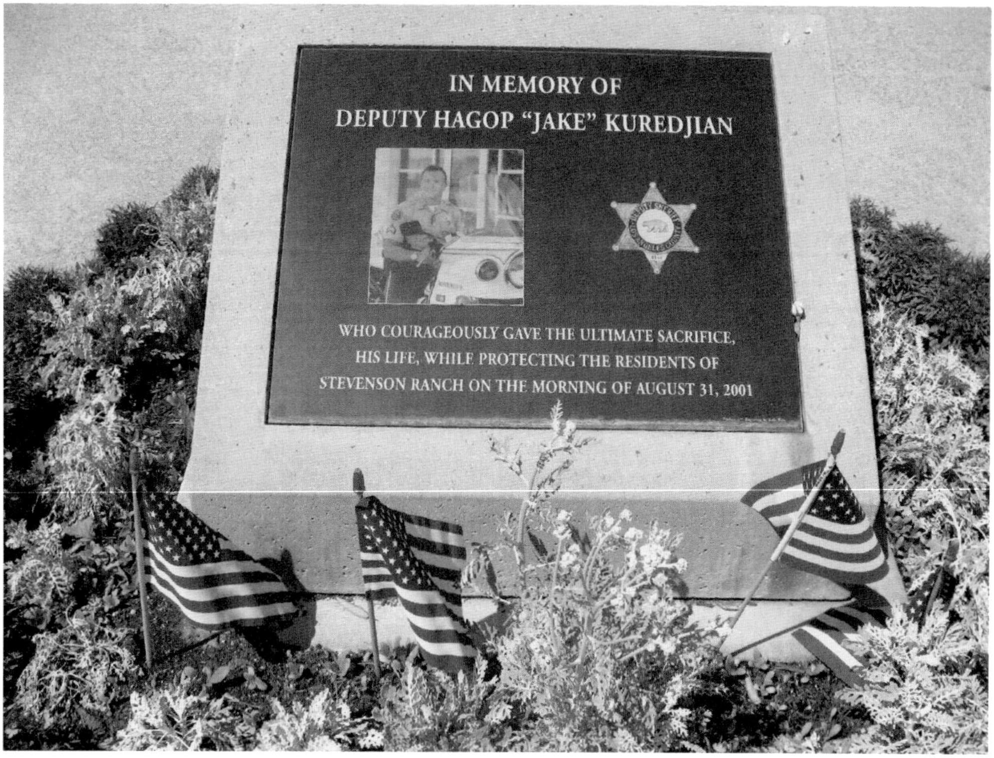

Jake Kuredjian and David March

In August 2001, L.A. County sheriff's deputy and Santa Clarita resident Hagop "Jake" Kuredjian was gunned down while assisting ATF agents serving a search warrant. Today, there is a memorial (above) and a park in Stevenson Ranch dedicated to him. Deputy David March was killed in the line of duty in April 2002 after stopping a car carrying attempted murder suspect Armando Garcia, who shot and killed March and fled to Mexico. March's widow, Teri, spent years lobbying to bring Garcia to justice. He was extradited to the United States in 2006 and received a life sentence. This memorial (below) at David March Park in Saugus contains a bell that once belonged to March's great-great-grandfather, who rang it every morning to call students to the school he built. It rang one last time at the park's dedication.

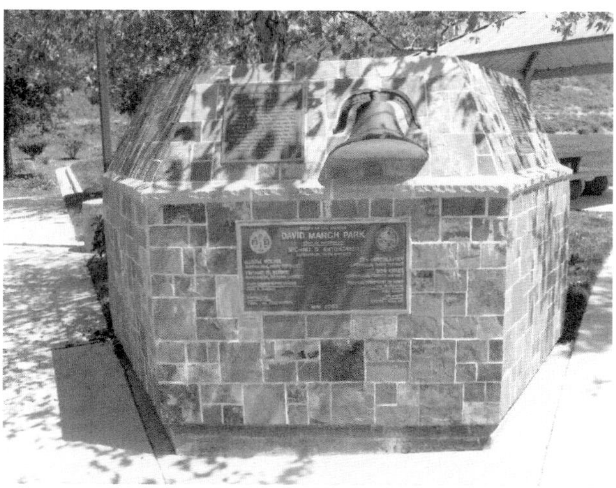

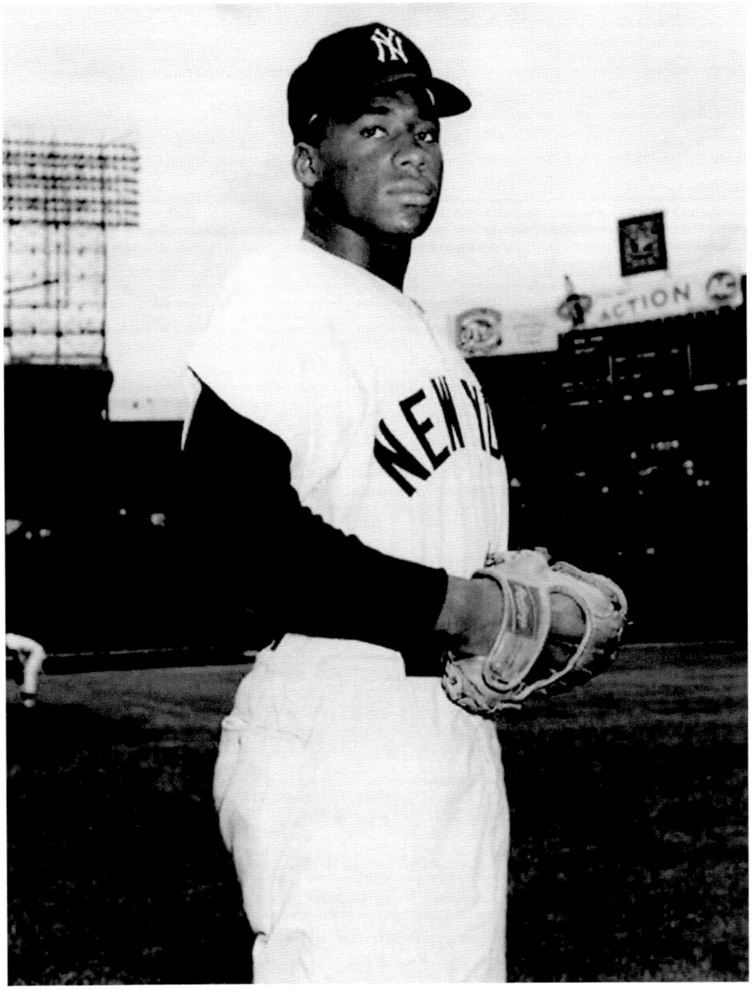

Al Downing, Bob Walk, and James Shields
At least three local men have pitched in the World Series. Hurler Al Downing (pictured in 1963), the man who gave up Hank Aaron's 715th dinger, appeared in three World Series games for the Yankees and Dodgers. Bob Walk won a game for the Phillies in 1980. In 2008, Newhall-native James Shields became the first and only Tampa Bay pitcher to ever notch a win in the series.

Duane Harte
Retired naval officer Duane Harte keeps busy shepherding a seemingly endless number of SCV organizations, including the Santa Clarita Valley Historical Society, the Friends of Mentryville (Mentryville pictured here in 2012), and the Canyon Theatre Guild. He is proud to emcee the yearly Memorial Day Celebration at Eternal Valley Cemetery, and to organize Newhall's Fourth of July Parade. Harte was the valley's Man of the Year in 2003.

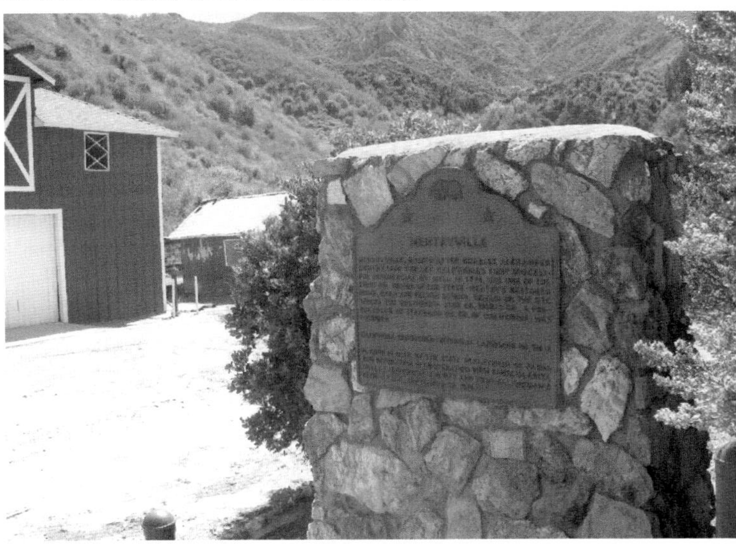

Barry Goldstein

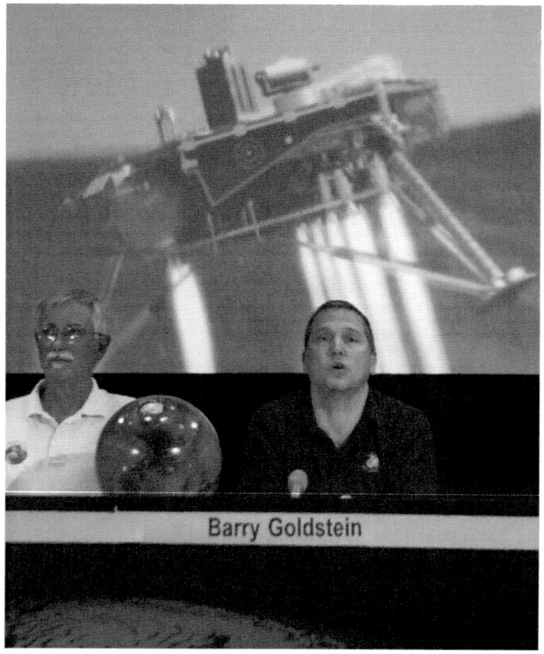

Santa Clarita resident Barry Goldstein joined NASA's Jet Propulsion Laboratory (JPL) in 1982. He was the project manager for the Mars Phoenix Scout program, dedicated to using the latest technologies to explore deep into the icy north polar region of Mars. Under Goldstein's direction, the Mars Phoenix Lander craft was credited with making the first successful landing in a Martian polar region. Goldstein is pictured briefing reporters at JPL in 2008. (Courtesy Reuters.)

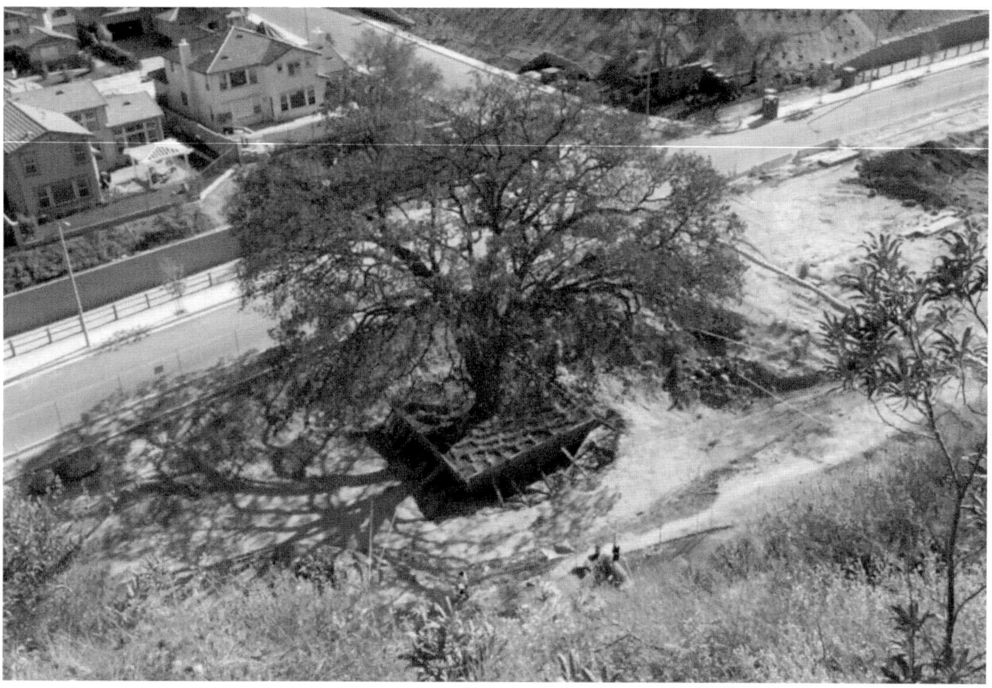

John Quigley

He just couldn't let the old tree die. In 2002, environmental activist John Quigley took up residence for 71 days on the upper branches of a 400-year-old California oak tree affectionately called "Old Glory." Quigley's actions brought national attention to the plight of Old Glory, and the developers who wanted to cut the old oak down eventually moved it to a nearby park, where it still lives today. Above is a May 2003 photograph of Old Glory being moved. (Courtesy savedoldglory.org.)

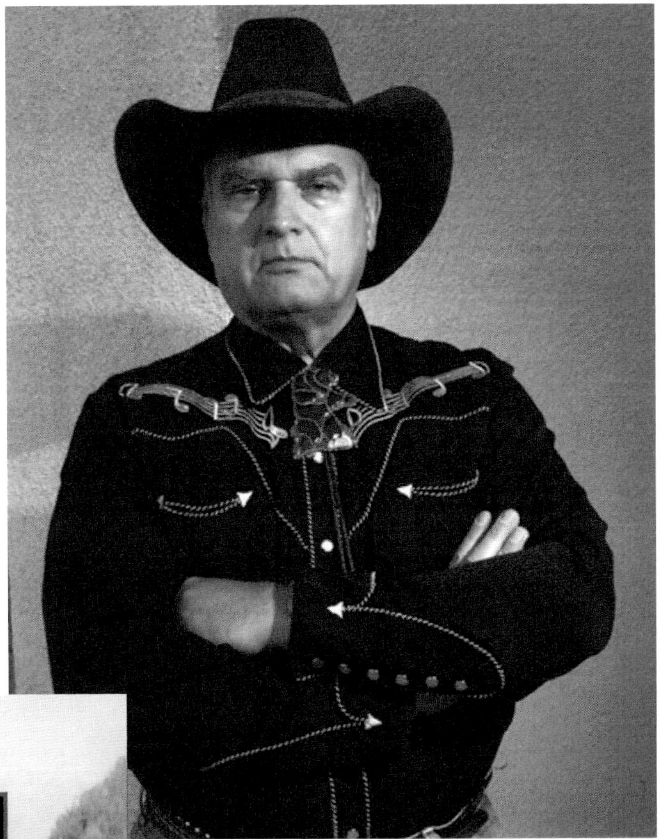

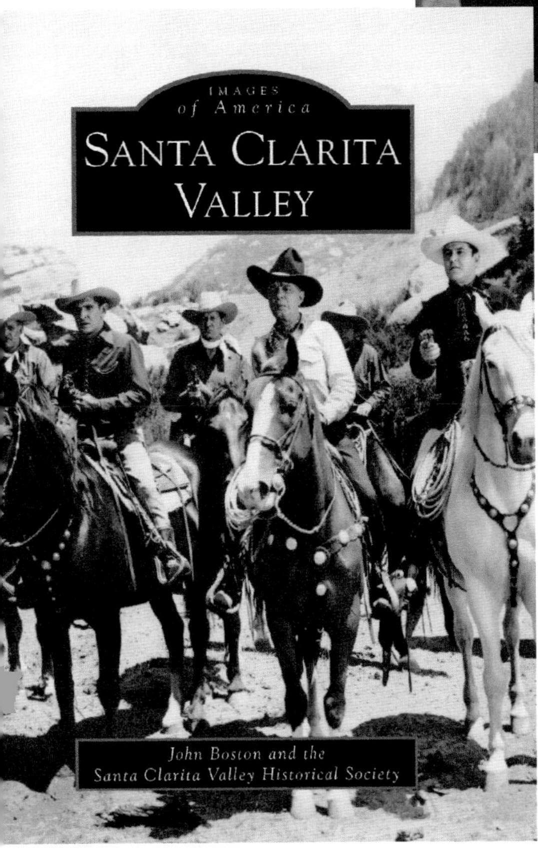

John Boston

John Boston (above), one of Santa Clarita's most beloved sons, has an impressive resume. A graduate of Hart High School in Newhall, Boston boasts 119 writing awards from high-ranking organizations and is the proud recipient of the Will Rogers Lifetime Achievement Award. He hosts a popular local radio show called *The Former Friends of John Boston* and was a frequent contributor to *The Santa Clarita Valley Signal* in Valencia. A highly-respected local historian and founder of *Santa Clarita Valley Magazine*, Boston recently authored Images of America: *The Santa Clarita Valley* (pictured left). A hilarious lecturer, "Mr. Santa Clarita" has for decades been chronicling the quaint and quirky characters who populate the Santa Clarita Valley. Resume aside, Boston claims his greatest accomplishment is being Indiana Boston's father.

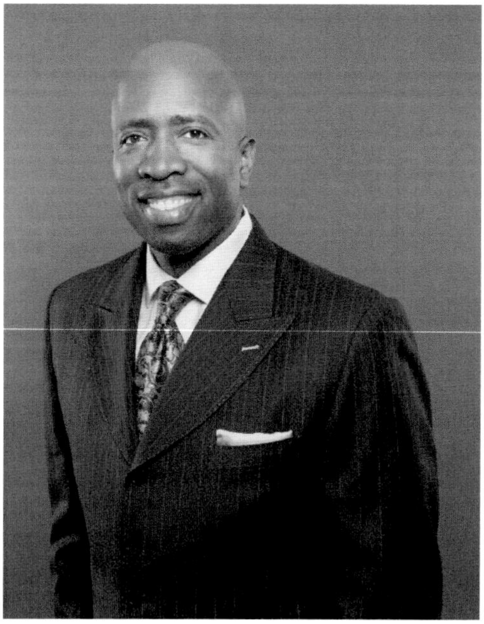

Kenny Smith

Retired NBA champion Kenny "The Jet" Smith is more than just a talking head who spars with Charles Barkley on TNT. As a point guard, he was instrumental in winning back-to-back championships for the Houston Rockets in 1994 and 1995. Today, the Stevenson Ranch resident "assists" inner-city youth through his Aim High Foundation, a charity committed to helping young people achieve their goals through sports and education.

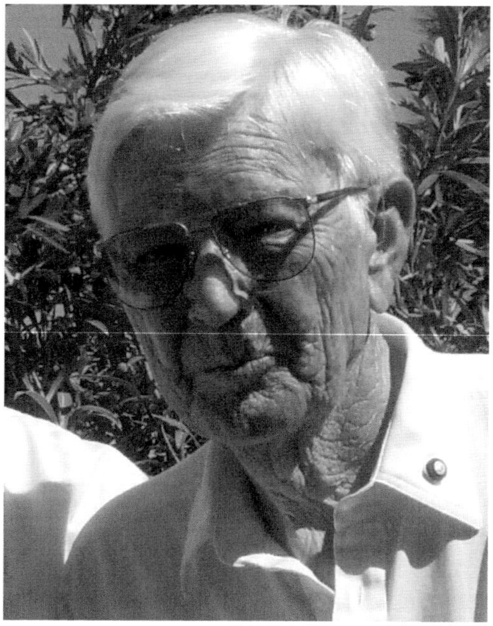

Harry Bell

Realtor Harry Bell enlisted in the Army Air Corps just after the bombing of Pearl Harbor. He flew 50 missions over Europe in World War II as a gunner on a B-24 bomber. He was named SCV Man of the Year in 2011 for 45 years of service to the SCV Rotary Club and for his part in the formation of the Henry Mayo Newhall Memorial Hospital. Bell was tragically killed piloting his small plane in July 2012.

Carl Goldman and Jeri Seratti-Goldman

Carl Goldman (left) and Jeri Seratti-Goldman (right) moved to the SCV in 1990 when they purchased what later became radio station KHTS AM-1220, Santa Clarita's "Hometown Station." They have worked tirelessly on local charitable projects ever since, including raising a staggering half-million dollars for the expansion of Providence/Holy Cross hospital; helping create the Michael Hoefflin Foundation to assist children and their families impacted by cancer; founding *Art of Healing*, which places local student's artwork throughout Providence's cancer wing; and *Habitat for Heroes*, which provides housing for Santa Clarita veterans. They also donated a statue to Providence ensuring that all cancer patients are greeted by an angel when entering the hospital. In honor of their numerous charitable contributions to the community, Jeri was named SCV Woman of the Year in 2005, and Carl was the SCV Man of the Year in 2008.

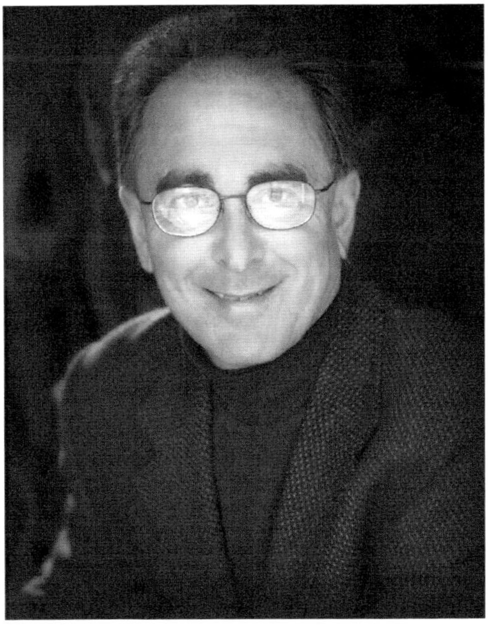

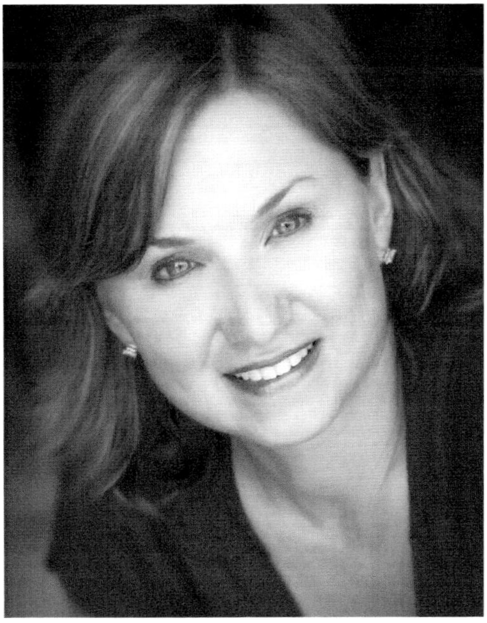

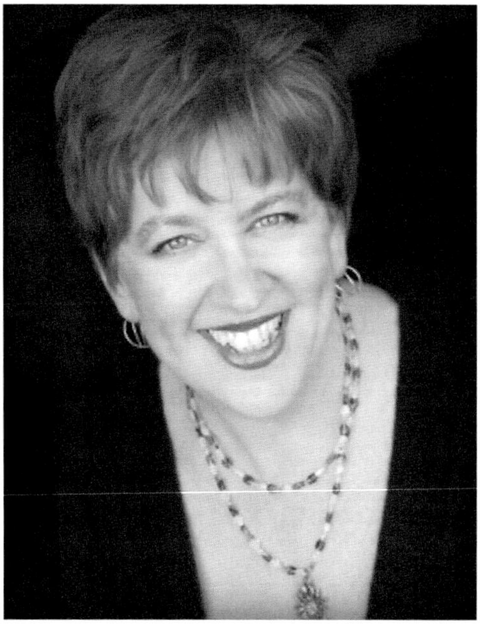

Carol and Frank Rock
Carol Rock has played a major role in the media, entertainment, and historical circles of Santa Clarita for many years. A past president of the Santa Clarita Valley Historical Society, she is currently news director at Santa Clarita's local radio station, KHTS. Carol's husband, Frank, is an accomplished muralist and the valley's "Dam Man"—one of the world's leading experts on the St. Francis Dam disaster.

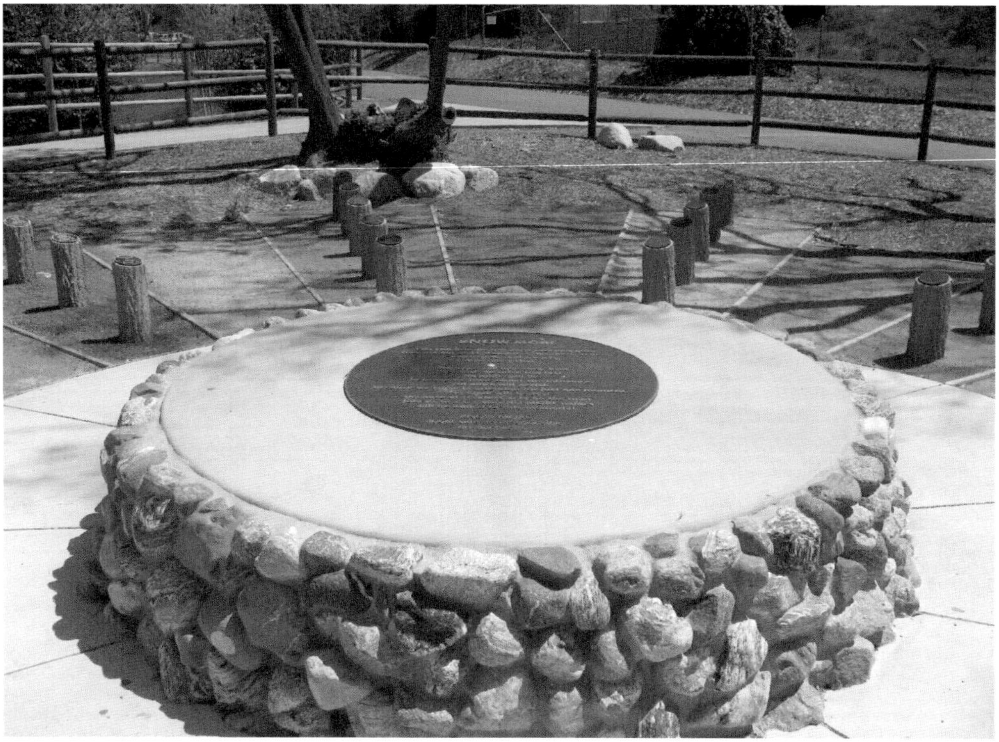

Tom and Alice Reynolds
Tom and Alice Reynolds endured the unthinkable. After losing two sons in an automobile crash caused by a reckless teen driver, they became the force behind the Youth Grove in Saugus's Central Park (pictured here), where local kids killed in traffic accidents are memorialized. The Grove currently has 82 tree stumps, each symbolizing a young life cut short.

Cary Quashen

As a high-risk teen counselor and president of ACTION Family Counseling, Cary Quashen (right) has dedicated his life to working with troubled youth and dysfunctional families. Quashen's signature take-charge persona and healing interventions are legendary among his clients. Through his "tough love" approach, Quashen has saved countless young lives and helped hundreds of families recover from the horrors of drug and alcohol addiction.

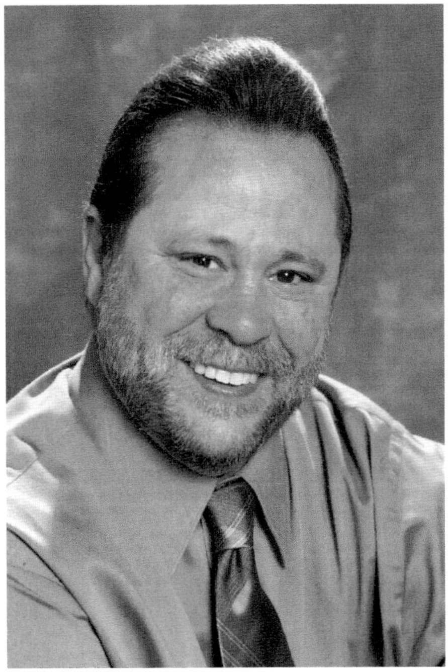

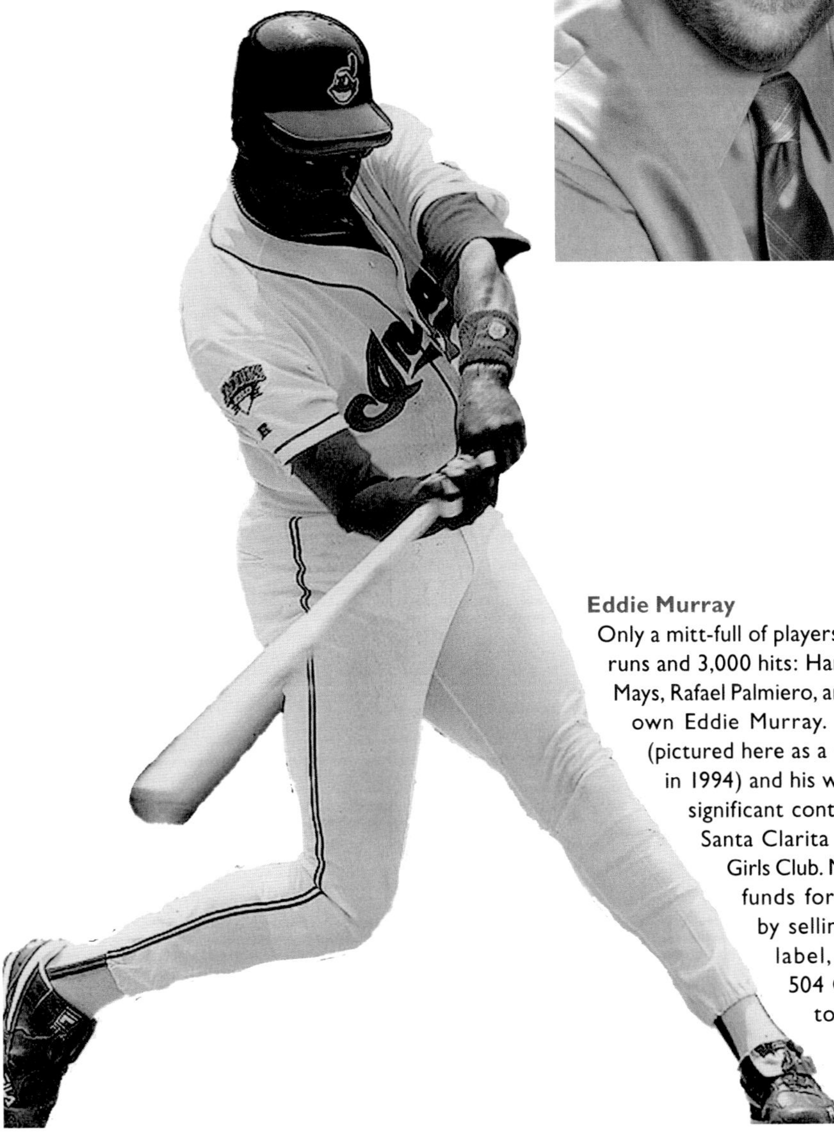

Eddie Murray

Only a mitt-full of players have 500 home runs and 3,000 hits: Hank Aaron, Willie Mays, Rafael Palmiero, and Santa Clarita's own Eddie Murray. "Steady Eddie" (pictured here as a Cleveland Indian in 1994) and his wife, Janice, make significant contributions to the Santa Clarita Valley Boys and Girls Club. Murray also raises funds for worthy causes by selling his own wine label, Eddie Murray 504 Cabernet, a nod to his 504 career home runs.

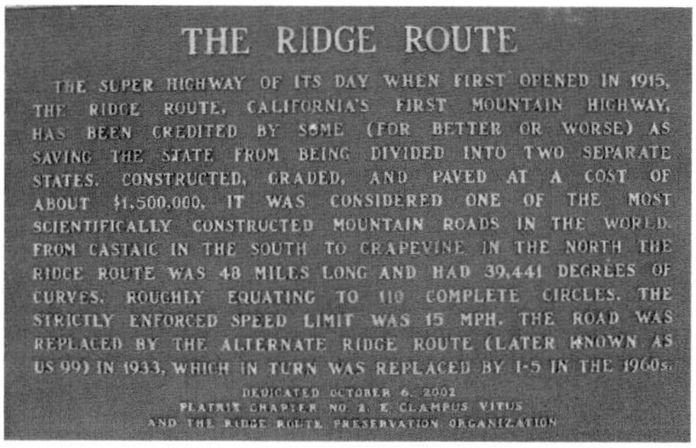

Harrison Scott

Between 1915 and 1933, a trip along the Ridge Route, a 20-foot-wide ribbon of concrete linking Los Angeles to Bakersfield, took 12 harrowing hours with nearly 700 curves in one 36-mile stretch. Despite its hazards, some historians feel it prevented California from splitting into two states. Harrison "Scotty" Scott rediscovered the route in 1991 and decided the historic road needed saving. Eight years battling bureaucracy culminated in National Register of Historic Places status for a 17.6-mile stretch of the highway in 1997. Scott is the executive director of the Ridge Route Preservation Organization. The group's volunteers invest "sweat equity" on the road one Saturday every month, hoping to open the once-forgotten thoroughfare as a park. The monument above is at the intersection of Interstate 5 and California 126. Below is a photograph of the construction of the road in 1915. (Courtesy Dept. of Transportation.)

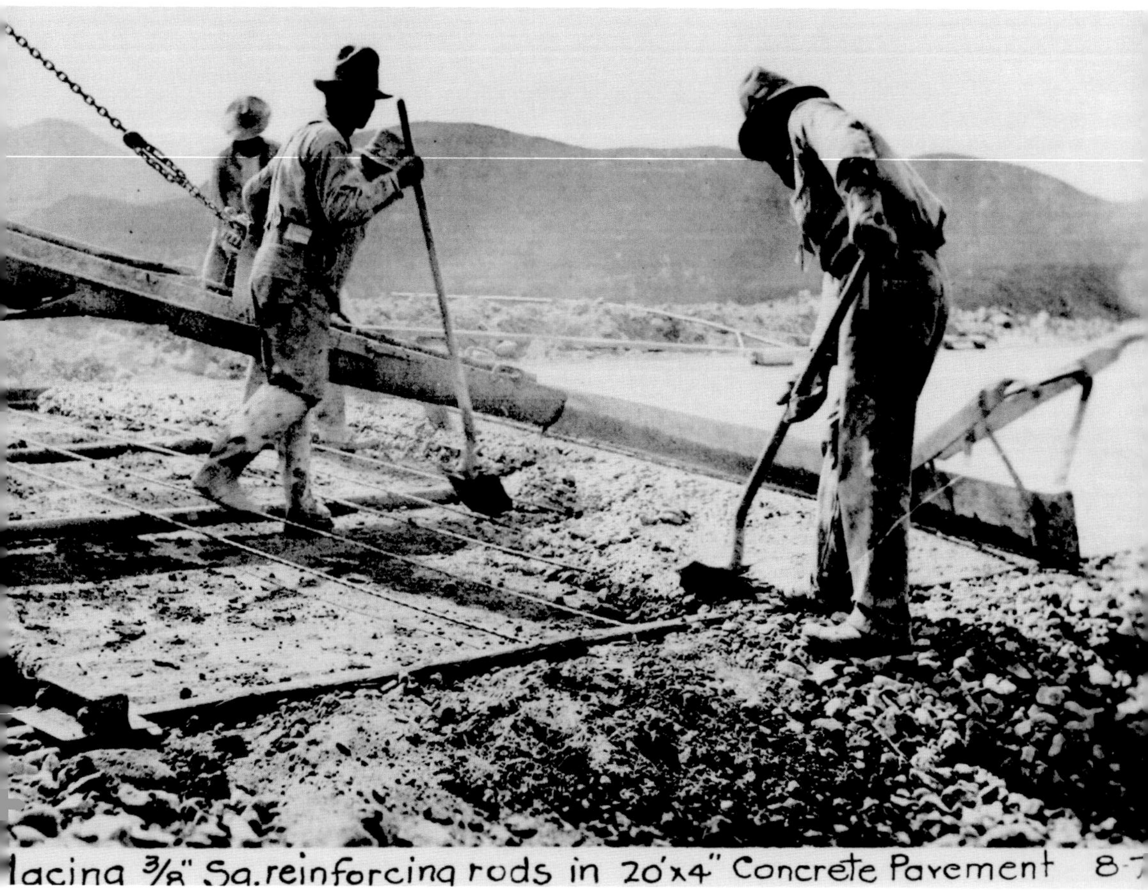

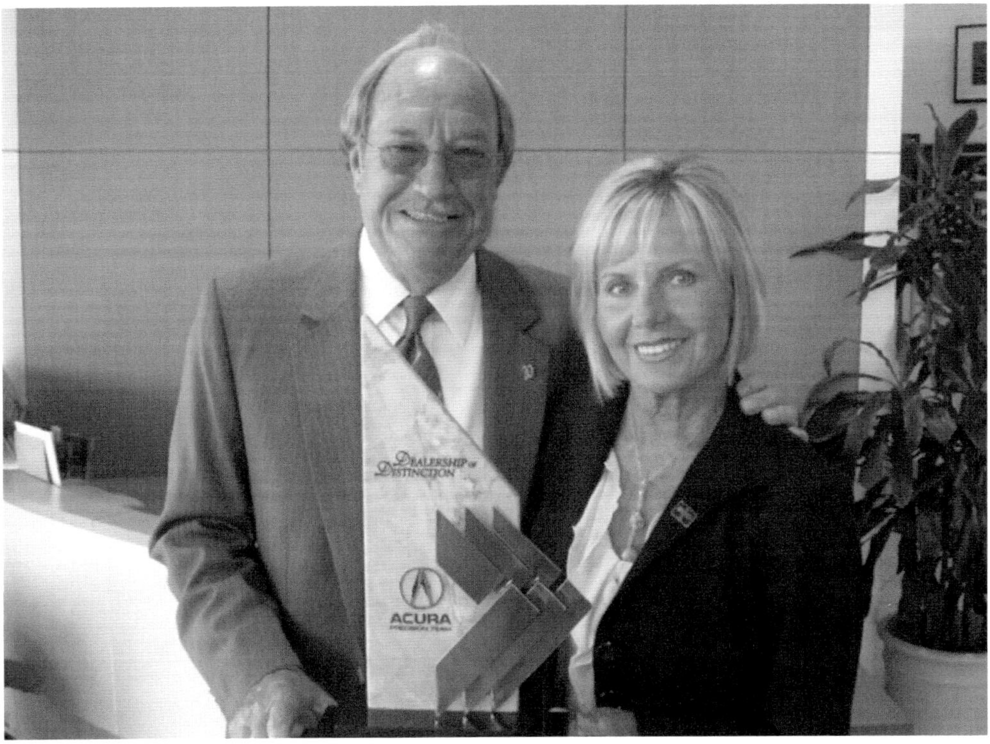

Don and Cheri Fleming

After serving in Vietnam, Don Fleming opened the country's first tanning salon in his native Texas. He began supplying other salon owners, including a young lady named Cheri from Woodland Hills. The couple (pictured above) married in 1984 and purchased a waning Acura dealership in Valencia in 1997, which they turned into a thriving business. Cheri has lived with rheumatoid arthritis since she was 28, and both the Flemings' mothers died of cancer. These brushes with disease inspire them to passionately fundraise for the Henry Mayo Newhall Hospital, the Arthritis Foundation, the Sheila R. Veloz Breast Imaging Center, and other local charities. For their philanthropic efforts, they were named Santa Clarita Valley's Man and Woman of the Year in 2004. Recently, the Flemings helped raise over $500,000 for the Santa Clarita Valley Boys and Girls Club (pictured below).

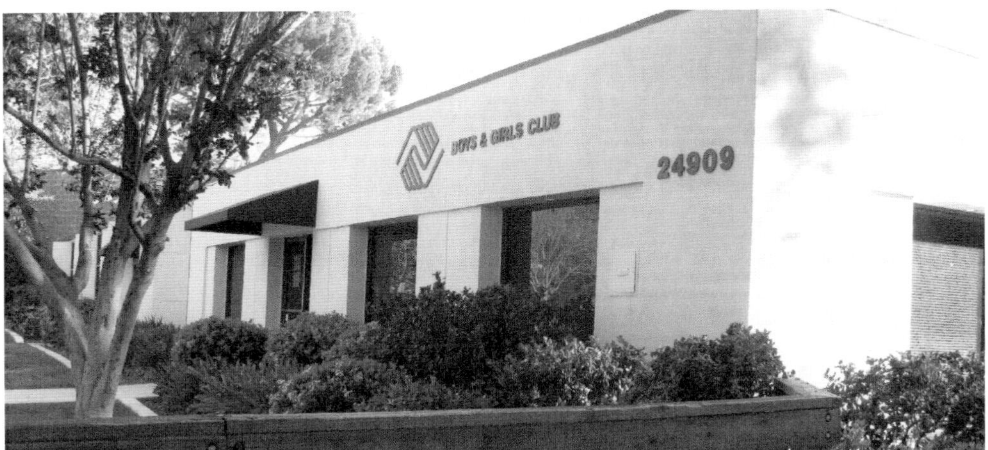

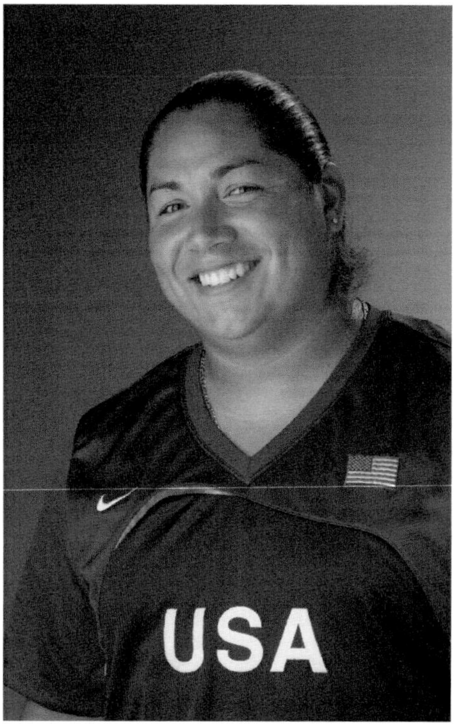

Crystl Bustos

Canyon Country's Crystl "Boo" Bustos (left) is an inspiration to female athletes around the world. Through superior athleticism and determination, Bustos has become one of the most honored female fast-pitch softball players ever, winning gold medals with the US Women's Softball Team in two separate Olympic Games (Sydney, 2000 and Athens, 2004). In Beijing, Bustos batted .500 and hit a record-breaking six home runs and 10 RBIs, earning the US team the silver medal. Bustos was voted MVP in the Women's Pro Softball League (WPSL) and won three Pan American gold medals. Since retiring from international competition, Bustos has sponsored a team called "Bustos Elite" and a softball league in Ohio for kids between the ages of 12 and 18 called "Bustos Ultimate." Below, teammates wait to mob Bustos as she crosses the plate. (Courtesy *Fresno Beehive.*)

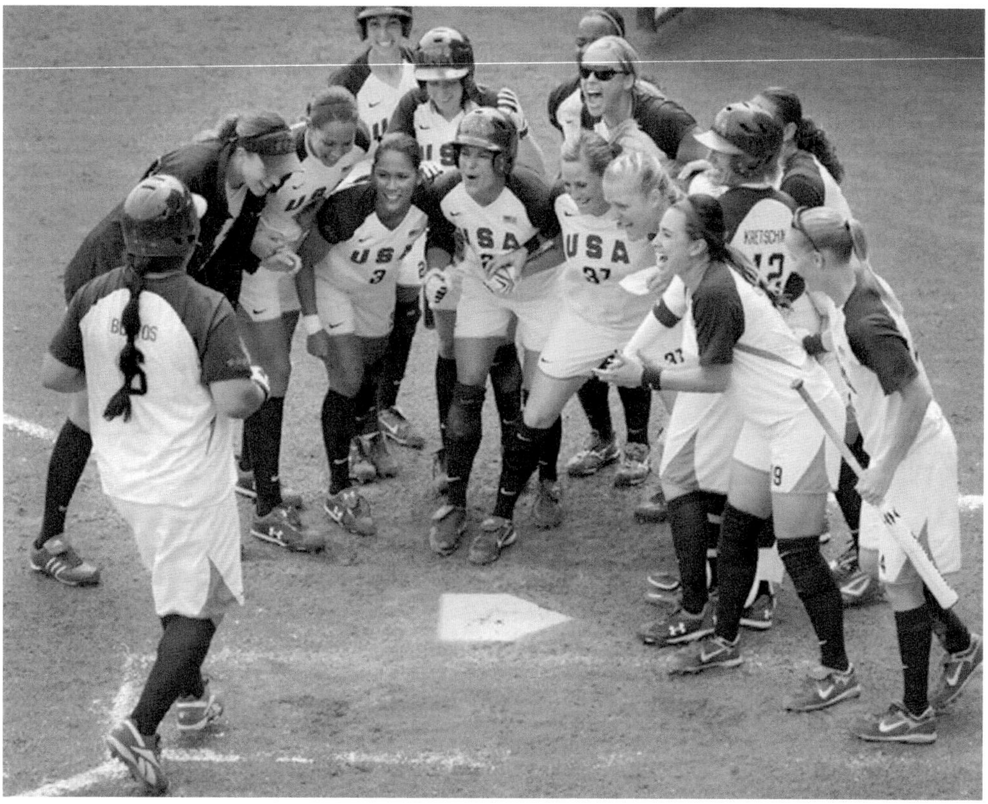

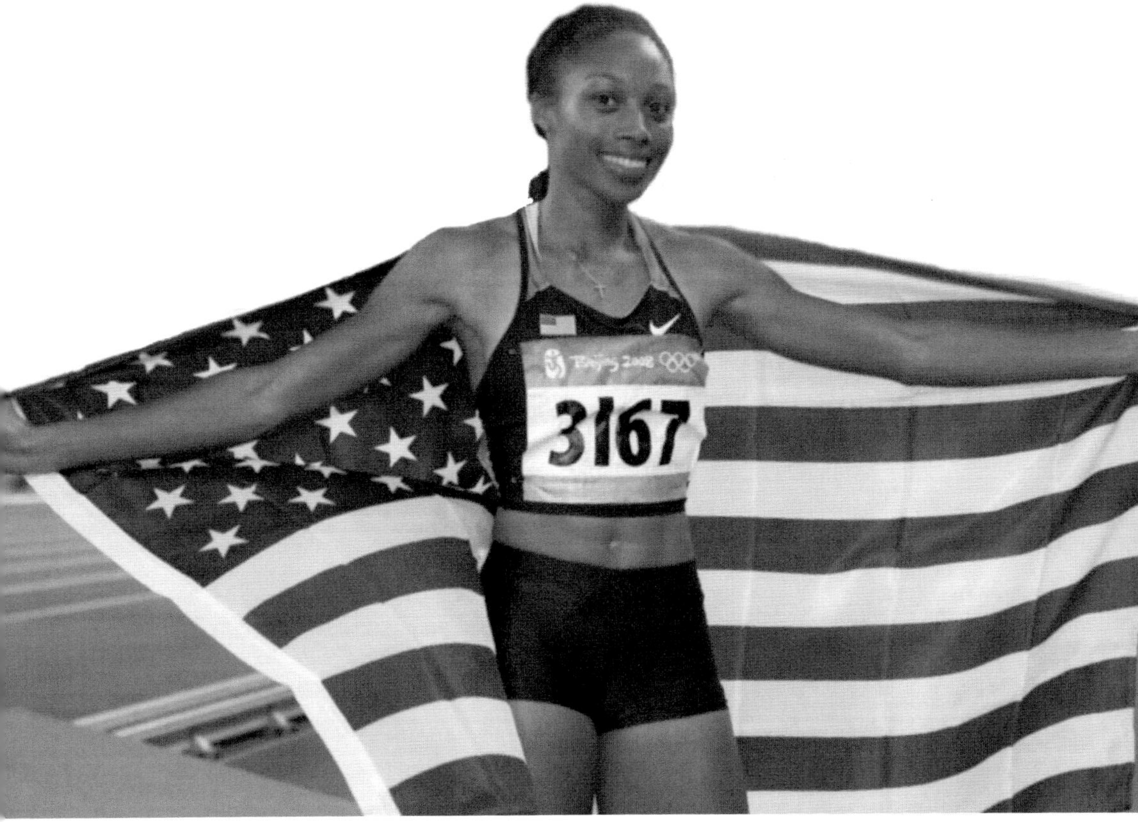

Allyson Felix and Lauren Fleshman
Santa Clarita sprinter Allyson Felix (above) and Canyon High School graduate and middle-distance runner Lauren Fleshman (right) have put SCV on the "winning track." Felix has won several world championships and captured Olympic gold in Beijing as a member of the 4x400 meter team. She is a proud member of *Project Believe*, a group of athletes committed to proving that drug-free champions do exist. Fleshman has won national titles in cross-country and middle-distance events. She has a popular running blog called AskLaurenFleshman.com and is the co-founder of Believe I Am, a web business that sells motivational sports merchandise.

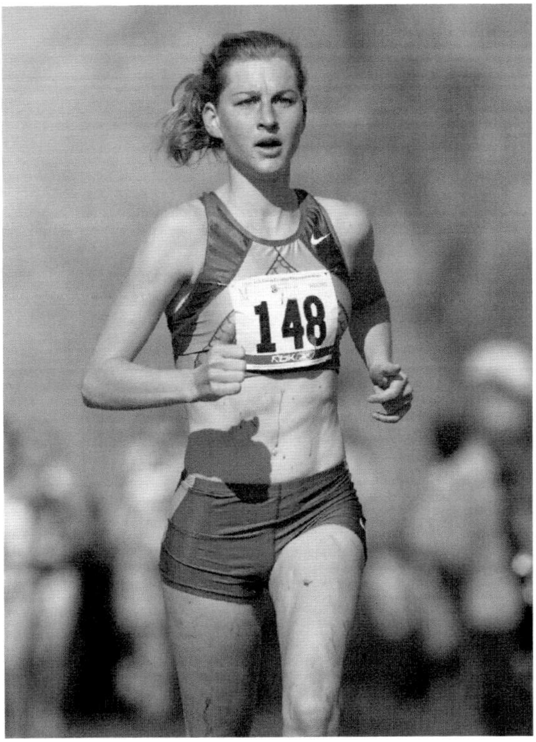

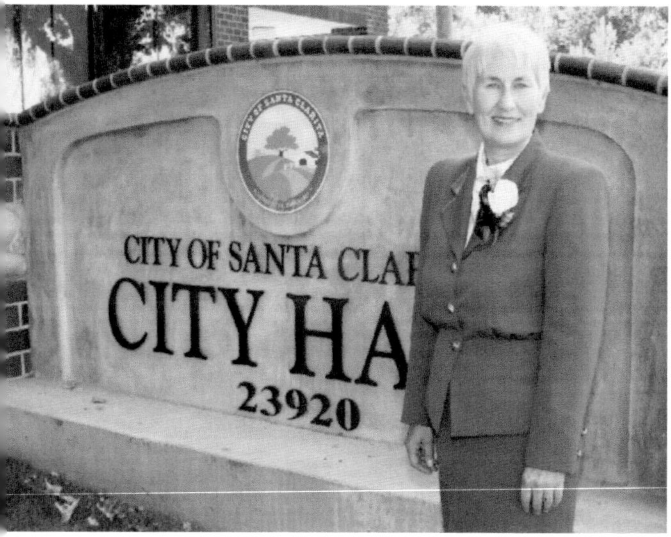

Laurene Weste

Laurene Weste (above) makes no secret of her love for local history, animals, and the environment. Originally from Burbank, where her father supervised music for Hollywood films, three-time Santa Clarita mayor Weste fell in love with the Santa Clarita Valley during numerous visits to Hart Park. She has served on the boards of the SCV Historical Society and Friends of Hart Park and helped save the historic oil town of Mentryville. It was through her project to preserve open space and to create a trail system in Santa Clarita that she met L.A. County planner James McCarthy, who she married in 1992. Below, from left to right, are Capt. Paul Becker, Jennifer Glover (holding son Landen Glover), Mayor Laurene Weste, and Councilmember Laurie Ender, who plant a tree in memory of fallen L.A. County sheriff's deputy Cameron Glover in 2010. (Courtesy City of Santa Clarita.)

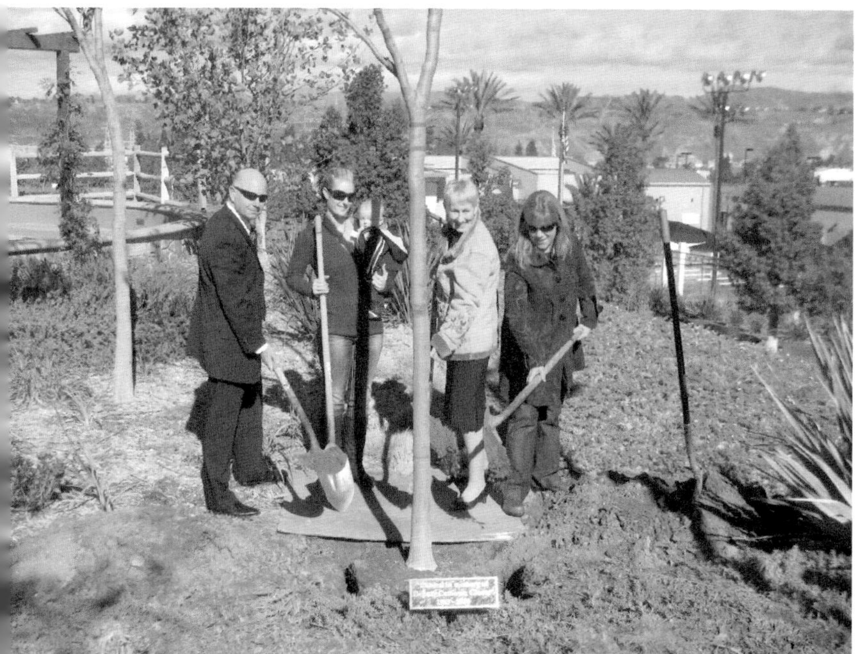

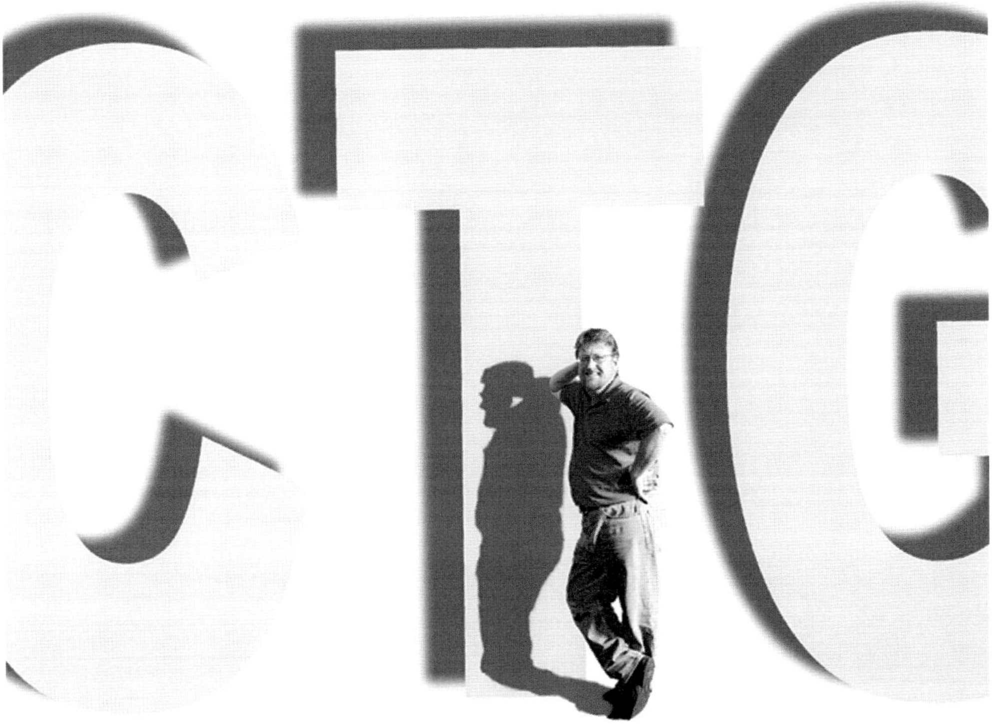

TimBen and Ingrid Boydston
TimBen Boydston came to Newhall's Canyon Theatre Guild in 1986 and has been their executive director for many years. Ingrid arrived in Hollywood as a 21-year-old, with little more than a suitcase and a dream. They met when Ingrid auditioned for a play and married the following year. Besides guiding the Guild, TimBen is currently a Santa Clarita City Council member, and Ingrid was the 1999 California Teacher of the Year.

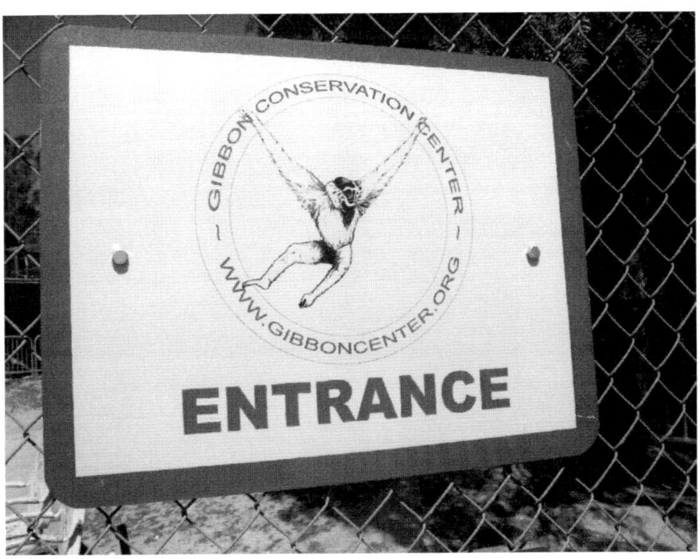

Alan Mootnick
A childhood fascination with primates led Alan Mootnick to establish the Gibbon Conservation Center in Saugus, the largest gibbon preserve in the Western hemisphere. Mootnick lived on the conservation grounds until his death in 2011. The Gibbon Conservation Center remains committed to furthering Mootnick's life's work. (Courtesy *The Santa Clarita Valley Signal.*)

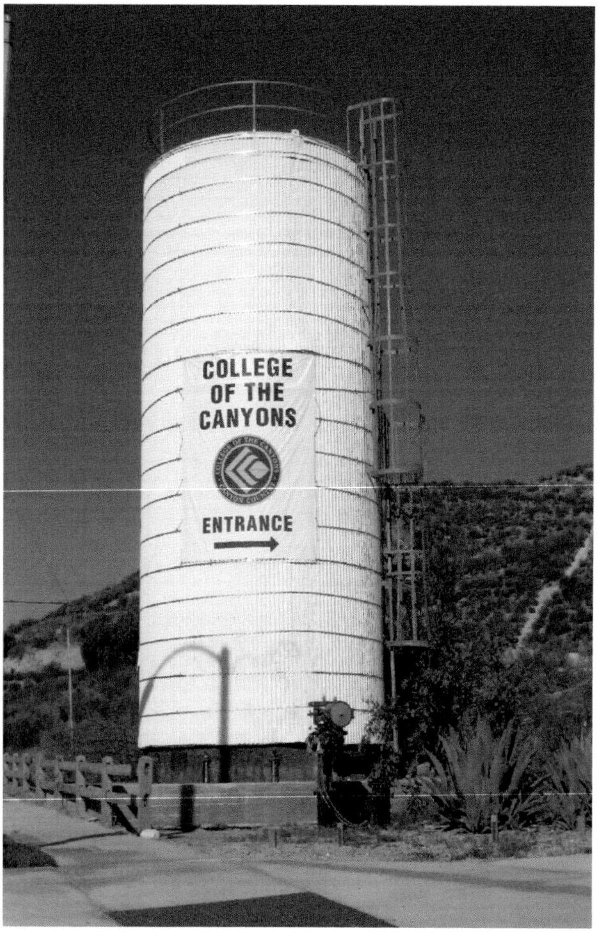

Dianne Van Hook

No one knows the value of a quality education better than College of the Canyons chancellor Dr. Dianne Van Hook. Since becoming the youngest chief executive of a community college in the state's history in 1988, Van Hook has brought millions of dollars in increased revenue into the college and obtained a $150-million commitment to expand 13 community college campuses across California. To broaden the higher education opportunities for working parents in the SCV, she oversaw the creation of a satellite campus in Canyon Country in 2007 (left). That same year, ground was broken on the Dr. Dianne G. Van Hook University Center (below), offering bachelor's, master's, and doctoral level degrees. For her accomplishments in improving women's education, Van Hook was named the Betty Ferguson Foundation's "Woman of Honor" in 2009. (Courtesy Dylan Lieberman.)

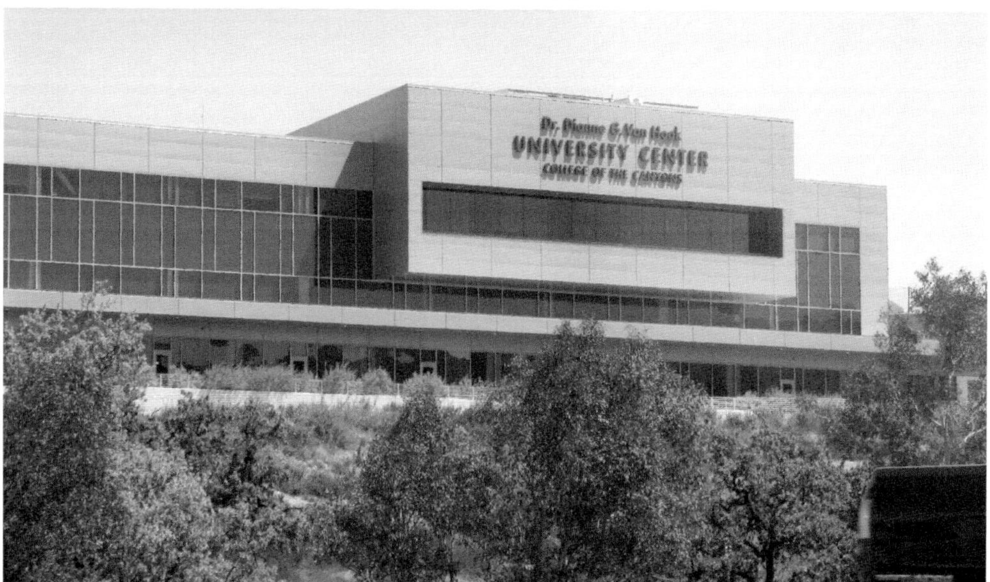

Ellie Laks

Santa Clarita Valley's four-legged residents have a champion in Ellie Laks. Laks realized a lifelong dream in 1999 when she founded the Gentle Barn in Canyon Country, a sanctuary for abused, neglected, and lonely farm animals. Laks, her husband, Jay Weiner, and the staff of Gentle Barn rehabilitate the animals with naturopathic healing and hours of cuddling. Celebrities like Ellen and Portia DeGeneres (below, with "Buddha" in 2010) support their cause by televising their visits to the facility. Scores of guests visit the ranch each weekend and hundreds of high-risk youth have gone through Gentle Barn's at-risk program. Some, who are incapable of accepting love from a human, have been able to bond with the animals, beginning the process of emotional healing.

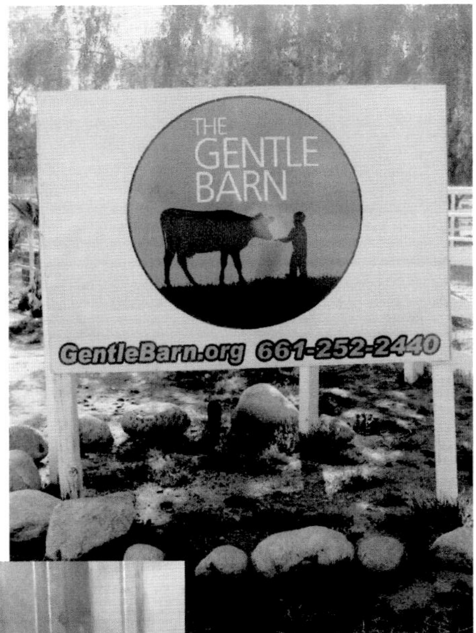

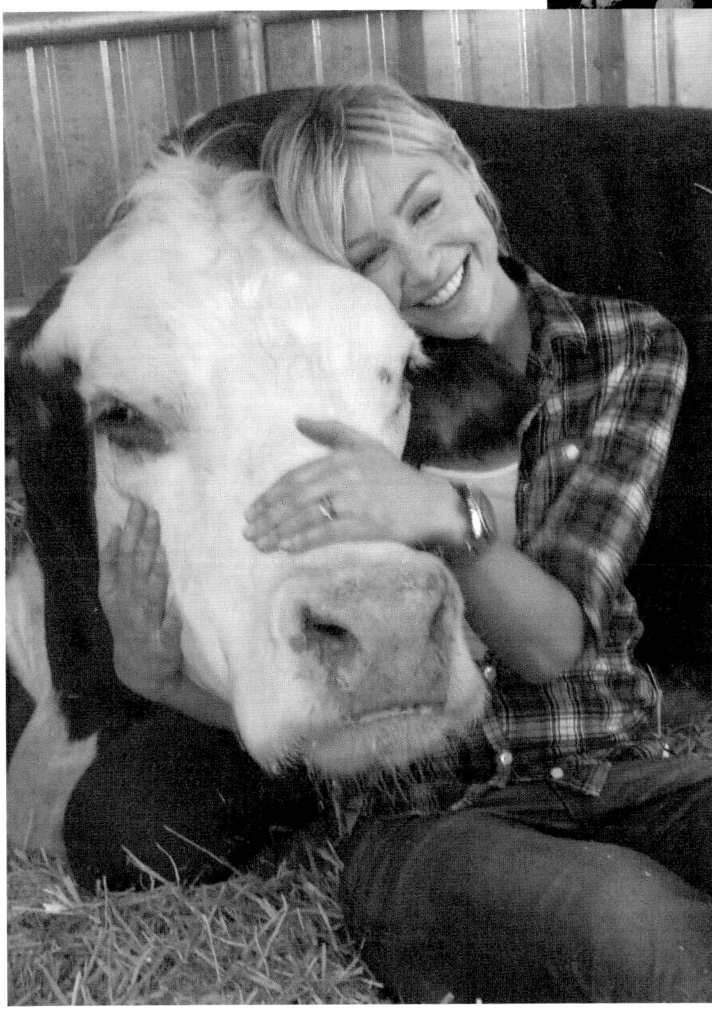

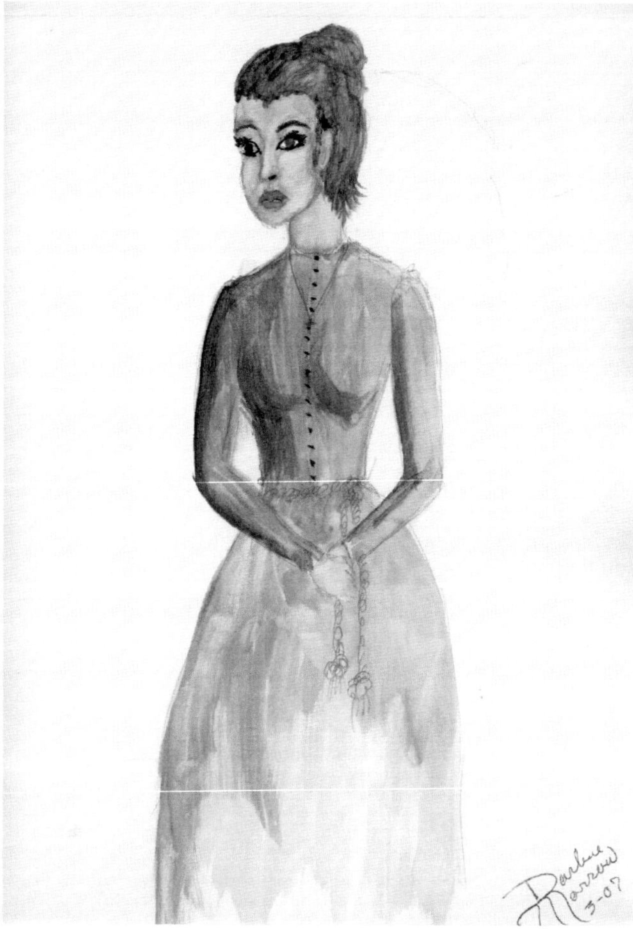

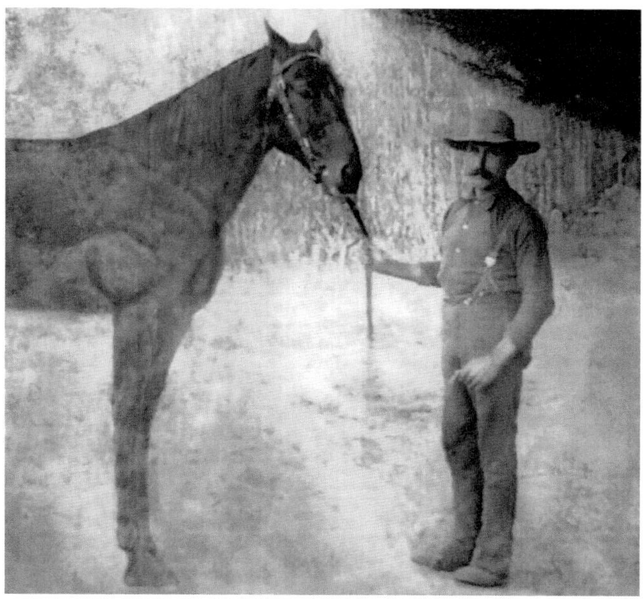

Martha
Not all of the area's contemporary legends are living. After the Newhall Ranch house was moved to Heritage Junction in 1990, witnesses began reporting ghostly sightings. A psychic was called in who reported making contact with a woman named Martha (or Marta), who was born in 1823. Martha is reportedly most often seen in 1880s-era dark blue clothing, earning her the nickname "the Blue Lady." She is said to sometimes be seen in the company of an eight-year-old boy named Timothy and a polite 19th-century cowboy named Rory MacGregor. Ghost hunters regularly investigate the house, and during Halloween, the supposedly haunted Newhall Ranch house becomes a popular attraction as . . . a *haunted house*! Above is a 2007 drawing of Martha by psychic Darlene Marrow. Below, this digitally-reconstructed photograph of a gentleman thought to be Rory MacGregor was found inside a wall of the Newhall Ranch house.

CHAPTER THREE

The Portrayers

Hollywood came calling in the 20th century, employing the vistas of the valley to re-create the colorful era of the Old West at the site of its recent passing.

The film history of the Santa Clarita Valley traces its roots to 1882, when novelist Helen Hunt Jackson spent the night at Rancho Camulos while doing research for her novel *Ramona*. Camulos was later used as the setting for a short 1910 silent film based on the novel, which starred "America's Sweetheart," Mary Pickford, and was directed by D.W. Griffith.

Film ranches sprouted like mushrooms in the valley. At singing cowboy Gene Autry's Melody Ranch, Gary Cooper stared down gunfighters in *High Noon*, and Matt Dillon sent dozens of Dodge City's bad men to Boot Hill. Scores of early Western stars like Bob Steele, Tom Mix, John Wayne, and local residents William S. Hart and Harry Carey honed their craft here and in other valley locations.

Stone-faced clown Buster Keaton filmed at Beale's Cut during the 1920s and Charlie Chaplin chose a site on Sierra Highway to draw the curtain down on the entire Silent Era. Previously, he had filmed a portion of *The Pilgrim* at Saugus's historic train station in 1923. Frank Sinatra later made it the intended site of a presidential assassination in 1954's *Suddenly*.

A local legend claims that actor James Dean ate his last meal at a restaurant near Castaic Junction on September 30, 1955, a few hours before his young life was snuffed out in a car crash near Paso Robles.

Not all of the SCV's "legendary locals" in the entertainment world are relegated to the past. Scores of entertainers make the valley their home, like Hollywood legend Tippi Hedren, who after appearing in the Alfred Hitchcock films *The Birds* and *Marnie*, set up a world-famous rescue center for lions, tigers, and other large cats called Shambala Preserve.

Every day, from SCV studios, film ranches, and locations, stories are still being told that are seen nightly on television sets and computer and movie screens around the world.

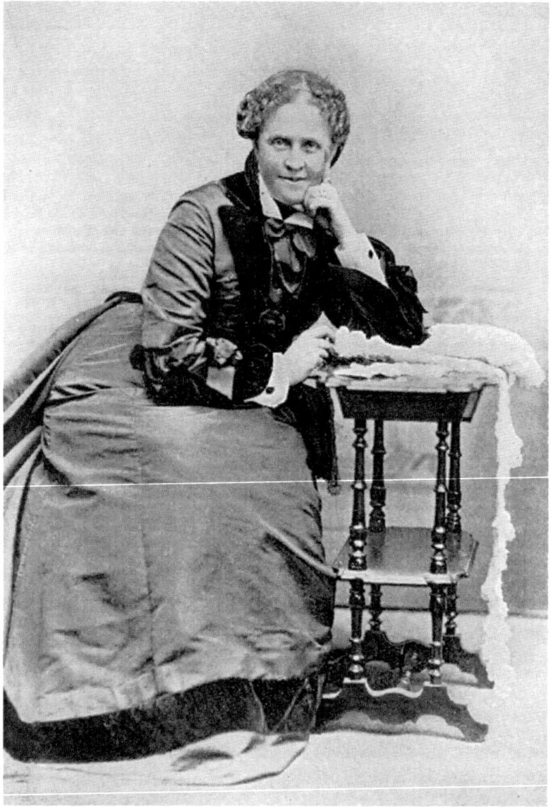

Helen Hunt Jackson

Rancho Camulos lord Ygnacio Del Valle died before seeing his property gain worldwide fame as the "Home of Ramona" following the publication of Helen Hunt Jackson's novel *Ramona*. Massachusetts-born Jackson (pictured above in the 1850s or 1860s) turned to writing after surviving the deaths of her parents, children, and first husband. After publishing several novels, she penned a dry 1881 historical treatise entitled *A Century of Dishonor*. Seeking to influence a wider readership, she wrote the novel *Ramona* three years later, intending the story to be received as an "*Uncle Tom's Cabin* for Indians." The underlying message was missed by most of the reading public, who were more interested in the tragic romance between Ramona and her Indian lover, Alessandro. Jackson had visited Rancho Camulos in 1882 while doing research for the novel, and its purported use as a backdrop painted a romantic image of the Mission and rancho period of old Spanish California. Camulos became a major tourist attraction due to the book's explosive popularity, and people all over the country became obsessed with seeing where the fictional character Ramona had once "lived." Shortly after the book's publication, the Southern Pacific added a stop on its Ventura line just outside the gates of the property. The Del Valle family initially welcomed the hordes of tourists and adroitly capitalized on their connection with the fictional heroine by marketing their locally-grown fruits and vegetables under the "Home of Ramona" brand. Towns, schools, and highways all over California clamored to be named after Ramona and the rest of the book's characters. Readers traveled cross-country to see anything that could be associated with its setting, including Ramona's supposed birthplace, marriage chapel, and even her gravesite. Sadly, Jackson died of stomach cancer only a year after her novel's publication. She is still remembered during Ramona Days at Rancho Camulos, which was designated a national historic landmark in 2000. Each April in Hemet—another Southern California town that boasts a link to *Ramona*—more than 400 fans participate in *The Ramona Pageant* theatrical production, portraying the love story between Ramona and Alessandro. *The Ramona Pageant* has been an annual event since 1923.

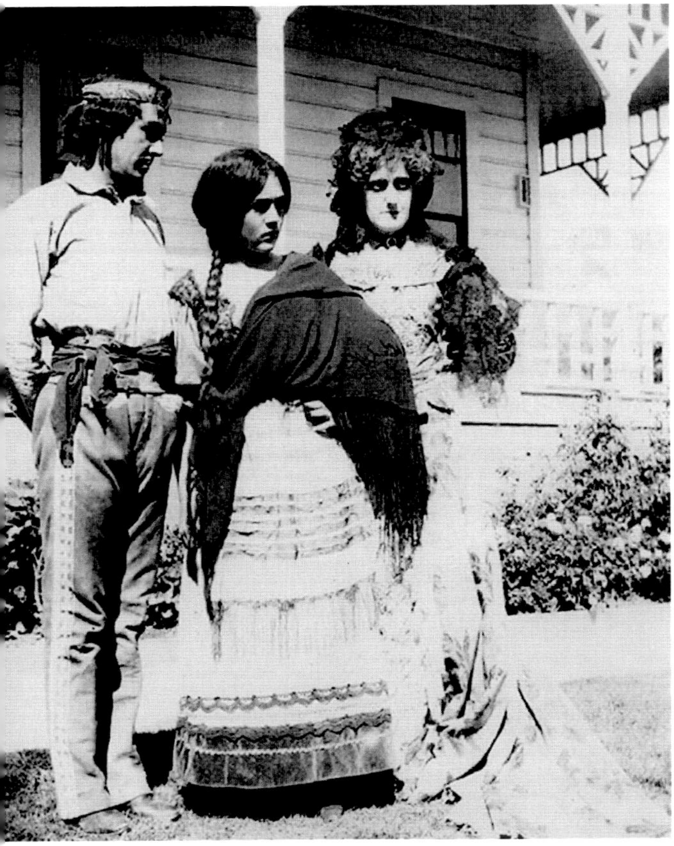

Mary Pickford and D.W. Griffith
In 1910, legendary silent film director D.W. Griffith, a fan of the novel *Ramona*, secured the story's filming rights for only $100 and boiled the 350-page novel down to a 17-minute one-reeler. Seventeen-year-old Mary Pickford, who was on her way to becoming "America's Sweetheart" at the time, was chosen for the lead role. Rancho Camulos had become so associated with the *Ramona* story that Griffith decided to film part of the movie there in May 1910 and made it the first location to ever receive a screen credit. Today, over a century after the filming of *Ramona*, the rancho and the surrounding hills look remarkably the same. From left to right, Henry B. Walthall, Mary Pickford, and Kate Bruce pose in Piru in 1910. Below, D.W. Griffith directs a movie around 1910.

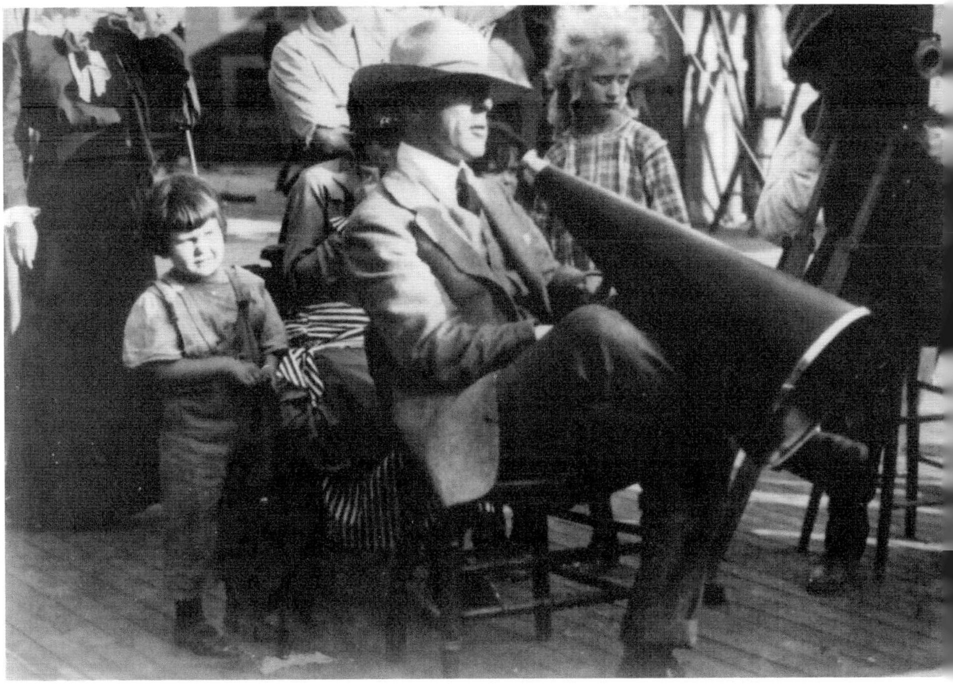

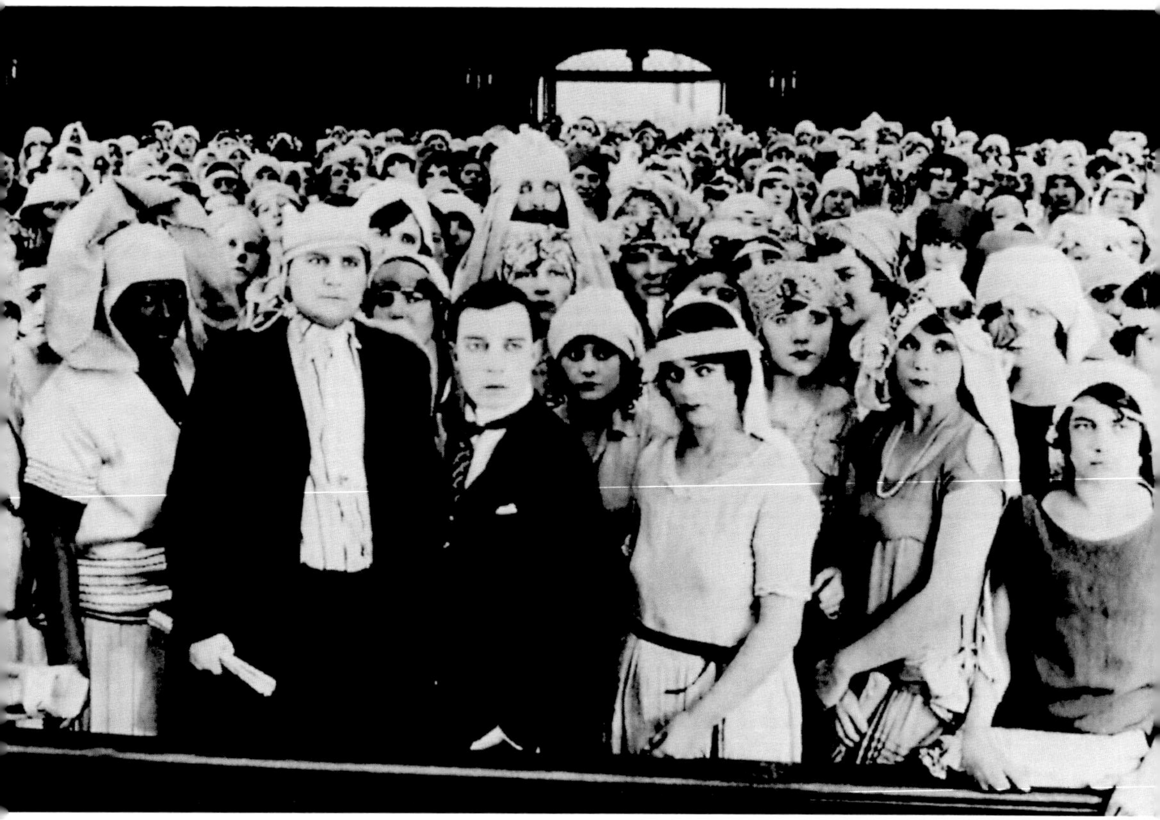

Buster Keaton

Stone-faced silent comedian Buster Keaton came to the Santa Clarita Valley in 1921 to make a film called *The Paleface*. In one scene, Keaton crosses a bridge constructed over Beale's Cut in Newhall to evade a group of hostile Indians. Beale's Cut was at one time a 90-foot-deep man-made slit carved through a mountain, which greatly aided travel to and from the San Fernando Valley. Keaton returned to Beale's Cut in 1925 while filming *Seven Chances* (pictured here). In this film, he plays a man who has to be married by seven o'clock or lose his fortune. He fails to find a bride by taking "seven chances" at proposing directly, and in desperation, places an advertisement in the paper to find a wife. A mob of women in wedding dresses pursue Buster throughout the remainder of the film, briefly chasing him through the cut. Beale's Cut has been used as a movie location many times in the past, most notably in *Stagecoach* (1939) starring John Wayne, and in *Three Jumps Ahead* (1923), a lost Tom Mix film where Mix appears to jump the expanse on horseback! In 1923, Buster's friend and rival Charlie Chaplin filmed part of *The Pilgrim* a few miles up the road from Beale's Cut at the Saugus Train Station. At that time, the station was located on Railroad Avenue across from the present site of the Saugus Café. Since then, it has been relocated three miles south to the Heritage Junction Historical Park in Newhall. This park sits inside the William S. Hart Regional Park, which contains the home and ranch of the former silent cowboy star William S. Hart. Ironically, Hart was the subject of a Western parody that Keaton filmed in 1922 called *The Frozen North*. Buster was angry at Hart for publicly condemning his friend Roscoe "Fatty" Arbuckle during Fatty's well-publicized scandal, which was brought on by the death of an actress at one of Arbuckle's parties. In *The Frozen North*, Keaton poked fun at the tough, melodramatic character that Hart most often portrayed in his films. Hart apparently did not find the satire all that funny and refused to speak to Keaton for years.

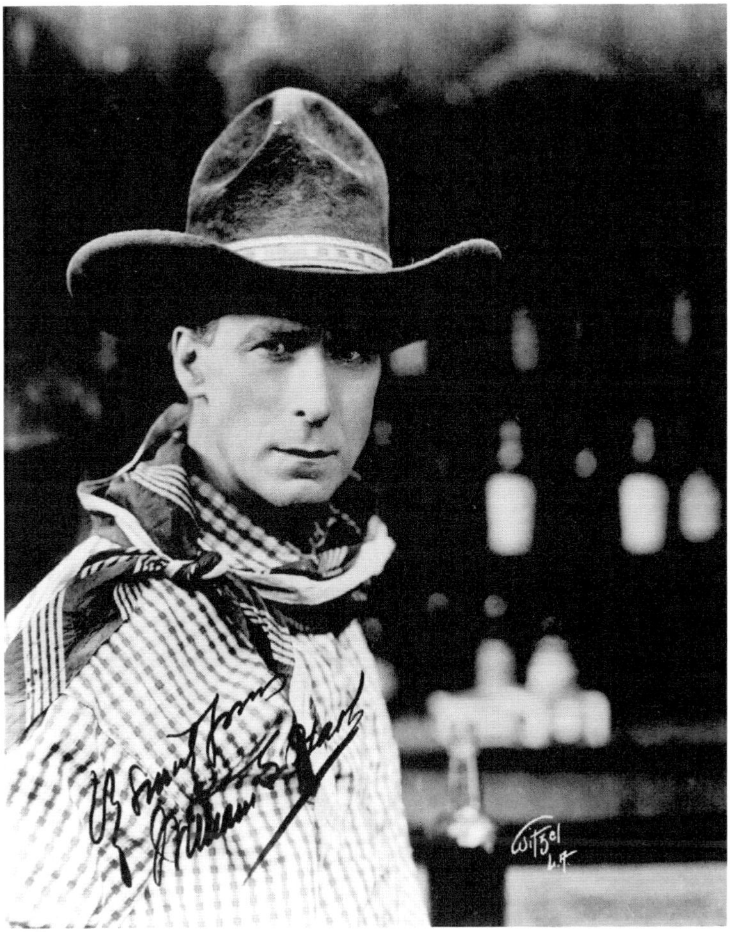

William S. Hart

Because of its rugged scenery and proximity to Hollywood, the Santa Clarita Valley hosted many of the early Western movies with stars like Hoot Gibson, Tim McCoy, Tom Mix, Harry Carey, John Wayne, and Newhall's most famous resident, William Surrey Hart (pictured here around 1920). "Two Gun Bill" Hart was born during the Civil War in New York and later achieved success as a Shakespearian stage actor. As a boy, Hart traveled throughout the country with his family, interacting with cowboys, Indians, and ranchers firsthand. As a witness to the Old West, Hart would later incorporate a more truthful and respectful account of this era into his films. At the advanced age of 49, he began his screen career for Thomas Ince's New York Motion Picture Company for $125 per week before moving to Hollywood. His movie career lasted from 1914 to 1925, during which time he was perhaps the most famous actor on the planet. In total, he made 65 films, all silent, that were known for their realism. He purchased a ranch in Newhall in 1921, and later, upon his retirement, built a hilltop Spanish Colonial–style mansion there called "La Loma de los Vientos" (The Hill of the Winds). Hart counted the legendary lawmen Wyatt Earp and Bat Masterson and famed Western artist Charles Russell among his friends. Active in civic affairs, in 1940 Hart built and financed the first theater in the valley on Spruce Street in Newhall. During his retirement, Hart turned to writing, penning a dozen novels and his autobiography, *My Life East and West*. He lived with his sister Mary Ellen at the mansion until his death in 1946. He was quoted as saying, "While I was making pictures, the people gave me their nickels, dimes, and quarters. When I am gone, I want them to have my home." A man of his word, as a final act of philanthropy, Hart willed his 265-acre ranch to the people of Los Angeles County to be used as a public park.

Wyatt Earp

The Santa Clarita Valley is where actors play Old West lawmen on screen, but it also has ties to real-life Tombstone lawman Wyatt Earp as well. A legend since the 1881 "Gunfight at the O.K. Corral," Earp (pictured here at age 75) spent his last years in the Los Angeles area and had a close friendship with the most famous citizen of Newhall, silent Western star William S. Hart. During the 25 years following the shootout in Tombstone, Earp and his wife, Josie, roamed the West, making stops in Dodge City, the Pacific Northwest, Colorado, Idaho, San Francisco, and San Diego. For a time during the Alaska Gold Rush, Earp ran saloons and gambling halls in Nome. The couple settled in Hollywood in 1906, where Earp served as a consultant on movie sets, meeting several famous actors, including William S. Hart. Earp had become increasingly frustrated with the way his life was portrayed in the media and began corresponding with Hart in 1920, hoping to get the star to set the record straight in a movie about his life. The correspondence grew into a close friendship between the two men, which lasted until Earp's death in 1929. Hart never completed a film production on the life of Wyatt Earp, but he did help the aging lawman find an author to write his life story, *Wyatt Earp, Frontier Marshal*, which was published nearly three years after Earp's death. Despite being sanitized by Earp's wife, it is still considered one of the definitive books on the life of the legendary lawman. Wyatt Earp died at the age of 80 in Los Angeles on January 13, 1929, and Hart and Tom Mix served as pallbearers at the funeral. Following the service, Hart wrote, "I have just returned from the funeral services of a very dear friend of mine, who has crossed the Big Divide: Wyatt Earp, the last of the really great gunmen-peace officers of the frontier."

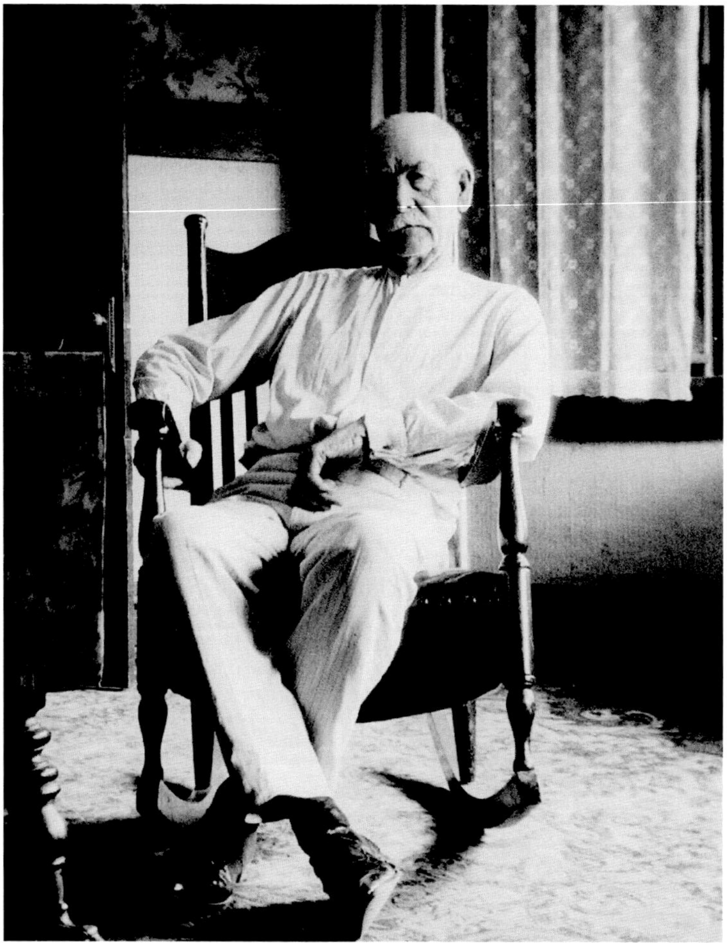

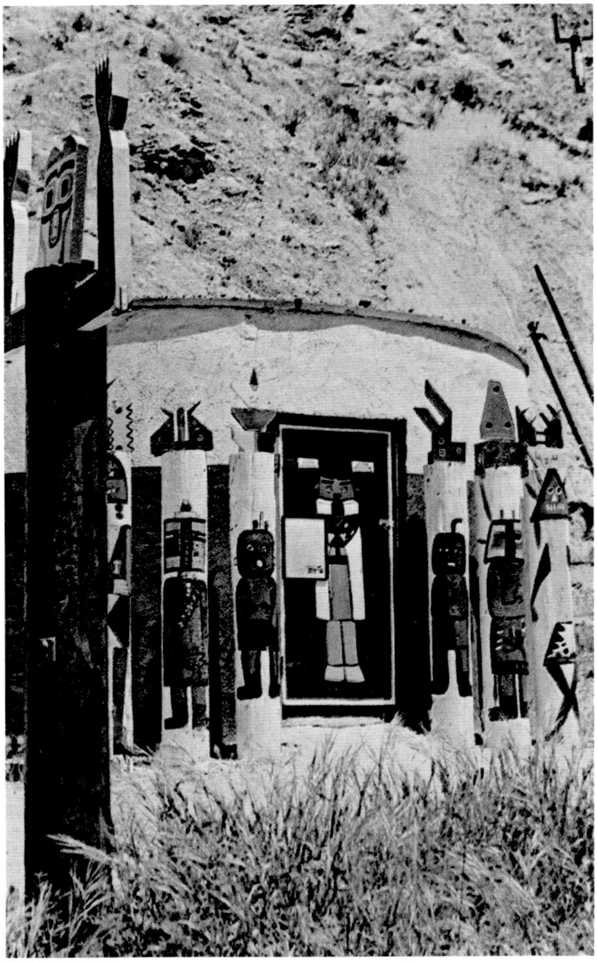

Robert Callahan

In 1928, advertising man Robert Callahan, a self-proclaimed *Ramona* fanatic, built a theme park in Culver City called Ramona Village, where he was accused by one critic of creating a "jazz commercial version" of California's past. Ramona Village closed during the Great Depression and Callahan built a new park on the site called Mission Village. It was destroyed in 1962 to make way for the Santa Monica Freeway, and Callahan then created a tourist attraction called Callahan's Old West at a remote location on Sierra Highway in Canyon Country. Pictured at right is a 1960s postcard of its trading post. After his death in 1981, Callahan's wife, Marion, donated remnants of Callahan's Old West to the SCV Historical Society, including the Ramona Chapel and Little Red School House (below). It can be seen today at Heritage Junction in Newhall.

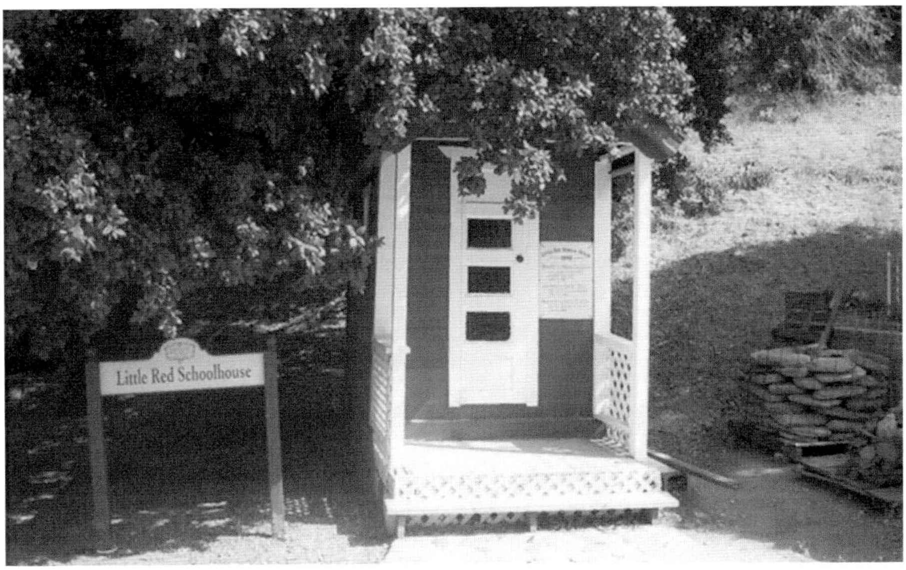

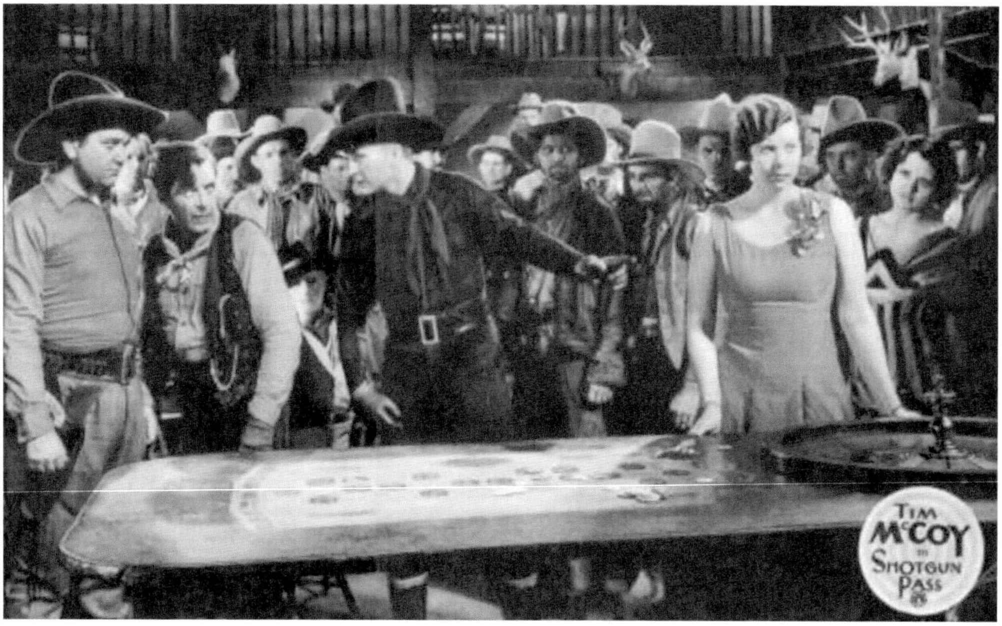

Ace Cain

When Ace Cain was not acting in B-Westerns, he ran a speakeasy in Saugus known as the Rocky Springs Country Club. Though children swam in his pool and teens danced to the jukebox, many believed Cain's establishment to be a house of ill repute because of the showgirls and "very friendly women" who frequented the club. Cain offered Rocky Springs's pool as a safe haven during evacuations caused by canyon fires, gave water to friends when their ranch pumps went dry, and was married to the same woman for decades. He is pictured (above) at far left in this lobby card from *Shotgun Pass* (1935), starring Tim McCoy. Cain is buried in an unmarked grave in Newhall's Eternal Valley Cemetery (below). (Top photograph courtesy Les Adams.)

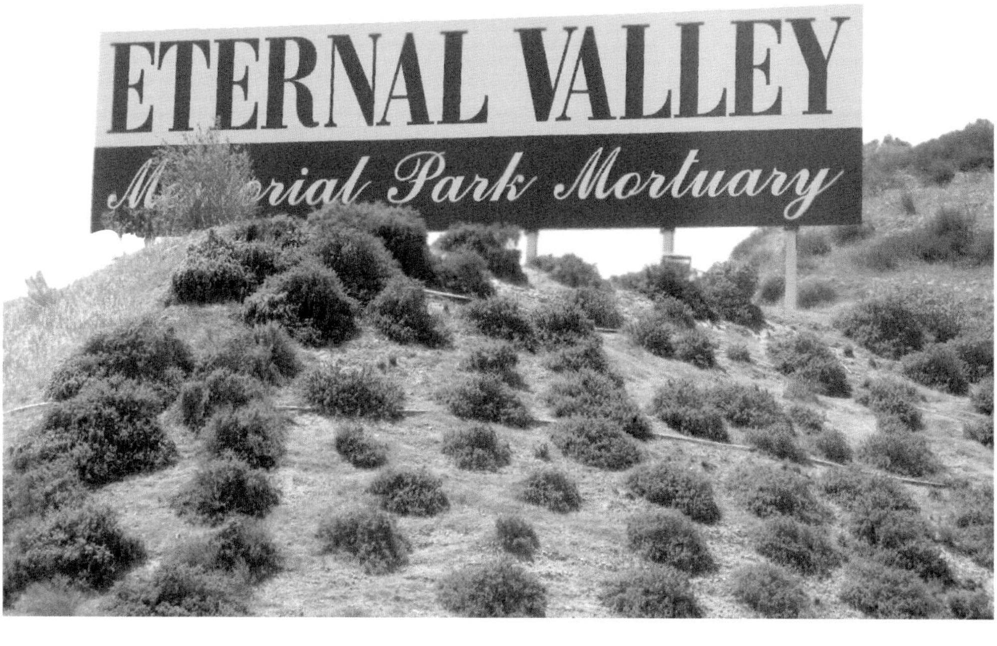

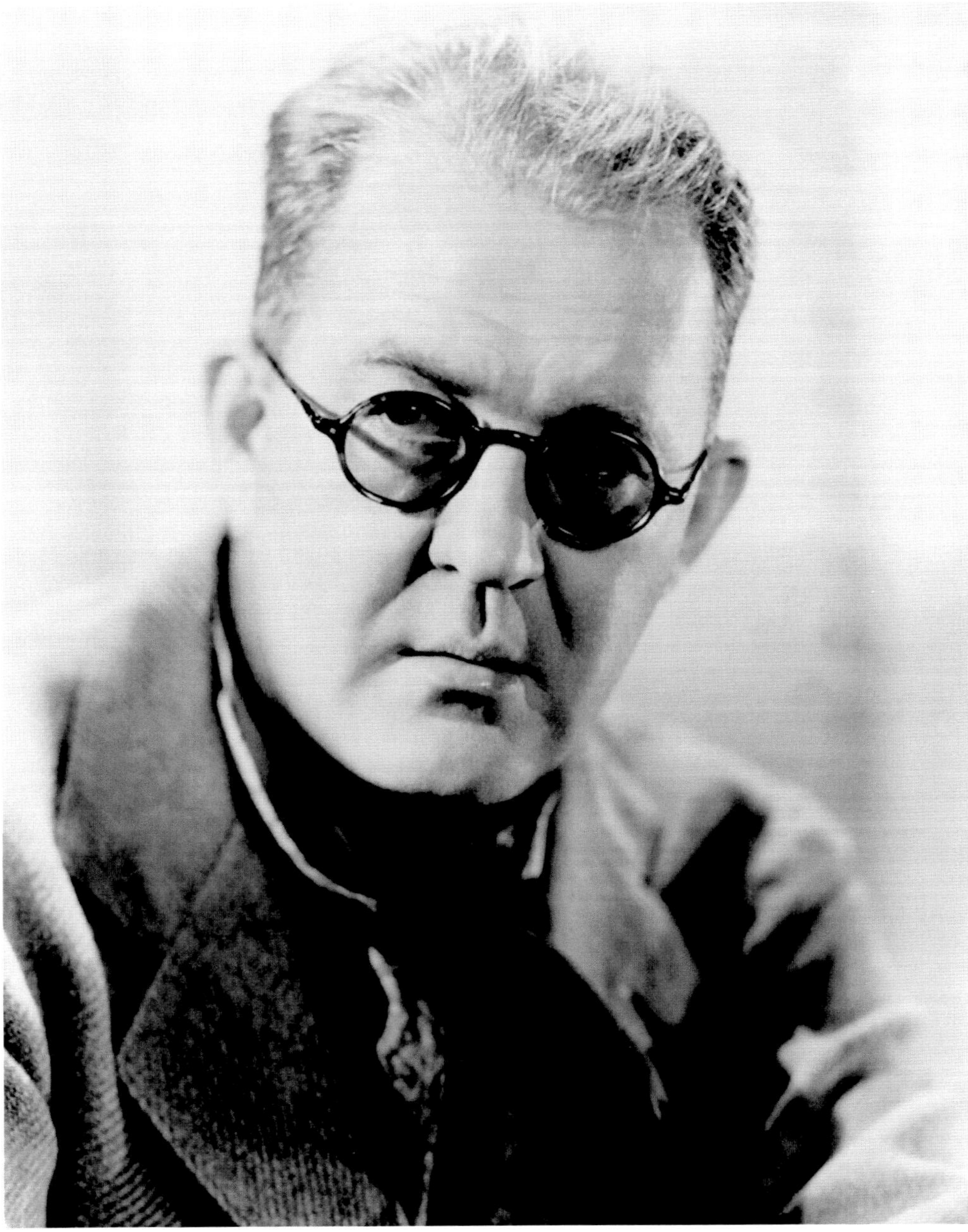

John Ford

Legendary director John Ford filmed four times at the man-made SCV slit in the mountains called Beale's Cut. Ford first arrived in 1917 to make *Straight Shooting* and was back for *Three Jumps Ahead* (1923). He returned the following year for *The Iron Horse* and again in 1939 for *Stagecoach*, the movie that made John Wayne a star. In a 1995 interview, Gene Autry recalled an exchange between Ford and Wayne that had taken place decades earlier at Autry's Melody Ranch in Newhall. After Wayne arrived on set late and hungover, Ford publicly berated him, denying Duke water on the hot set. Secretly, on Ford's orders, Autry slipped Wayne a shot of bourbon. Years later, Duke sent Autry a signed picture that read, "To Gene Autry. A lot of water has gone under the bridge. And whiskey too."

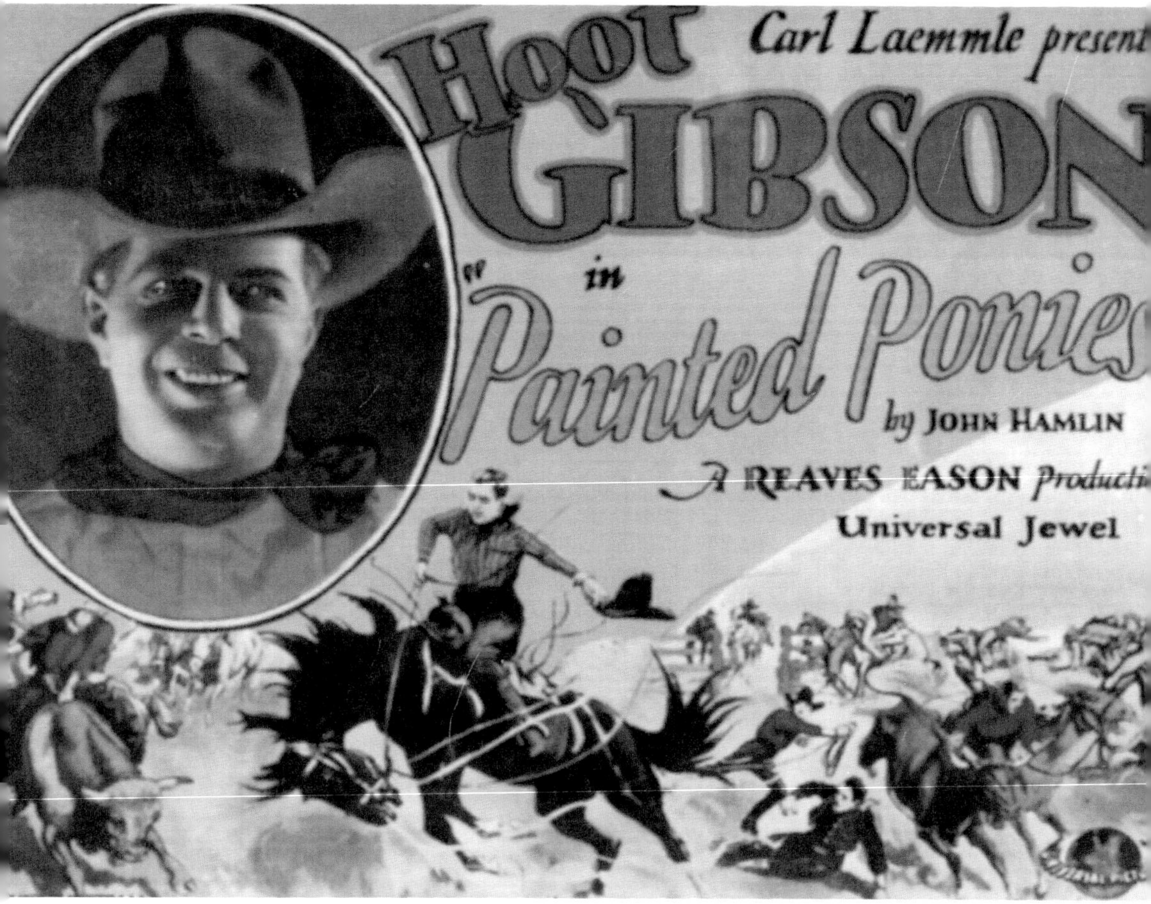

Hoot Gibson

Like his cinematic peer and Santa Clarita Valley neighbor, Gene Autry, Edmund Richard "Hoot" Gibson (1892–1962) began his working career as a telegraph operator. As a young delivery boy for the Owl Drug Company, Gibson earned his nickname when he became affectionately known as "Hoot Owl," which was later shortened to Hoot. A love of horses coupled with his superior riding ability made him a world rodeo champion and landed him a job in the motion picture industry as a stunt rider in D.W. Griffith's *Two Brothers* in 1910. In part because of his friendship with Santa Clarita Valley resident Harry Carey, Gibson soon became a sought-after silent star at Universal Studios. Gibson's homely-yet-handsome looks and winning smile perfectly filled the character gap between the dashing Tom Mix and the austere William S. Hart and appealed to people of all ages, especially women. He successfully weathered the industry's transition from silents to talkies and continued to star in several Universal films. Gibson made a fortune during the 1920s but saw his film career decline during the Depression. Bad investments and broken marriages threatened to ruin him financially. In 1930, Gibson bought part of the Baker Ranch and Rodeo in Saugus (located at the present-day Saugus Swap Meet) for $250,000, but the bank later foreclosed on the mortgage. An abandoned barn that Gibson erected can still be seen on the property. Gibson toured for years with various circuses and spent time as a greeter at a Las Vegas casino. He appeared in the occasional film until 1959, but by the early 1960s, the millions he had made during his career were gone, and he was dying of cancer. He was later honored with a star on the Hollywood Walk of Fame and inducted into the Western Performers Hall of Fame. He also earned a spot on Newhall's Walk of Western Stars. A saddle he used in the rodeo in 1934 can be seen in the SCV Historical Society museum at the Saugus Train Station at Heritage Junction in Newhall. The poster is from Gibson's *Painted Ponies* (1927).

Charlie Chaplin

In the summer of 1935, silent screen comic Charlie Chaplin came to Sierra Highway in the Santa Clarita Valley to film the final scene of his silent comedy classic *Modern Times*. In the film, Chaplin, playing his most legendary character "The Little Tramp," with Paulette Goddard at his side, walks down the empty road in search of adventure. This iconic scene (below) was pivotal in the history of motion pictures, as it was the last time the Little Tramp was ever seen on film. Since *Modern Times* was the last major silent motion picture made at that time, this scene brought the curtain down on the entire Silent Era. Chaplin had been to the valley before. In 1923, he filmed part of *The Pilgrim* at the Saugus Train Station. At right is the sign that hangs on the "Chaplin Door" at the station, which Charlie walks through in the film.

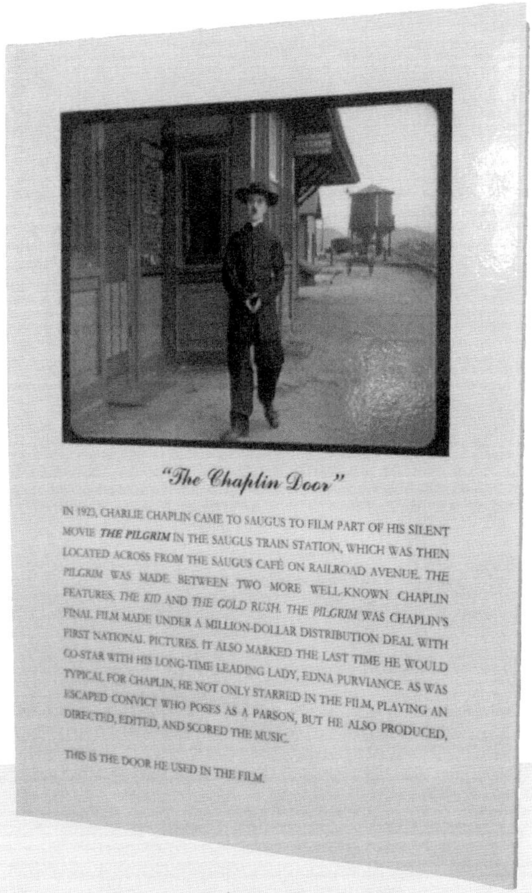

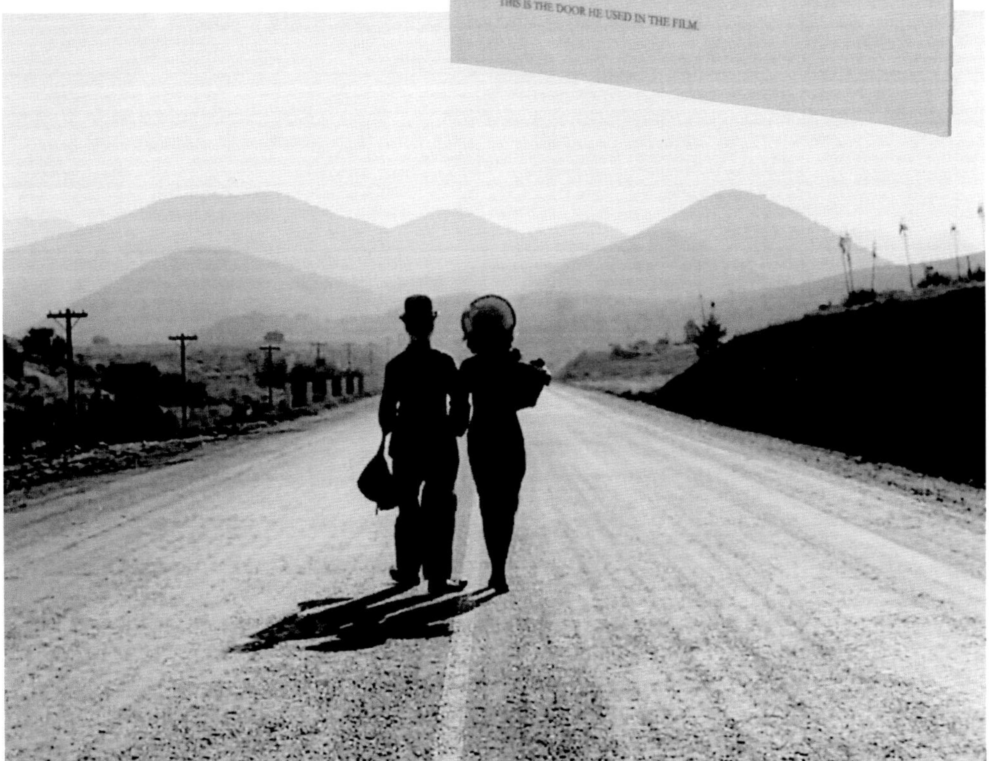

Charles and Maria Sotelo

To commemorate the 75th anniversary of the release of the epic silent comedy *Modern Times*, the Santa Clarita Valley Historical Society, the William S. Hart Park and Museum, and the Los Angeles County Museum of Natural History jointly hosted a silent film festival in February 2011 called *ChaplinFest* at William S. Hart Park and Heritage Junction in Newhall. Hollywood luminaries Tippi Hedren (who appeared in Chaplin's final film, *A Countess From Hong Kong*) and Leonard Maltin appeared at the festivities where a large black granite plaque commemorating the film's anniversary was unveiled. The plaque's creators, Charles and Maria Sotelo of High Desert Monuments in Hesperia, California, donated their time to the monument's creation. Plans are in motion to place the monument on Sierra Highway at the site of the final scene. The Sotelos are pictured posing next to their creation (right and below).

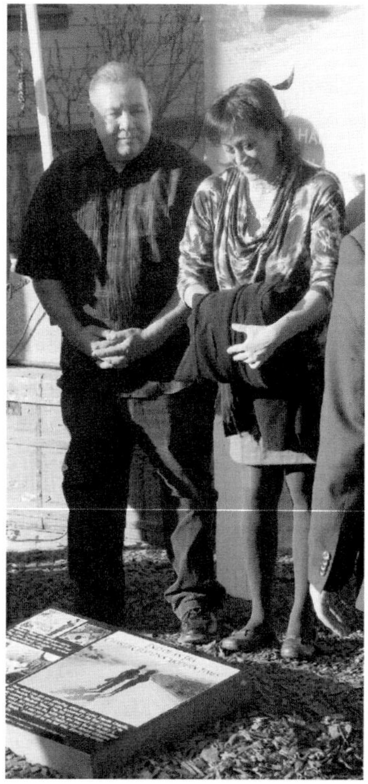

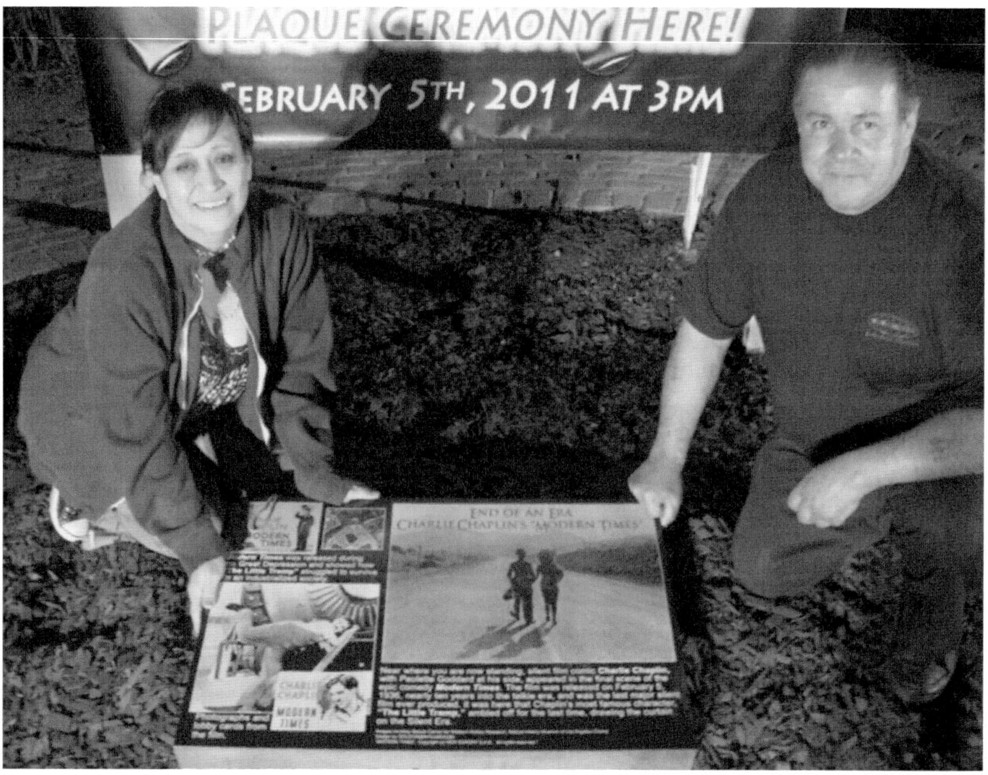

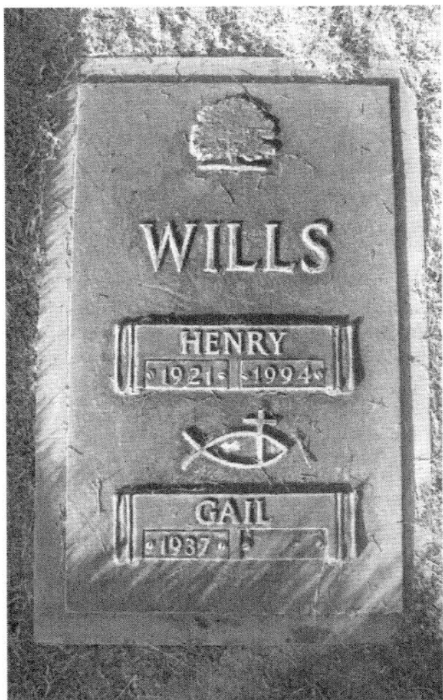

SCV Stuntmen

Despite decades of hard spills, many of the valley's famous stunt people lived to a hoary age. Jack Williams, who began his career at the age of four, lived to be 85. Rodeo champion, stuntman, and Cowboy Hall of Fame inductee Andy Jauregui died at the age of 87. Legendary Yakima Canutt, who was somehow able to beat the odds by living to be 90, created one of cinema's most famous action sequences when he slid under the horse team in *Stagecoach* (1939). Steven Spielberg paid homage to the scene in *Raiders of the Lost Ark*. Pictured below, Andy Jauregui stands with William S. Hart at the Jauregui Ranch in 1938. At left is the grave of SCV stuntman Henry Wills, who made over 1,500 horse falls during his long career, and died one day past his 73rd birthday.

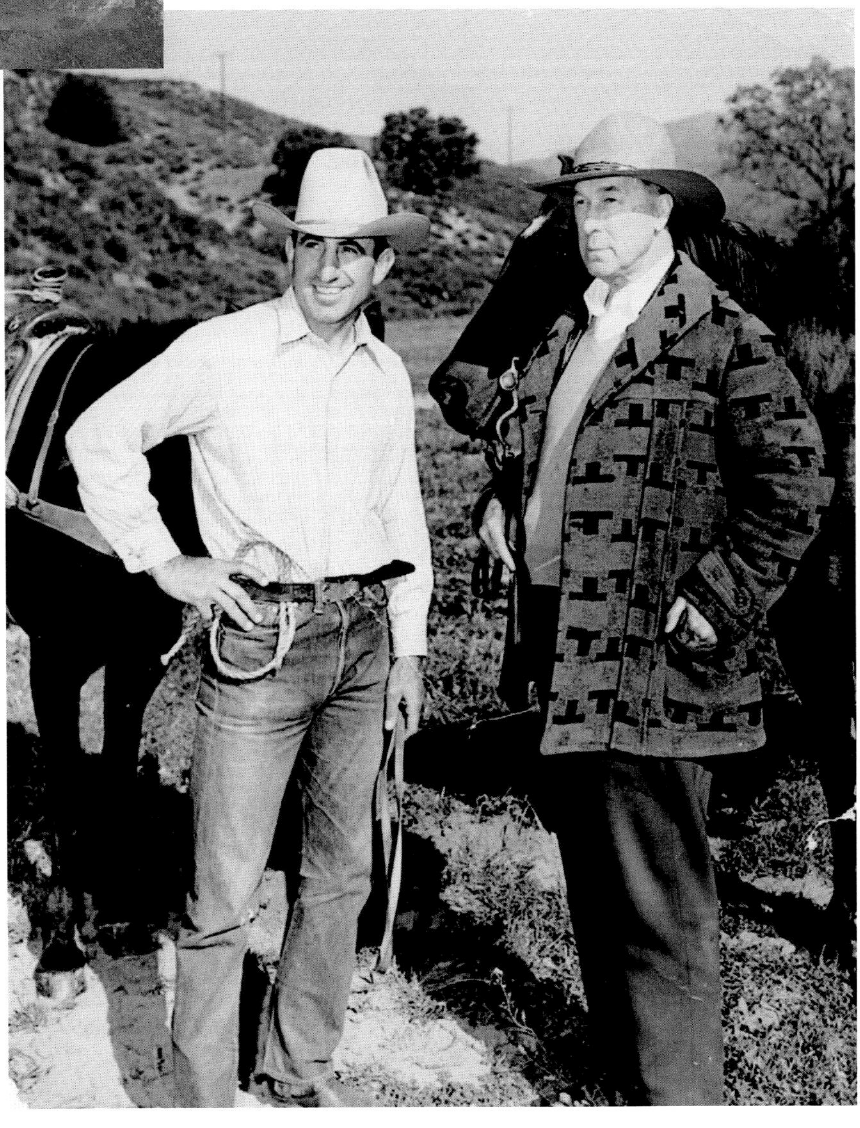

Tom Mix

Once the biggest film star in the world, former nickelodeon cowboy hero Tom Mix died on October 12, 1940, when the car he was driving plunged into a washed-out gully south of Florence, Arizona. His sturdy aluminum suitcase struck him on the head, crushing his skull. Mix had an exciting biography, which seemed to get more colorful with each telling. He claimed to be a child of the West, with one-quarter Cherokee ancestry, and to have been one of Teddy Roosevelt's "Rough Riders" in the Spanish-American War. He also reported that he had been a Texas Ranger and US Marshal before becoming a film star. In truth, Mix was born in 1880 in Pennsylvania, and though he did enlist in the Army in 1898, he remained stateside and never saw combat. He served as a lawman, but never in Texas, and instead of pinning on a marshal's badge, Mix found employment as a local constable in Oklahoma and Kansas. But to Mix's credit, and unlike many Western film stars, he *was* a cowboy, earning his spurs for a time on the largest ranch in America, where he became an expert rider and shooter. Fame came quickly to Mix after his first film in 1910. By the 1920s, he was making $7,500 a week and oversaw the construction of several Western film sets called "Mixvilles" around Southern California, including one in downtown Newhall. Mix's film career ended with the coming of talkies, but his fame continued in radio on the *Tom Mix Ralston Straight Shooters* program. It is estimated that Mix made over $6 million during his film career (which translates to roughly $400 million today), but spent most of it on high living and costly divorces (he was married five times). He was not quite penniless at the time of his crash, but it may have been better for him if he had been, because the suitcase that killed him was filled with money, traveler's checks, and jewels. Mix is pictured here in a white hat (far left) in Newhall during the filming of *Tom Mix in Arabia* (1922).

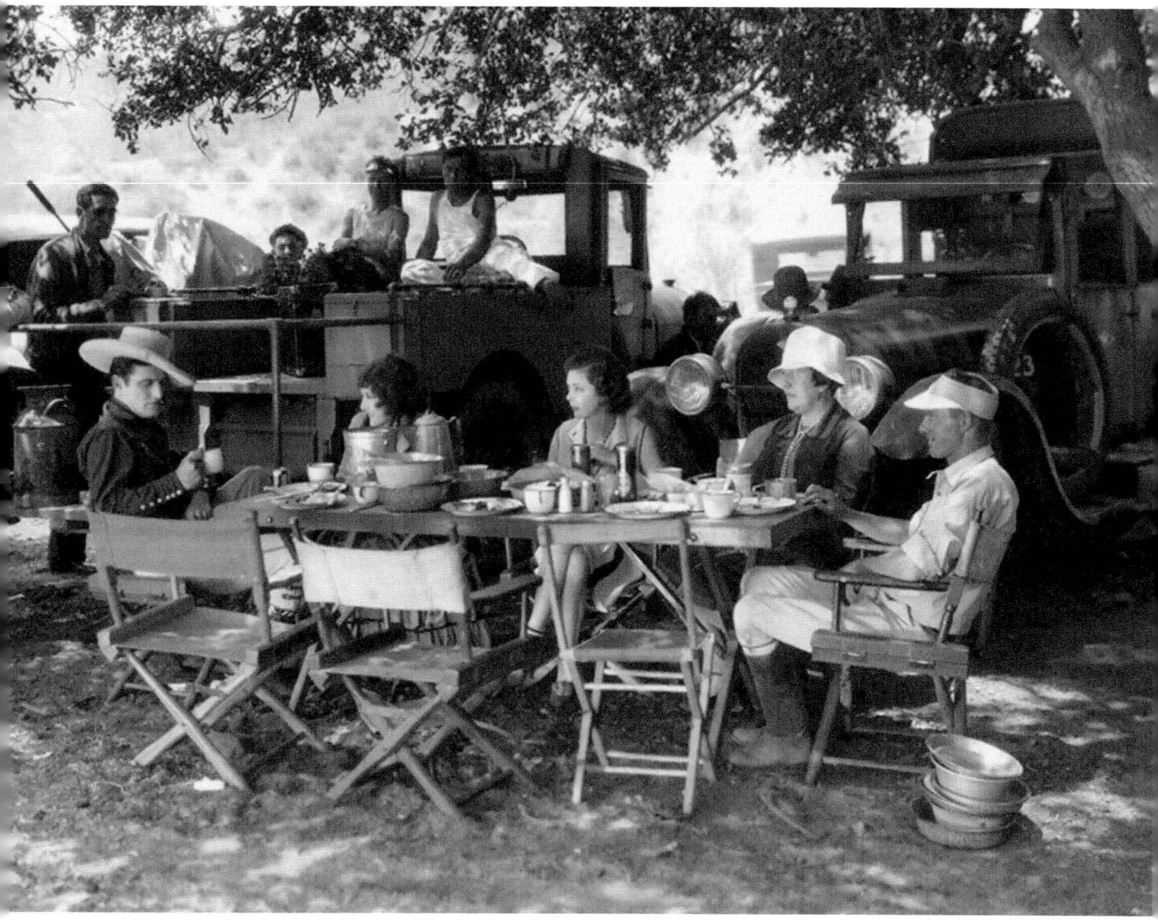

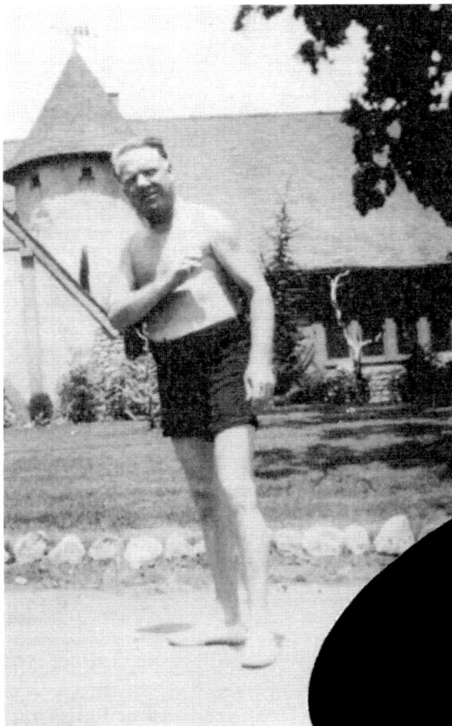

W.C. Fields

For a time in the 1930s, comedian W.C. Fields lived in Newhall in one of the houses built by fellow vaudevillian Charlie Mack, who, along with comic George Moran, made up the comedy team the "Two Black Crows." Mack and Moran performed in blackface, an overtly racist and demeaning depiction of African Americans that was popular at the time with white audiences. At roughly the same time, Al Jolson filmed part of the early talkie *Mammy*, which was a film about a blackface singer, in Newhall. Fields came back to Newhall in 1940 to film part of *My Little Chickadee* at Melody Ranch alongside Mae West. Fields is pictured at left in front of the Mack house in 1935. It still stands on Eighth Street in Newhall.

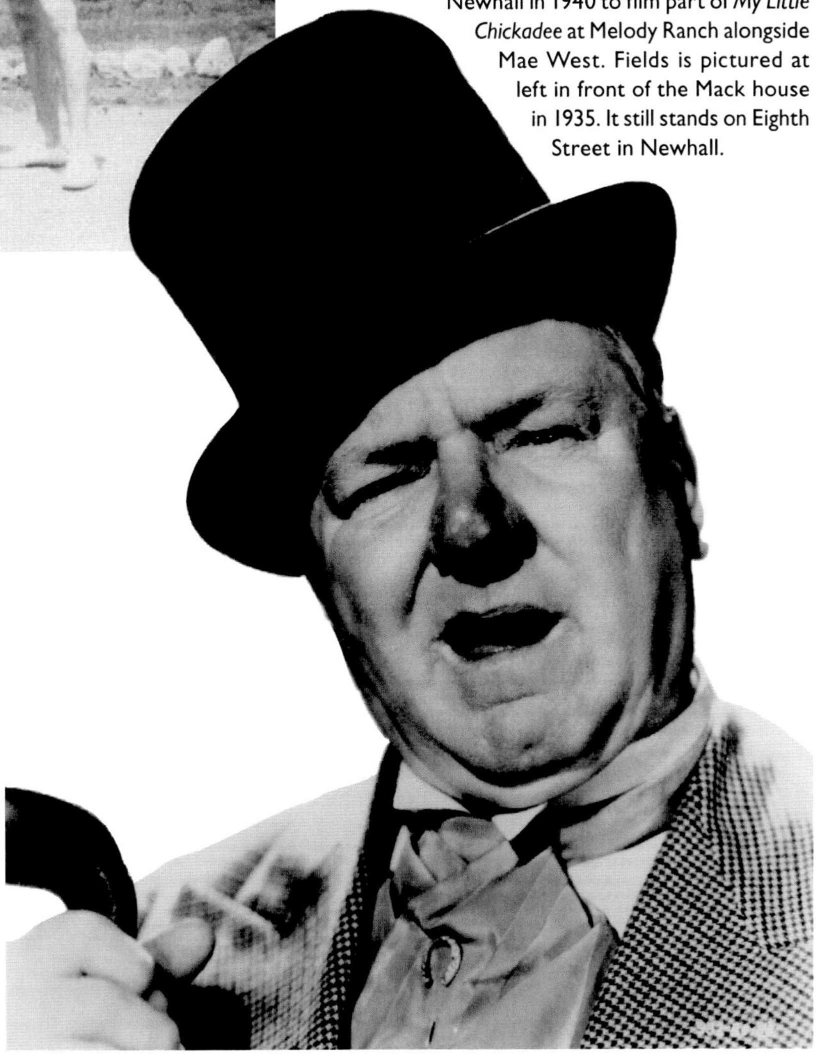

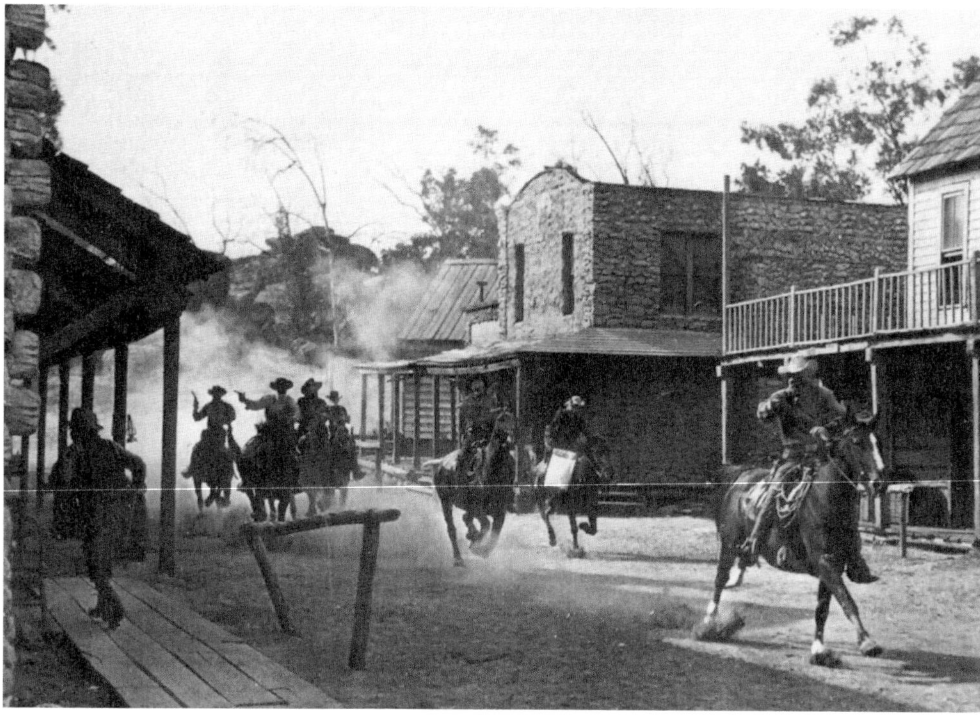

Ernie Hickson

In the early 1930s, artist and set designer Ernie Hickson built an authentic Western town in Placerita Canyon for producer Trem Carr using wood he acquired from ghost towns. In 1936, Hickson purchased his own 10-acre plot of land and reportedly dragged his original Western town to the new location, where he rebuilt the sets. It became known as Monogram Ranch and eventually expanded to a full-feature Western studio on 110 acres. Hundreds of B-Westerns were made at the ranch, which was later renamed Placeritos Ranch, and Hickson became a popular member of the community by opening up his sets to the public for Fourth of July celebrations. Singing cowboy Gene Autry had long coveted the property and purchased it a year after Hickson's death in 1952, renaming it Melody Ranch. Above is a publicity photograph for *Waco* (1952), starring Bill Elliot, which was filmed at the ranch. Below is Melody Ranch shortly before the 1962 fire.

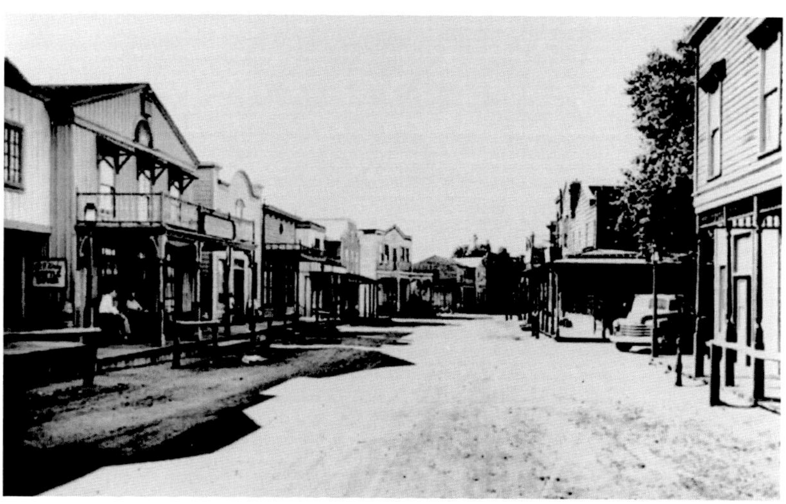

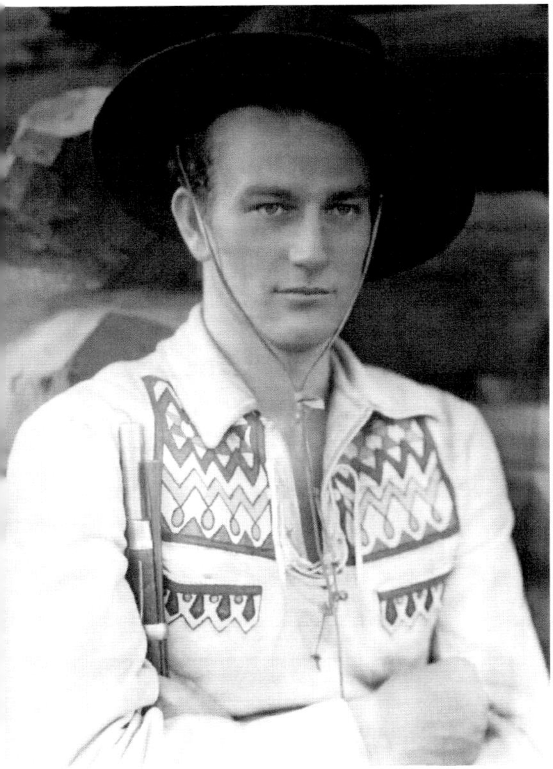

John Wayne and Bob Steele

When one thinks of singing cowboys, Roy Rogers and Gene Autry immediately spring to mind . . . but John Wayne? Lots of filmmakers used Ernie Hickson's Newhall sets to make Westerns, including writer-director Robert N. Bradbury. Bradbury often cast his son Bob in his films. Bob —who used the stage name Bob Steele—got his Glendale High School buddy "Duke" Morrison a job in one of his father's movies. A short time later, Morrison, now known as John Wayne (pictured at left in 1930's *The Big Trail*), was warbling as "Singin' Sandy" Saunders in 1933's *Riders of Destiny*. Wayne couldn't sing a note, and it is possible that Steele's twin brother, Bill, dubbed Duke's singing voice on film. (In *Riders of Destiny*, Duke chases down some bad guys on the rubble of the St. Francis Dam.) Below is an undated publicity photograph of Bob Steele.

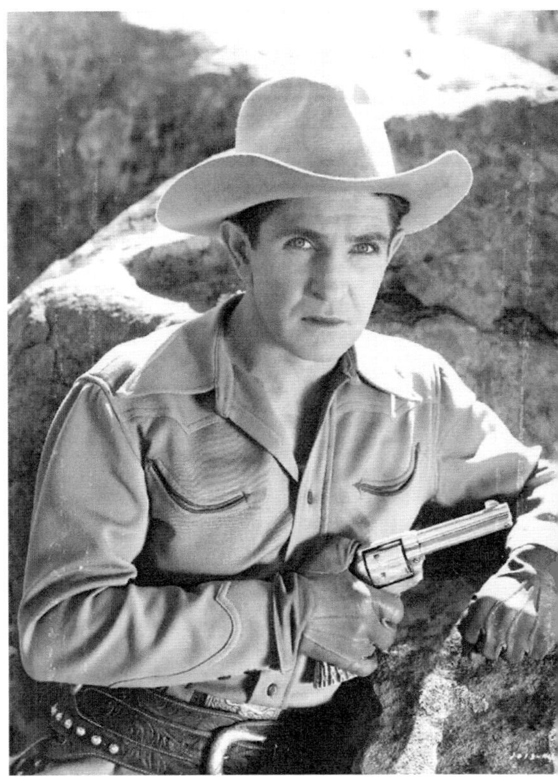

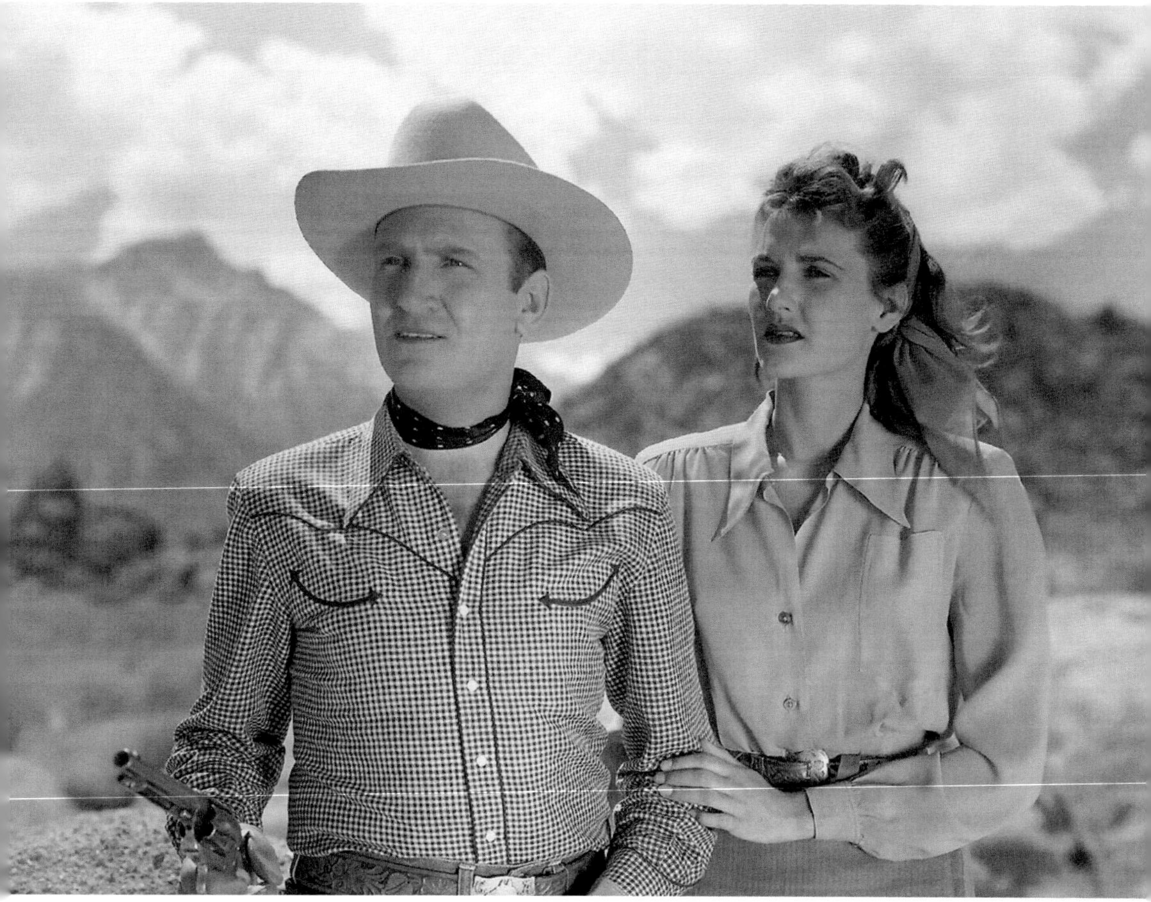

Gene Autry

Of the more than 2,400 performers who have been immortalized with terrazzo and brass stars embedded into the Hollywood Walk of Fame, only singing cowboy superstar Gene Autry has a star in each of the five featured categories of film, television, music, radio, and live performance. Orvon Grover Autry, who for decades owned Newhall's Melody Ranch, was born in Texas in 1907 and grew up on a ranch across the Oklahoma line. Autry signed his first recording contract in 1929 and hosted his own music show for four years on WLS-AM in Chicago, where he met singer-songwriter Smiley Burnette. Hollywood came calling, and Autry headed west to make dozens of enormously successful singing cowboy films over the next 20 years atop his horse Champion, with Burnette often cast as his singing sidekick. Autry recorded more than 600 songs and sold over 100 million records. His biggest hits were in the Christmas music category, where he struck gold with "Santa Claus Is Coming To Town," "Here Comes Santa Claus," "Frosty the Snowman," and "Rudolph the Red-Nosed Reindeer." A wise investor, Autry was the longtime owner of LA's KTLA television station as well as the American League baseball team that is today known as the Los Angeles Angels of Anaheim. Melody Ranch in Newhall, another former Autry property, has been seen on screen in hundreds of Westerns, including many made by Autry. He acquired it in 1953 and used it daily for film and television production until August 1962, when a brushfire burned most of it to the ground. For the next three decades, the property served as a retirement home for his horse Champion. In 1991, brothers Renaud and Andre Veluzat purchased the ranch and re-created the Western town from old photographs. It has since been home to dozens of commercials, films, and television shows. Autry passed away at the age of 91 on October 2, 1998, just three months after the death of his friend and rival, Roy Rogers. Gene is pictured here with another SCV resident, Peggy Stewart, in *Trail to San Antone* (1947).

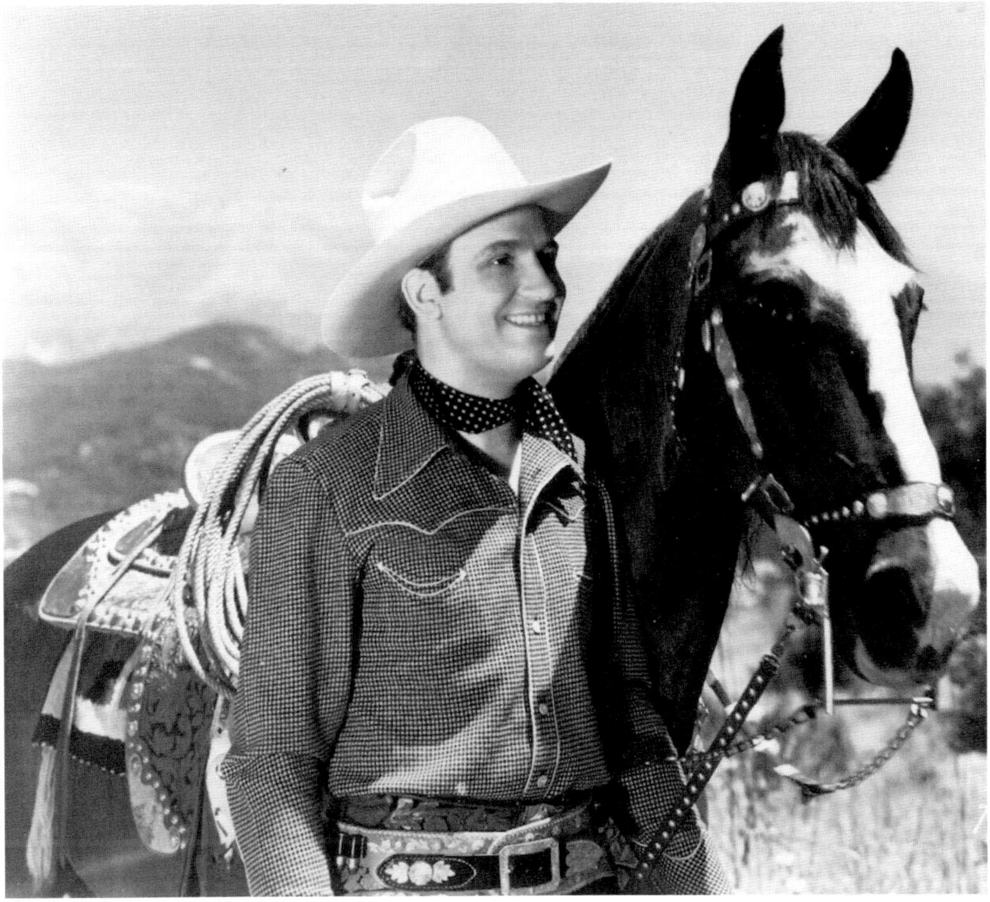

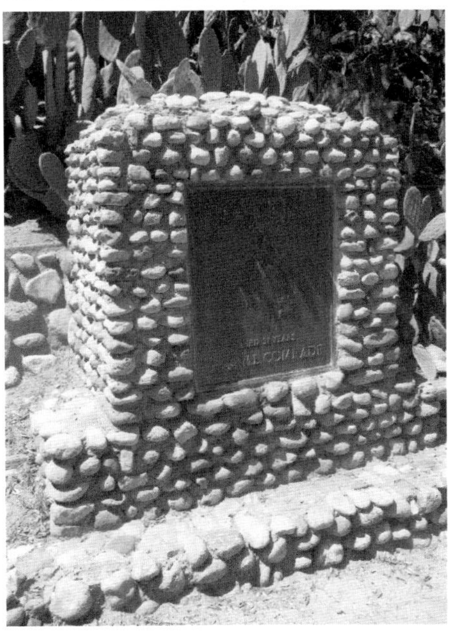

Champion, Tony, and Fritz
Without cowboys there would be no Westerns, and without horses there would be no cowboys. Gene Autry's horse, Champion (pictured above with Autry in 1938), achieved such celebrity status that for two years he had his own television show. Tony was the equine companion of cowboy actor Tom Mix. The two appear to jump Beale's Cut in Mix's 1923 film *Three Jumps Ahead.* (It was likely an example of cinematic visual trickery. Legendary SCV stuntman Andy Jauregui may have been aboard Tony that day.) Tony's hoofprints can be seen next to Mix's autograph outside Grauman's Chinese Theatre in Hollywood. He died two years to the day after Mix was killed in an automobile accident. William S. Hart's beloved pinto pony Fritz is buried on the grounds of Hart's Newhall ranch (left). The photograph above is of Gene and Champion in *Prairie Moon* (1938).

Harry Carey

Harry Carey (seen at right in a signed photograph from the 1930s), who is said to have discovered John Ford and been John Wayne's idol, was one of the earliest stars of Western silent film. Carey's rugged frame and gravelly baritone later carried him successfully into the sound era. He later purchased a large ranch in Saugus (today, the Tesoro Adobe Historic Park) with actress-wife Olive Golden. Their son, Harry Carey Jr., appeared alongside his mother and father in two films, *Red River* and *The Searchers.* In the final shot of *The Searchers*, John Wayne holds his right elbow with his left hand, a frequent Carey pose, in tribute to his late friend. Wayne later said that at the close of the scene, he and Carey's widow wept. Below is a photograph of Carey's trading post on his ranch. (Courtesy Anita Ruby Kellogg; enhanced by Audrey Erickson.)

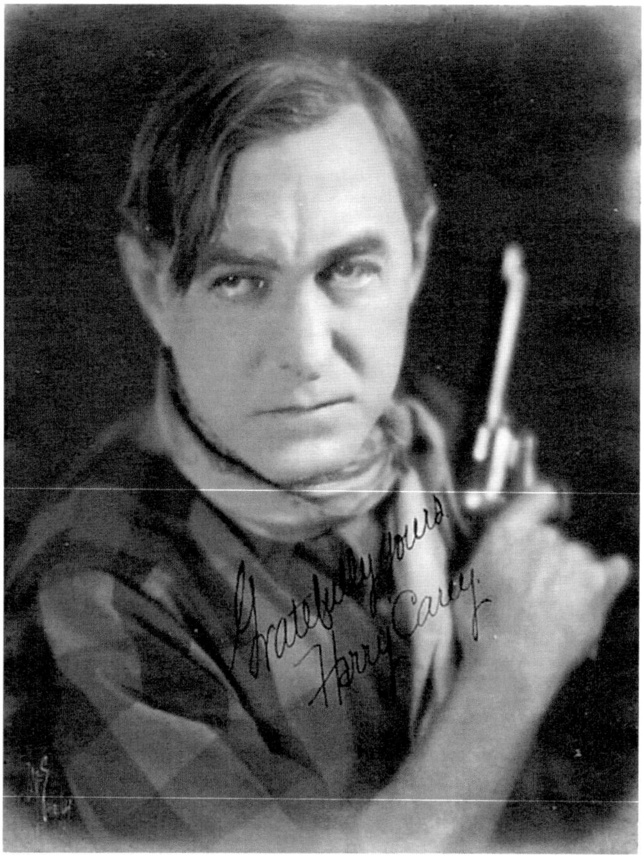

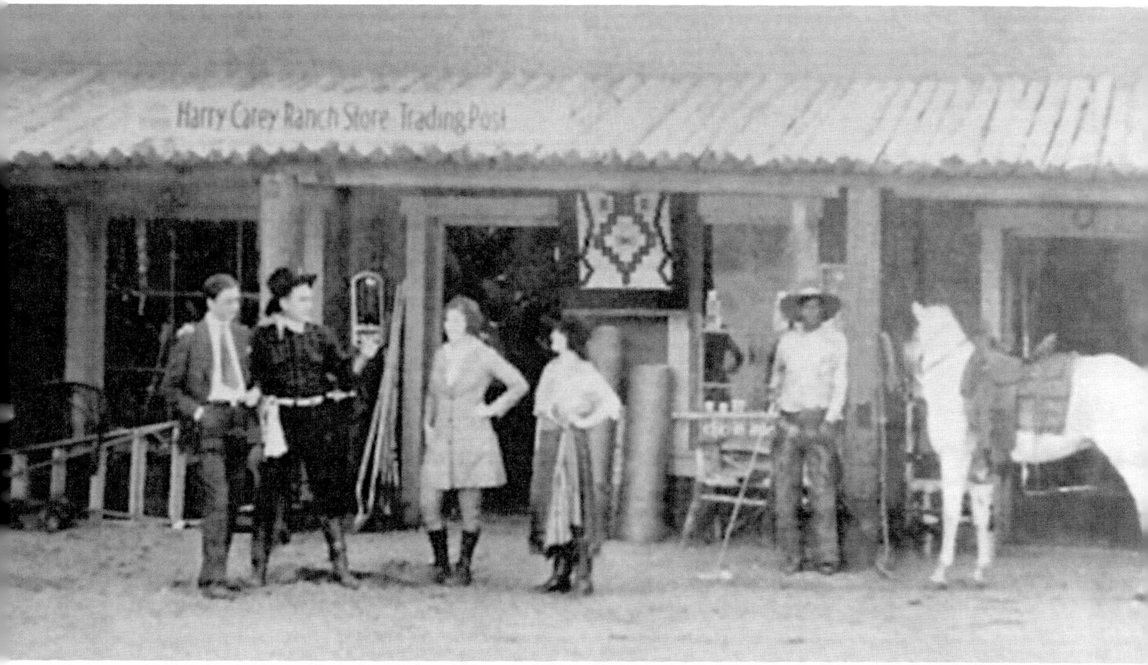

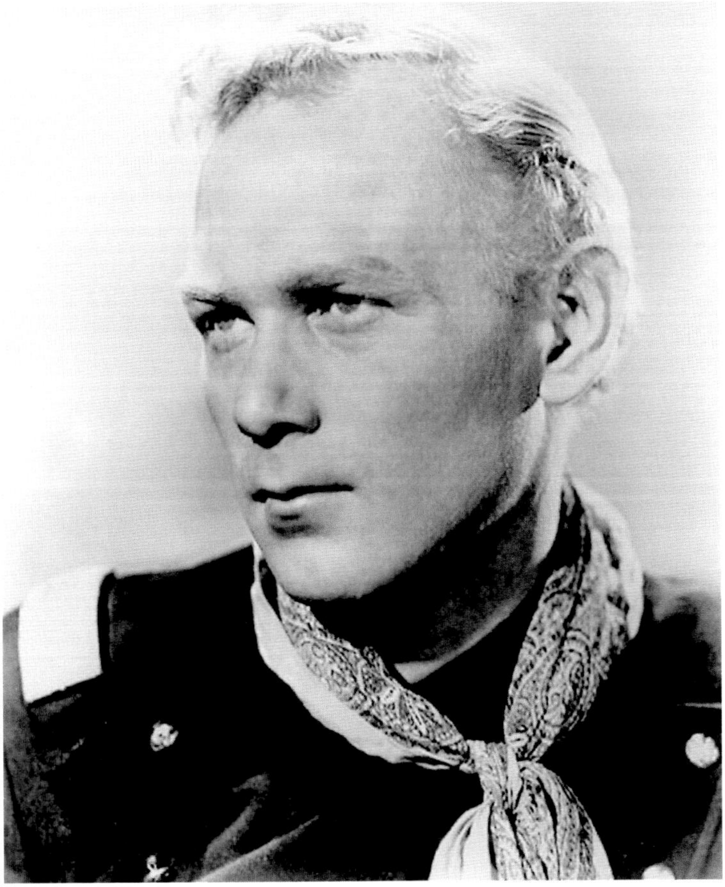

Harry Carey Jr.

Harry Carey Jr. (above), known to his friends as "Dobe" (pronounced *Dobey*, short for the red adobe color of his hair), was a respected character actor like his father and appeared in more than 90 films. Dobe (above) and his sister, Ella "Cappy" Carey, enjoyed happy childhoods on their parents' ranch in Saugus. Visitors today can still see "Dobe" carved into a surrounding wall at the ranch.

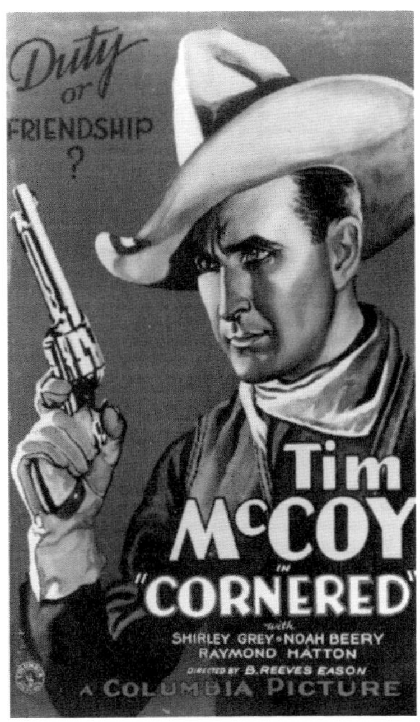

Tim McCoy

Michigan-born film star Tim McCoy (right) took to the West like a rustler to cattle, appearing in dozens of Westerns over a 40-year career, many filmed in the SCV. McCoy was married to Danish reporter Inga Arvad, who was investigated by the FBI after appearing alongside Adolph Hitler at the 1936 Munich Olympics. In the 1940s, she reportedly had an affair with John F. Kennedy. The poster comes from the 1934 film *Cornered*.

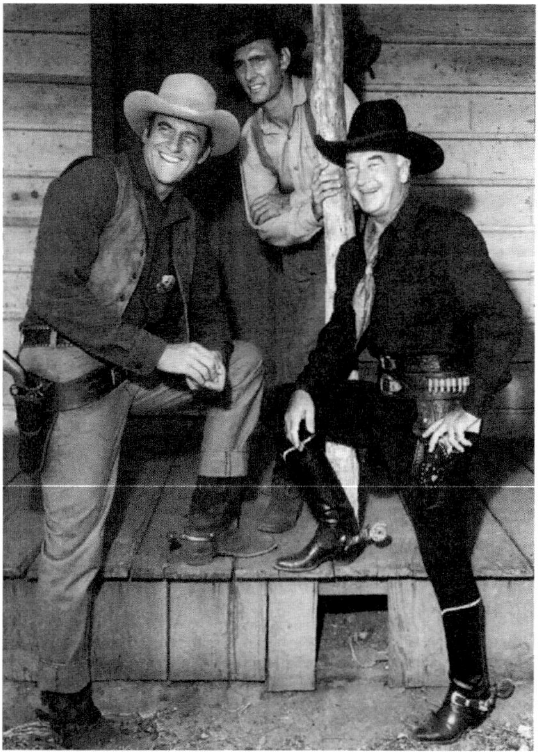

William Boyd
After starring in dozens of Hopalong Cassidy movies, William Boyd mortgaged everything to purchase the rights to the Hoppy films and character. Barely able to survive, Boyd and his wife Grace lived for a time at Gene Autry's Melody Ranch. When television came along, Boyd's big gamble paid off in a major way, earning him millions. From left to right are James Arness, Dennis Weaver, and William Boyd at Melody Ranch.

Tor Johnson
A "tor" is a large pile of rocks. At six-foot-four inches and 400 pounds, Swedish-born actor Tor Johnson *looked* like a large pile of rocks. Johnson, who is buried in Newhall's Eternal Valley Cemetery, became a 1950s schlock film fan favorite in Ed Wood's *Plan Nine From Outer Space* (1959). His "gentle giant" nature contrasted sharply with the monsters he played on film, proving that this "pile of rocks" had a heart of gold. He is pictured here carrying Mona McKinnon in a scene from *Plan Nine*.

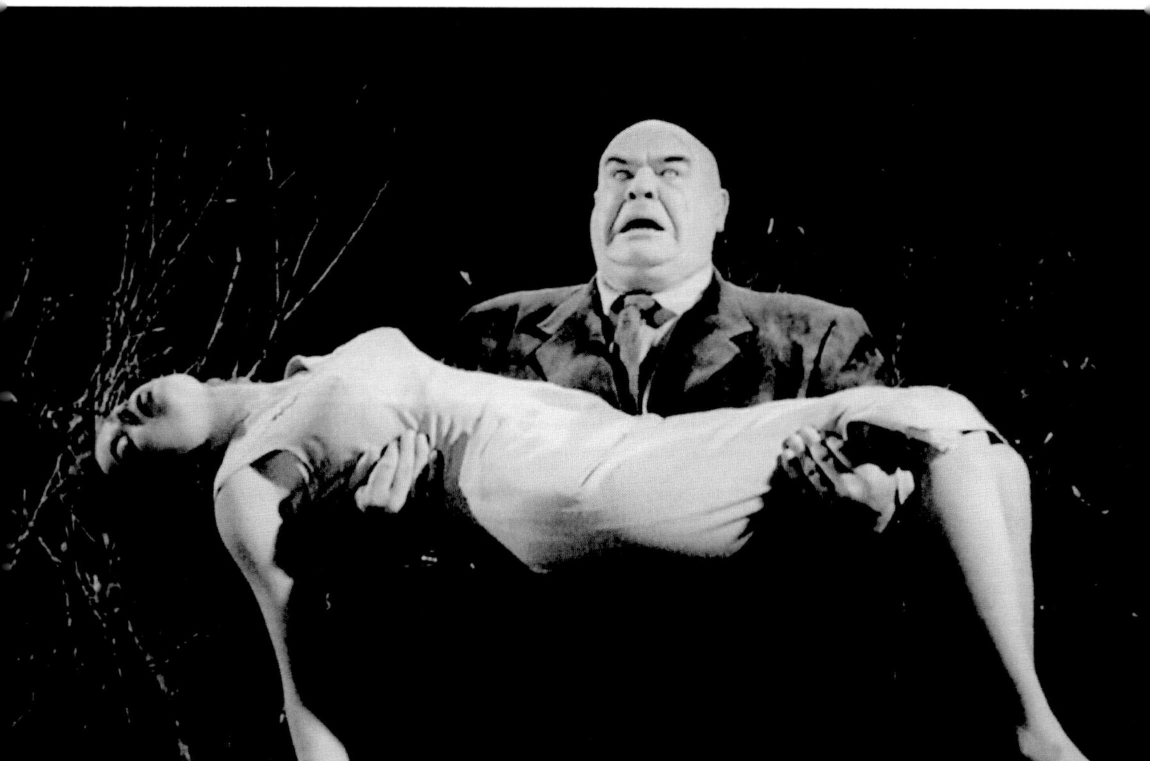

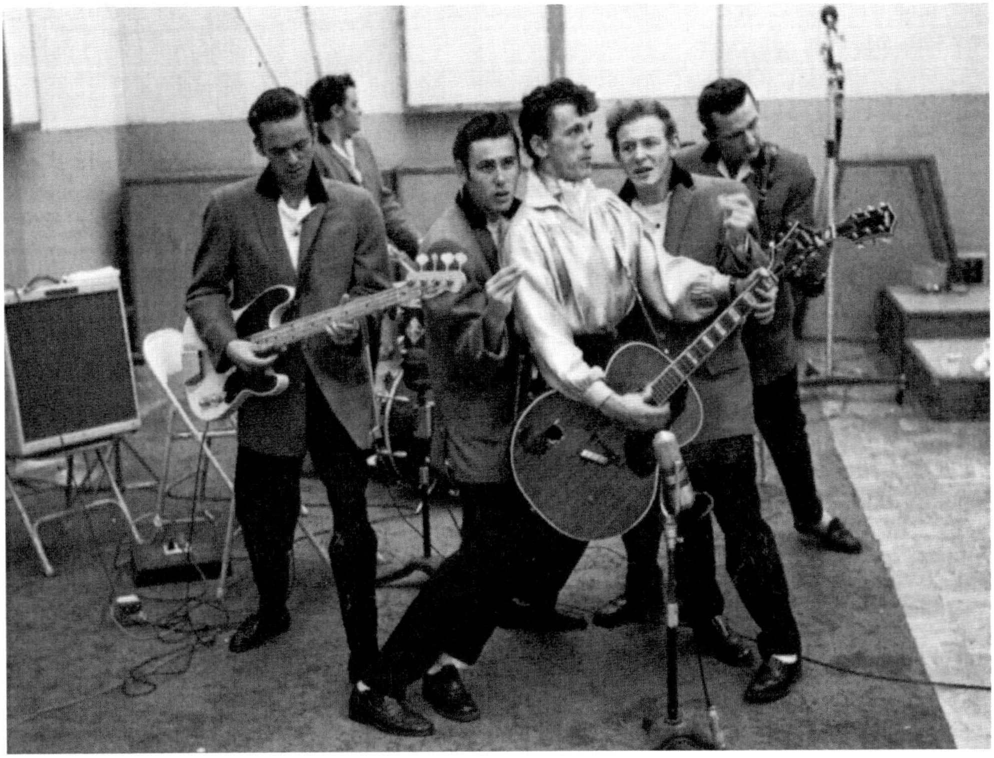

Gene Vincent

While the song "Be-Bop-A-Lula" is familiar to most fans of rock-and-roll, the story of the ditty's singer and co-author, permanent Santa Clarita Valley resident Gene Vincent, has largely been forgotten. Gene Vincent, whose real name was Vincent Eugene Craddock, was born in Virginia in 1935 and began playing guitar at the age of 12. He left school early to join the Navy, where he was stationed in Korea. After returning stateside, he was involved in a serious motorcycle accident that shattered his leg, leaving him with a permanent limp and chronic pain for the rest of his life. He wrote "Be-Bop-A-Lula" in the hospital while recovering from the injury. During the frantic months after the song's release in June 1956, Gene and his band, the Blue Caps, recorded an album, played numerous concerts, and appeared in *The Girl Can't Help It*, the first rock-and-roll feature film. Gene had a few follow-up hits, but nothing approached "Be-Bop-A-Lula" in popularity. With his career stalling in America, he went to Europe, where he was greeted as a hero by his legions of fans, which included a group of lads from Liverpool. Paul McCartney later wrote that "Be-Bop-A-Lula" was the first record he ever bought. The song helped bring the nucleus of the Beatles together when, as a 15-year-old, McCartney played it for John Lennon in a tryout for a spot in Lennon's band, The Quarrymen. Just before "Beatlemania" set the world ablaze, the group met and befriended their idol in Hamburg where Gene helped them craft their sound. Vincent spent the following years recording and touring, but years of heavy drinking, bad relationships, and poor management had compromised his finances and wrecked his health. He was visiting his parents in October 1971 when he was rushed to a hospital in Saugus, where he died from a bleeding ulcer. He was laid to rest in Newhall's Eternal Valley Cemetery. Recently, "Be-Bop-A-Lula" was listed as one of the "500 Songs That Shaped Rock and Roll" by the Rock and Roll Hall of Fame in Cleveland, where Gene was posthumously inducted in 1998. Vincent is pictured here, fourth from the left, with other members of the Blue Caps, at a recording session in Hollywood in the late 1950s.

Del Shannon

Gene Vincent is not the only Rock and Roll Hall of Famer to have ties to the Santa Clarita Valley. Del Shannon (pictured in 1974), who scored a number-one hit with 1961's classic single "Runaway," lived and died in Canyon Country's Sand Canyon district. The story of the song begins in the late 1950s in Battle Creek, Michigan, where Charles Westover played guitar at a local club. Westover, using the stage name Del Shannon, tried out an organist from Ann Arbor named Max Crook who played his own hand-made early synthesizer, which he called a Musitron. The tune for "Runaway" grew out of an impromptu jam session. Shannon wrote the lyrics the next day between tending customers at the carpet store where he worked. It became an immediate local hit, and soon the men and their wives were braving icy roads to New York for the recording session. They recorded "Runaway" and three other songs in only three hours with the help of some session musicians. Back in Battle Creek, Shannon presented the first copy of *Runaway* to the owner of the carpet store for letting him write the lyrics on company time. Within three weeks, the single was released, and on April 24, 1961, it reached the top of Billboard's charts where it would remain for a month. "Runaway" sold millions of copies, and secured Shannon's place in the Rock and Roll Hall of Fame in 1999. Like Vincent, Shannon's first hit was by far his most popular, and his later career was hampered by heavy drinking. At the end of his life, he was rumored to be replacing Roy Orbison, who had recently passed away, in the band The Traveling Wilburys, joining Tom Petty, George Harrison, Bob Dylan, and Jeff Lynne. But it was not to be. On February 8, 1990, Shannon, who suffered from depression, shot himself at his home just off Sand Canyon. His wife blamed Prozac for his death and later unsuccessfully sued Eli Lilly & Company, the drug's manufacturer.

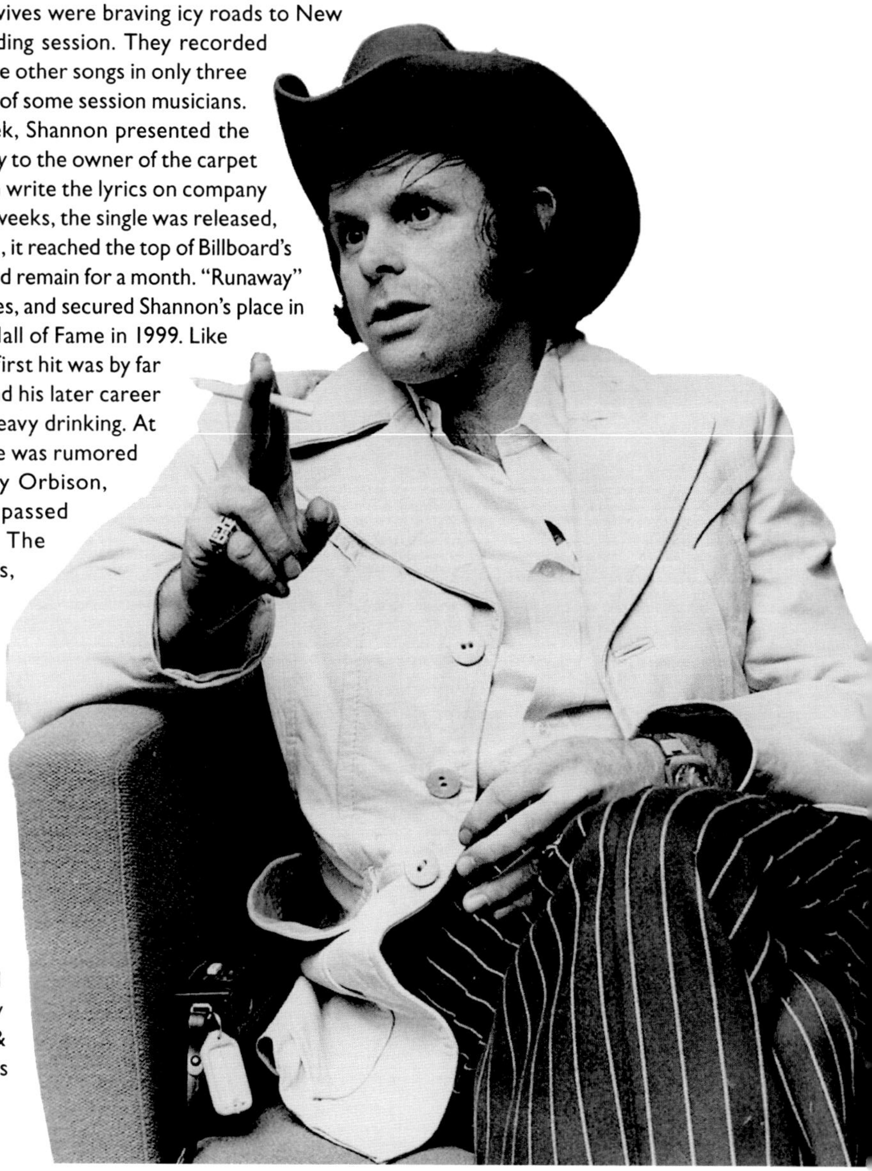

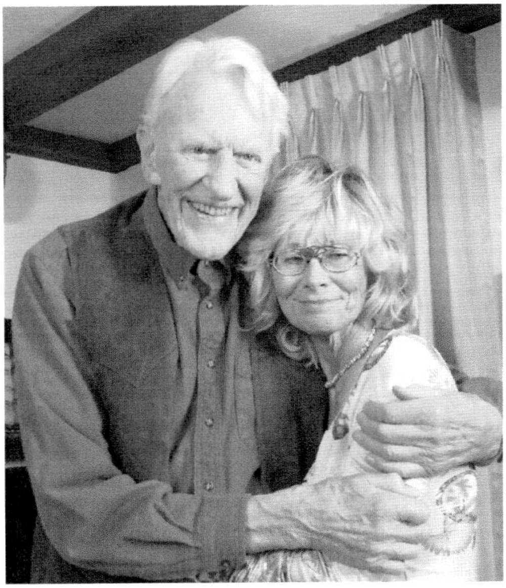

James Arness

For 20 years, millions of television viewers invited James Arness into their homes each week. The long-running Western *Gunsmoke*, which filmed for a time in the SCV, made a star of the Minnesota-born Arness, who made it to Hollywood after being machine-gunned by Nazis in World War II. After a stint as a beach bum, Arness landed parts as a "heavy" due to his imposing six-foot-seven-inch frame. John Wayne put Arness under contract and recommended him for the role of Marshal Dillon on *Gunsmoke*. Arness was reluctant to take the part, but Wayne proved persuasive and even filmed a teaser for the first episode to introduce America to the man who would become a generation's friend and role model. At left is an April 2006 photograph of Arness and his wife, Janet. Below, Dennis Weaver and James Arness appear in *Gunsmoke* at Melody Ranch in 1956.

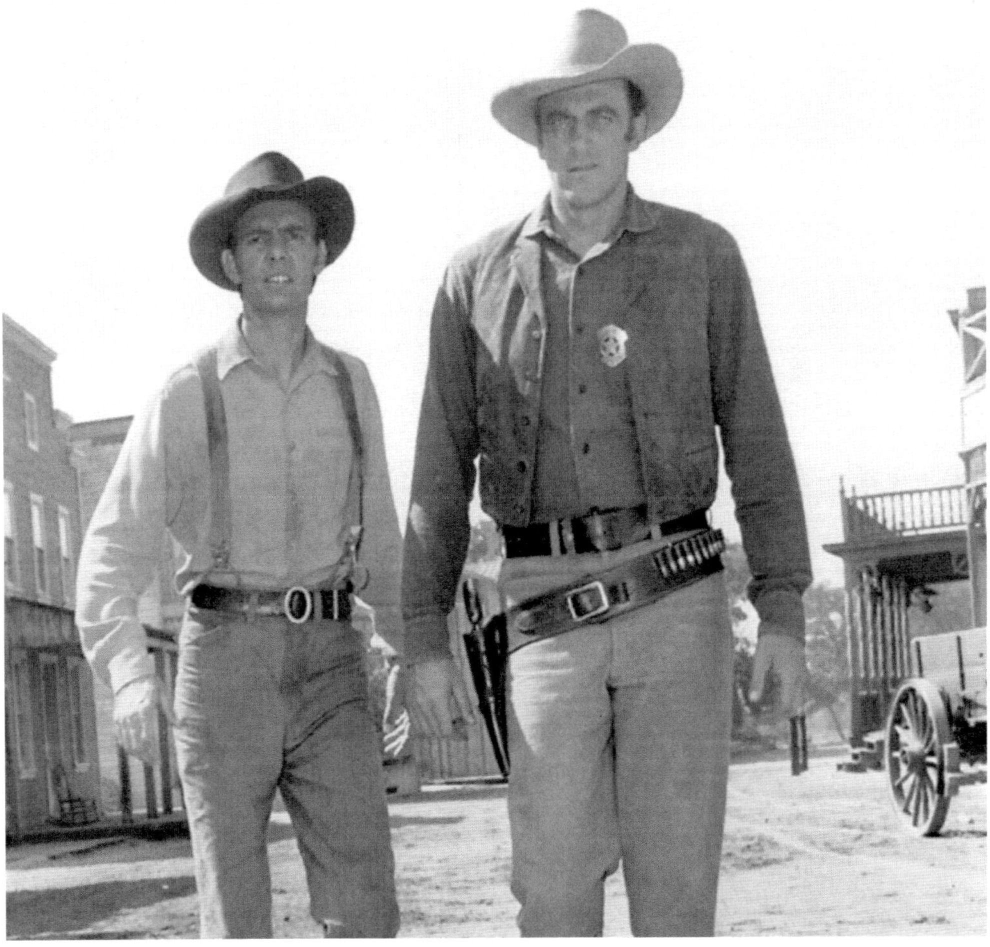

Eternal Valley's Hall of Famers

It is one thing to achieve success in the music business, but quite another to be inducted into a particular genre's hall of fame. As previously mentioned, Newhall's Eternal Valley Cemetery is the resting place of Gene Vincent, a 1998 inductee into the Rock and Roll Hall of Fame and the very first performer chosen for the Rockabilly Hall of Fame. Two other musical legends who were also inducted into halls of fame are buried nearby. Near the top rests musical legend Cliffie Stone, born Clifford Snyder, a country singer, musician, disk jockey, record producer, author, and music publisher. As the host of the *Hometown Jamboree* radio program from 1946 to 1960, he helped launch the careers of dozens of country musicians. The multi-tasking Stone was signed by Capitol Records in Hollywood as both an artist and as head of its country-and-western division. At the end of his life, he was kept busy directing local legend Gene Autry's vast publishing empire. Stone was awarded a star on the Hollywood Walk of Fame at the corner of Sunset and Vine, and was inducted into the Country Music Hall of Fame in 1989. On the far south side of the cemetery, in the Garden of Meditation, rests singer Roy Brown (pictured here in the 1940s). Roy James Brown was born in New Orleans in 1925 and began his career as a gospel singer. He later switched to the blues, and is now considered to be a pioneering voice in rock-and-roll history. Brown recorded his most famous song, *Good Rocking Tonight,* in 1947. *Good Rocking Tonight* was later covered by Elvis Presley, Paul McCartney, and a host of other singers. A dazzling showman, Brown helped pave the way for later performers like Little Richard and Jerry Lee Lewis. His fortunes declined during the 1960s to the point that he was forced to sell encyclopedias to make ends meet. He died in 1981, the same year he was inducted into the Blues Hall of Fame.

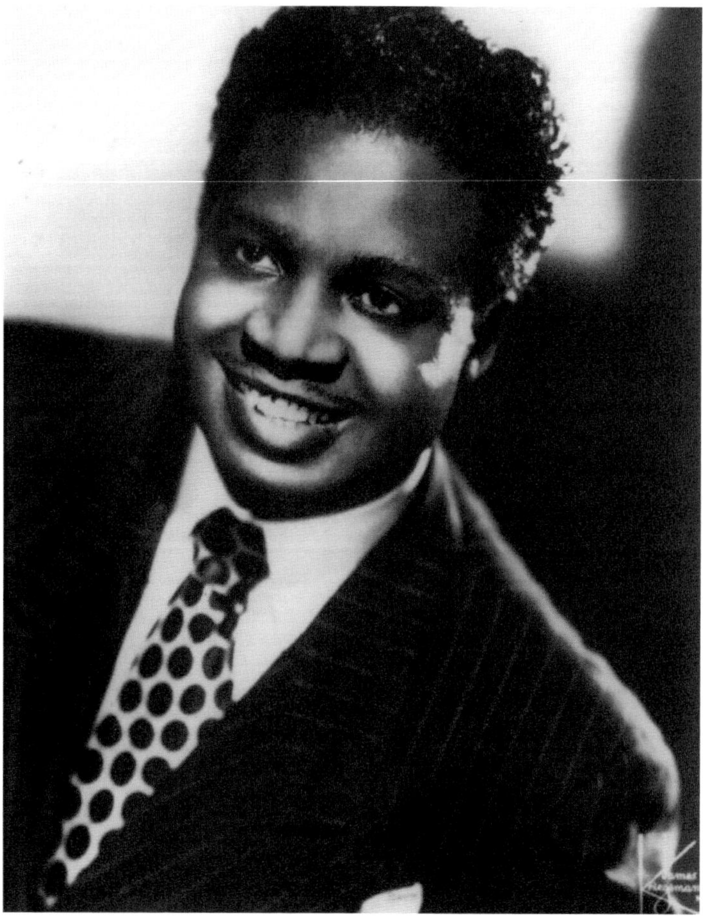

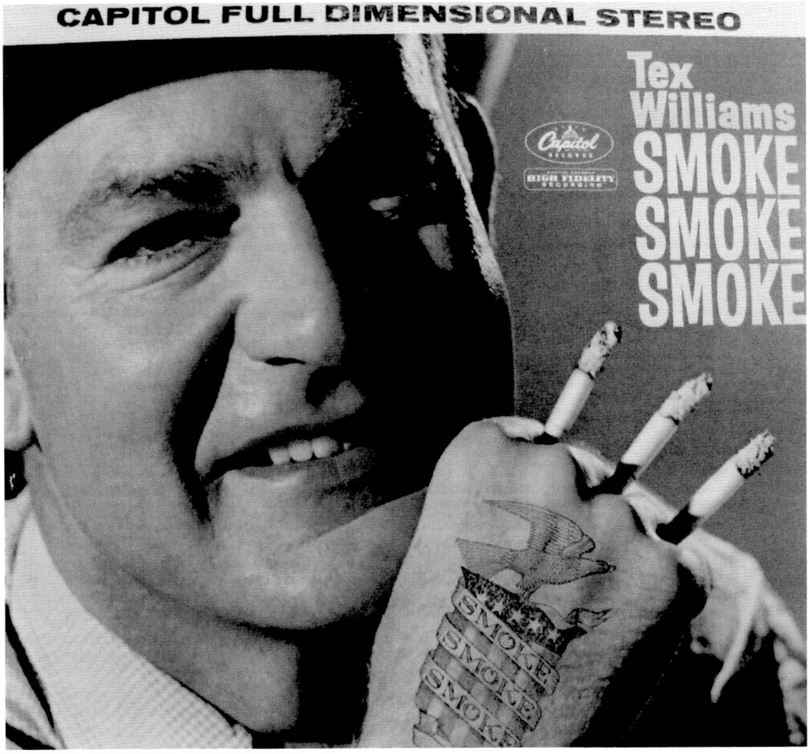

Tex Williams

Eternal Valley is also the permanent home of country singer-songwriter Tex Williams. Born Sollie Williams in Illinois in 1917, Tex moved to Los Angeles after high school and earned his first film role in a 1943 Joe E. Brown movie. During the 1940s and 1950s, he starred in a series of low-budget Western musicals for Universal, known as "oaters." Williams struck musical gold in 1945 as lead singer of the Spade Cooley Orchestra with their single *Shame On You*. Eternal Valley neighbor Cliffie Stone later offered Williams his own recording contract and Tex left Cooley to form Tex Williams and His Western Caravan. In 1947, their single "Smoke! Smoke! Smoke! (That Cigarette)" became Capitol Records' first million-selling record. Pictured above is Williams's "Smoke" album cover. At right is a picture of his grave at Eternal Valley Cemetery in Newhall.

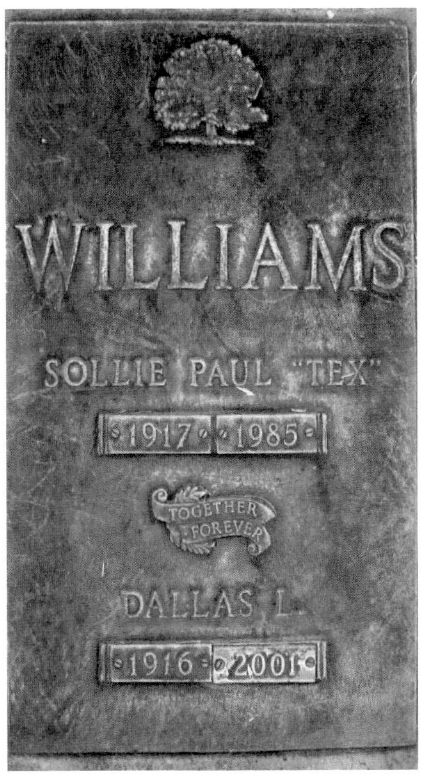

Frank Sinatra

Frank "Ol' Blue Eyes" Sinatra is remembered for being a lady-killer in his films, but what is forgotten is that he once played a would-be president killer as well. The time was October 1954, and the city of Newhall was still small enough to pose as the setting for the sleepy fictional town of Suddenly in the movie of the same name. In the film, Sinatra and a group of hired killers pose as FBI agents who take a group of people hostage in a house overlooking a train station where they intend to shoot the president when he de-trains. *Suddenly* (see poster at left) came on the heels of Sinatra's Oscar-winning performance in *From Here To Eternity.* The film used many locations sprinkled around downtown Newhall and Saugus. Many still exist, including the Benson house on Eighth Street and the Saugus Train Station, which is no longer at the site it occupied in the film but today can be found in Heritage Junction inside the William S. Hart Park. Rumors circulated that Lee Harvey Oswald watched *Suddenly* shortly before assassinating Sinatra's friend John F. Kennedy. This was not the case, but it is possible that Oswald saw the film on its initial release in theaters nine years earlier. The film was pulled from distribution after the Kennedy assassination and was largely forgotten. It again became a subject of controversy in the mid-1980s when a poorly colorized version was released, which turned Sinatra's famous blue eyes brown. The Saugus Train Station has been seen on-screen many times over the years going back to 1923 when silent clown Charlie Chaplin used it as a location in *The Pilgrim.* A few years later, Al Jolson sang the song "Mammy," in the film of the same name, from the back of a train parked at the station. Scenes from an early serial called *The Hurricane Express,* starring a young John Wayne, were also filmed here, and nearly a decade after the station was moved to Heritage Junction, John Cusack came here to film a scene from *The Grifters* (1989).

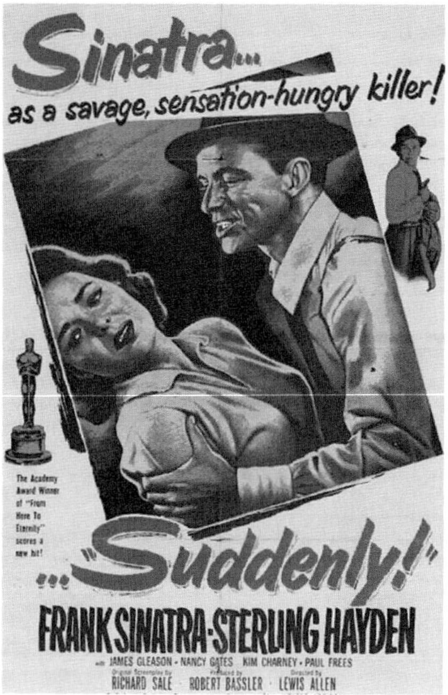

James Dean

Despite only making three films, James Dean (pictured opposite in *Giant*) remains one of the most popular actors in Hollywood history. It is known that he passed through the Santa Clarita Valley on September 30, 1955, just hours before his young life ended in a tragic automobile accident. But some believe he ate his last meal here at Tip's Restaurant in Saugus. An avid racing enthusiast, Dean celebrated the completion of his third film, *Giant*, by purchasing a Porsche 550 Spyder. He nicknamed it "Little Bastard" and decided to drive it up to Northern California to compete in races at the Salinas Airport. That final morning, Dean left Los Angeles with Rolf Wütherich, a 29-year-old mechanic, riding shotgun. They drove along Highway 99 and by some accounts stopped for lunch at a Tip's Restaurant at the corner of the present-day intersection of the Old Road and Magic Mountain Parkway. A waitress named Althea McGuinness, or one named Audrey, or perhaps both, might have served Dean that day. McGuinness's story was reported by former Tip's manager Carmen Cummings in an article in *The Santa Clarita Valley Signal* in September 2005, claiming, "Yes, he did stop there on his last day. He sat at the counter. We all recognized him." After his purported meal, Dean proceeded north up Highway 99 into the San Joaquin Valley where he was ticketed by California Highway Patrol officer Otie Hunter for speeding. He turned west onto US 466 (today California 46) heading towards Paso Robles. Just outside of Cholame, the road meets Highway 41 in a "Y" intersection. Approaching from the opposite direction was a black and white 1950 Ford Custom Tudor coupe driven by 23-year-old Donald Turnupseed. Turnupseed turned left onto 41 but did not see the approaching Porsche in time. The two cars collided in a horrific near-head-on crash with Dean's car ending up crumpled along a fence by the side of the road. He was pronounced dead on arrival at Paso Robles War Memorial Hospital.

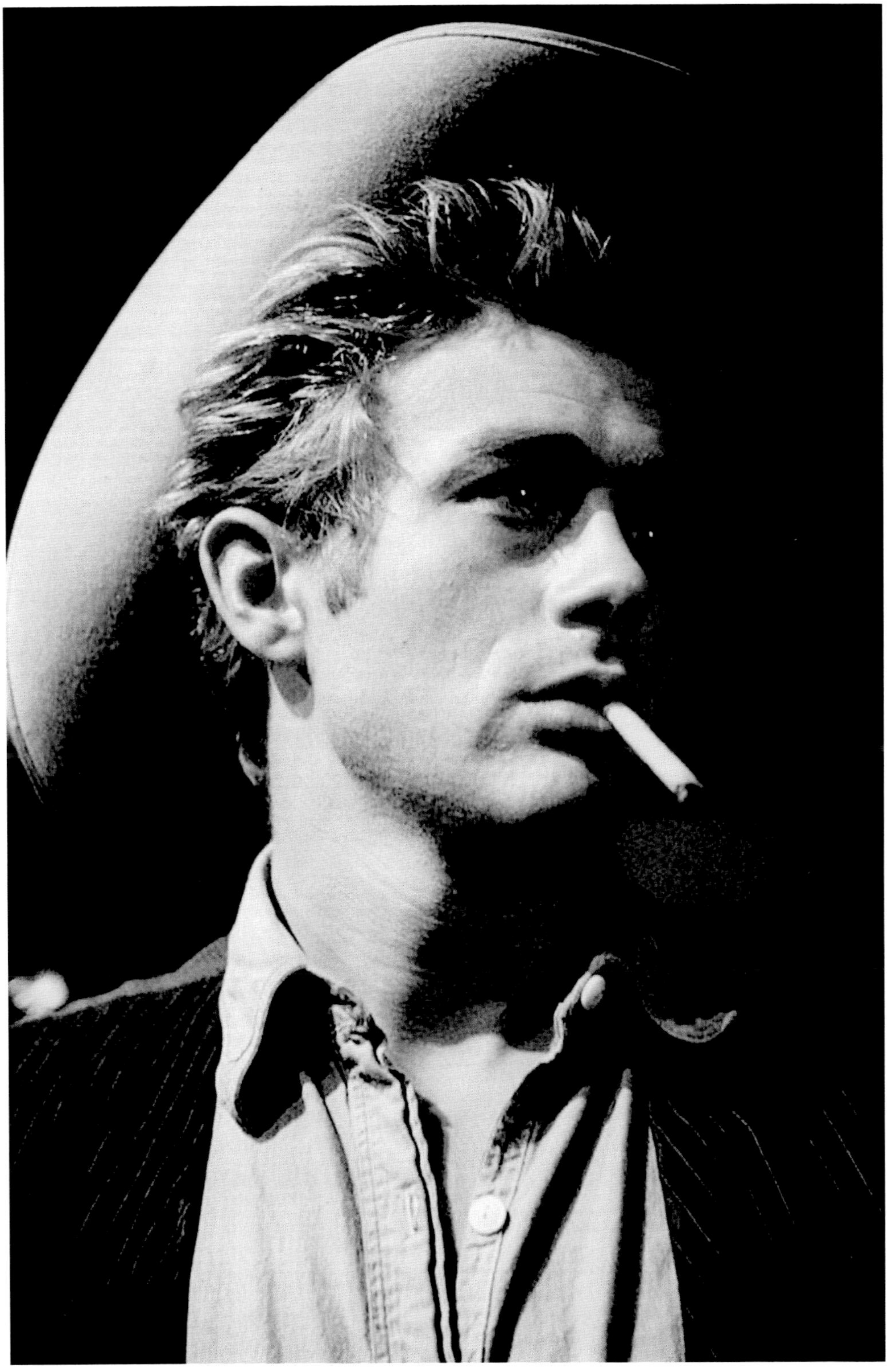

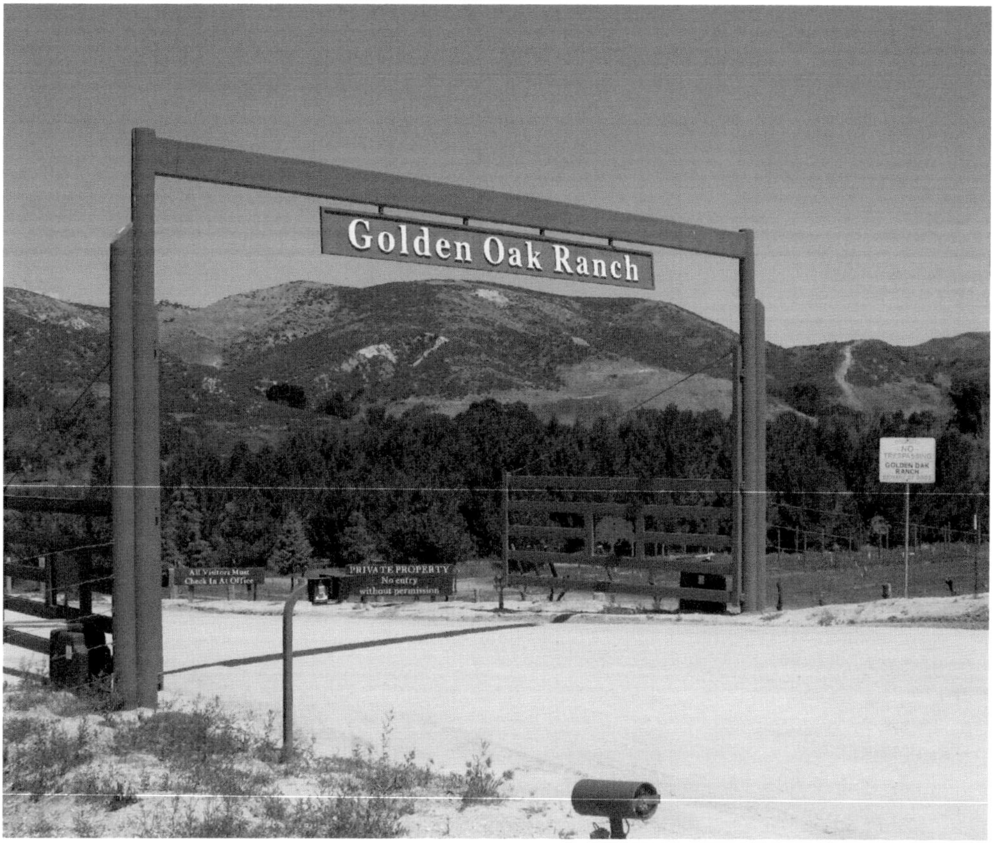

Walt Disney

Film production returned to the original site of Trem Carr's ranch in Placerita Canyon in 1959 when legendary producer Walt Disney purchased the property for $300,000. He named it Golden Oak Ranch in reference to the nearby "Oak of the Golden Dream," where Francisco Lopez made the first California gold strike in 1842. Disney built a new Western town near the site of the one constructed by Ernie Hickson in the 1930s, and it was quickly put into use on episodes of the *Mickey Mouse Club* and *Zorro.* Disney was a frequent visitor to the ranch, spending numerous weekends at his cabin on the grounds. For a time during the Cuban Missile Crisis, the cabin even served as the headquarters for the entire Walt Disney corporate empire. The ranch later showed up on *Bonanza, The Apple Dumpling Gang*, and notably as the Peabody farm in *Back to the Future*. In recent years, it has often been spotted on television and in the *Pirates of the Caribbean* movie franchise. Today, Golden Oak Ranch is one of the most popular filming sites in the county, with over 300 shooting days logged most years. A working ranch, Golden Oak provides produce for the Disney commissary in Burbank and for local food banks. In 2009, the Walt Disney Company announced its plan to create Disney|ABC Studios at the Ranch, building 12 new soundstages with several support facilities and offices at Golden Oak. When completed, the proposed project is expected to create nearly 3,000 new jobs and make a half-billion-dollar annual economic impact throughout the county. The plan calls for only six percent of the current 890-acre ranch to be developed, leaving the majority of the property in its current pristine state. One of Walt's early experiments at the ranch went awry when the bison herd he imported stampeded, going AWOL for several days. After they were rounded up, Disney donated them to the William S. Hart Park in Newhall, where their descendants can still be seen today.

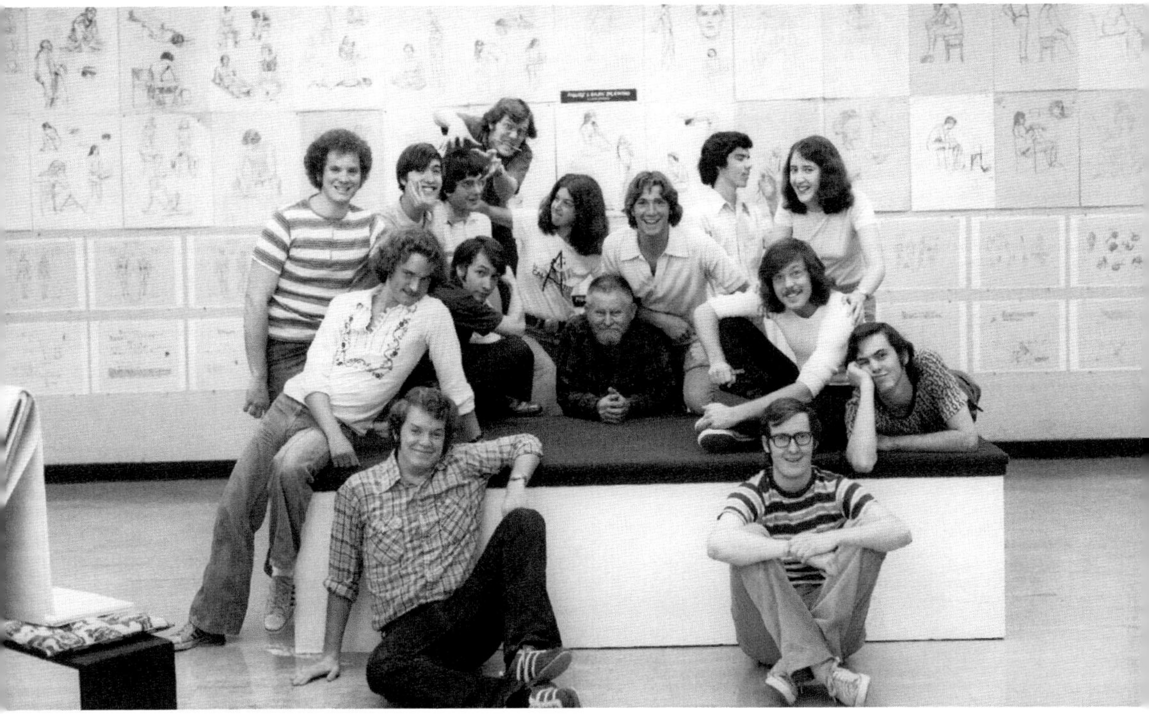

Walt Disney, Educator
Walt Disney's estate paved the way for the California Institute of the Arts in Valencia. A short list of alums includes Pee-Wee Herman, Tim Burton, and Stephen Hillenburg, the man who brought a certain sponge who lives in a pineapple under the sea to T-shirts everywhere. Pictured is the 1976 CalArts animation class with future Pixar creative forces John Lasseter, top, with pencil in mouth, and Brad Bird, middle row, second from right. (Courtesy David Johnson.)

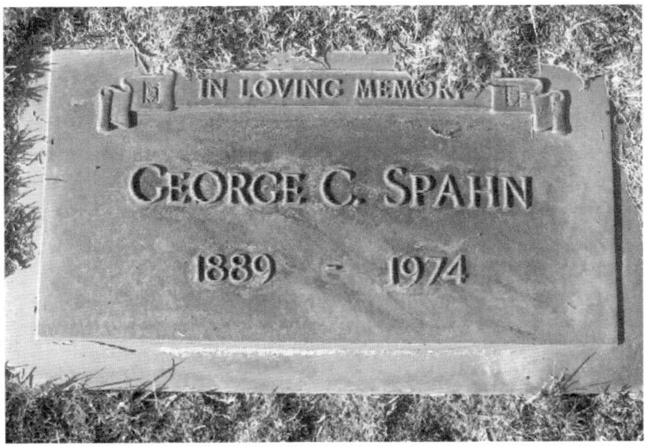

George Spahn
A film ranch in nearby Chatsworth with a gruesome history has connections to two Santa Clarita Valley men. In August 1969, while Charles Manson's "Family" was carrying out the vicious Tate and LaBianca murders, 80-year-old George Spahn, who is buried in Newhall (left), housed the gang at the ranch, allegedly in exchange for "keeping company" with the Family's women. The same ranch once belonged to SCV silent film star William S. Hart.

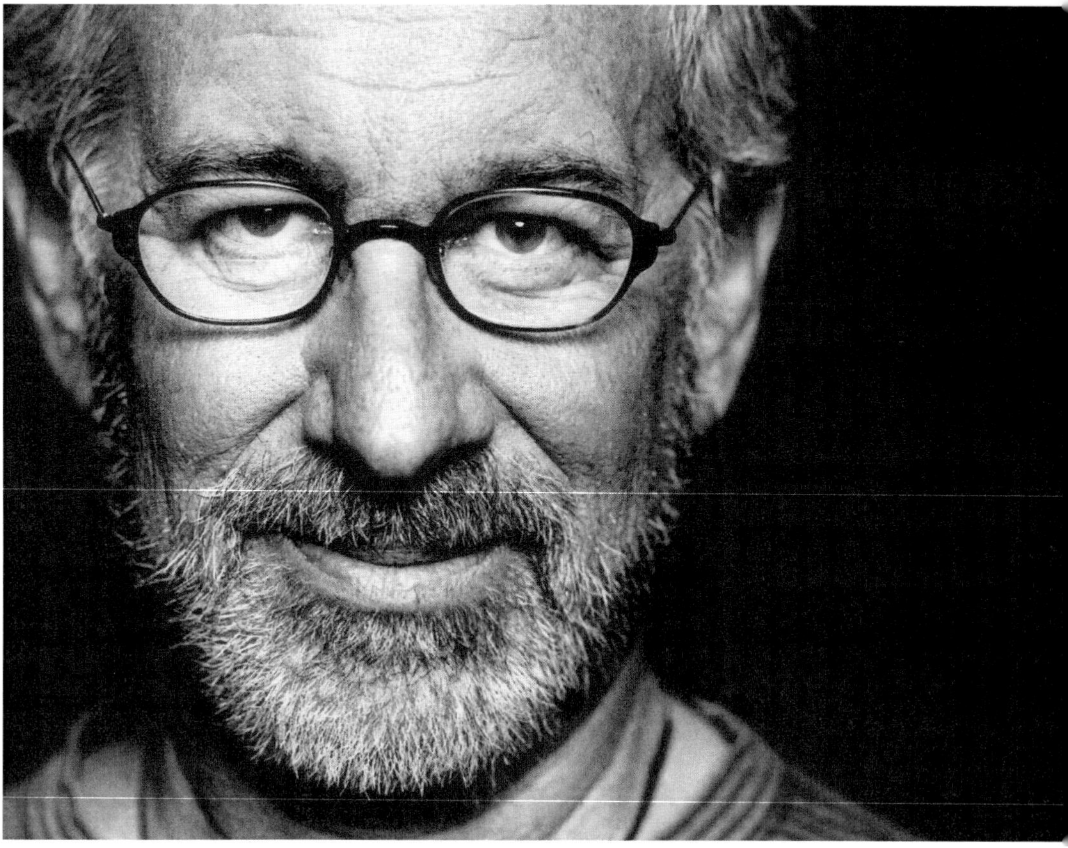

Steven Spielberg

In 1971, producer-director Steven Spielberg went a long way toward introducing the term "road rage" into the popular vernacular when he came to the Santa Clarita Valley to make his first film, the psychological thriller *Duel.* The movie is a simple story about a traveling salesman, played by Dennis Weaver, who is stalked in his red 1971 Dodge Valiant by a menacing rusty gasoline tanker truck. The driver of the truck is never seen, and the motive for the chase is never made clear. Spielberg was only 25 when he made the film. It was based on a story written by science-fiction and fantasy author Richard Matheson, who got the idea when he experienced road rage from a truck driver on the day that JFK was assassinated. Most of the film was shot over 13 days in and around the Acton area of the Santa Clarita Valley, far from the urban encroachment of Los Angeles (at the time). Since 1971, much of the open chaparral has been covered with tract housing, but a few of the locations still look much as they did back then. The tunnel used during the school bus scene is near Acton on Soledad Canyon Road. Nearby is Le Chene, a French restaurant on Sierra Highway north of Canyon Country, which was known as Chuck's Café in the film. It was here that Weaver's character confronts the man he believes to be the driver. The gasoline truck used in the film was a 1955 Peterbilt 281, which carried license plates from several states to subtly imply that the trucker had killed other drivers. It was destroyed at the film's conclusion when it tumbled down the face of Box Canyon at Mystery Mesa in Canyon Country, which is visible from Vasquez Canyon Road. For the film's theatrical release, additional scenes were shot that required the acquisition of additional trucks. At least one of the vehicles still exists today in a private collection in North Carolina. The roar that the truck makes when it tumbles over the cliff was later incorporated into Spielberg's film *Jaws* during the death of the shark. As the director later stated, it was "my way of thanking *Duel* for giving me a career."

Vic Morrow

Every day, as thousands of blue jean–clad thrill-riders stream through the turnstiles at Six Flags Magic Mountain theme park, few, if any, are aware that just outside the gates is the site of one of the worst filming disasters in Hollywood history. On July 23, 1982, a helicopter crash on the set of *Twilight Zone: The Movie* (see poster at right) killed 53-year-old veteran Hollywood actor Vic Morrow and two child actors. The tragic incident happened at Indian Dunes Park, a 600-acre ranch that was a frequent filming site for movie and television productions. Morrow, father of actress Jennifer Jason Leigh, was best known for the World War II television drama *Combat!*, which aired from 1962 to 1967. *Twilight Zone: The Movie* consisted of four segments, one in which director John Landis cast Morrow as a raving bigot who finds himself transported into the "Twilight Zone," where he is mistaken for different ethnicities; first as a Jew pursued by SS troops, then as a black man about to get lynched by the Ku Klux Klan, and finally as a member of the Viet Cong under attack by American troops. Morrow's character was to be redeemed by saving two Vietnamese children from an air attack that blows up their village. But something went terribly wrong. Despite concerns about safety and child labor law violations, filming of the climactic air attack scene began at 2:20 a.m., with Morrow taking his place in the Santa Clara River with a child under each arm. Landis ordered a helicopter to fly low as explosives were set off, launching fireballs into the night sky, causing the pilot to lose control. The helicopter plunged into the river on top of Morrow and the children, killing all three instantly. Landis was later charged with three counts of manslaughter and after a lengthy trial was acquitted by a jury in May 1987. He went on to direct hit films like Eddie Murphy's *Coming to America* and *Beverly Hills Cop III*. The tragic helicopter scene was cut from *Twilight Zone: The Movie*, which opened to dismal reviews in June 1983, with *Time* magazine critic Richard Corliss commenting, "the story hardly looks worth shooting, let alone dying for."

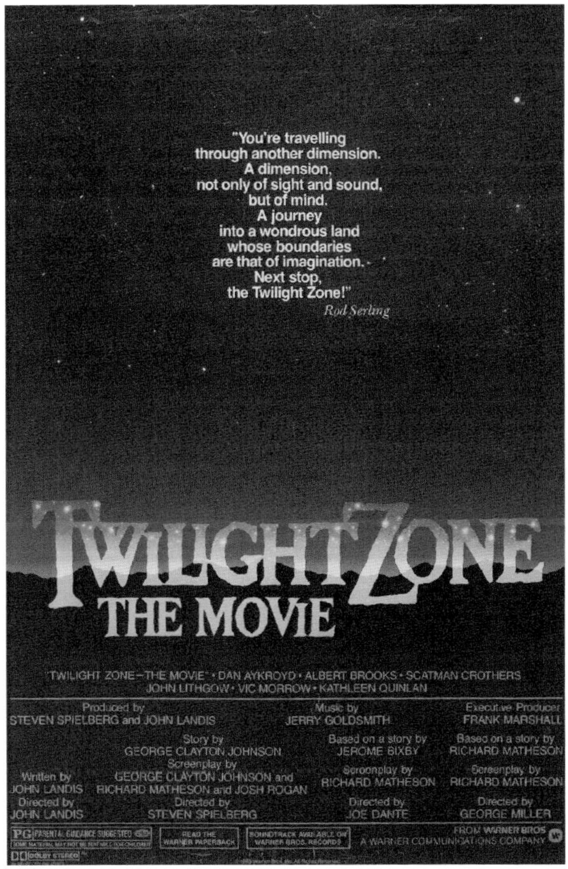

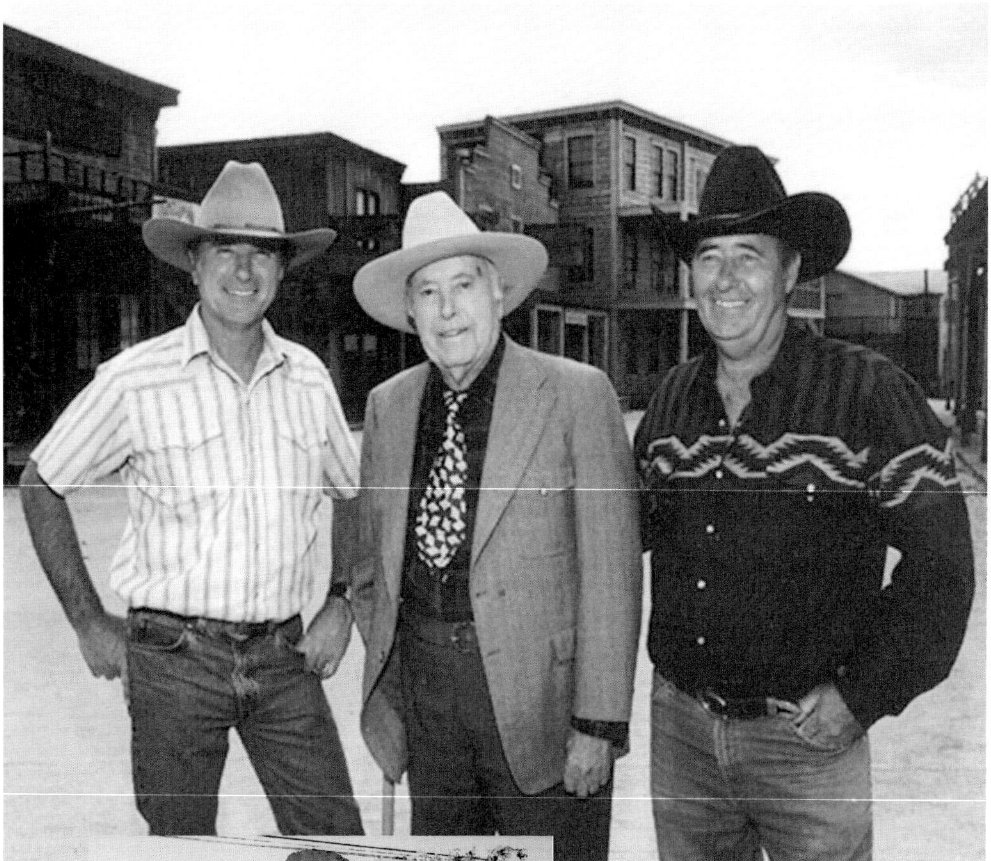

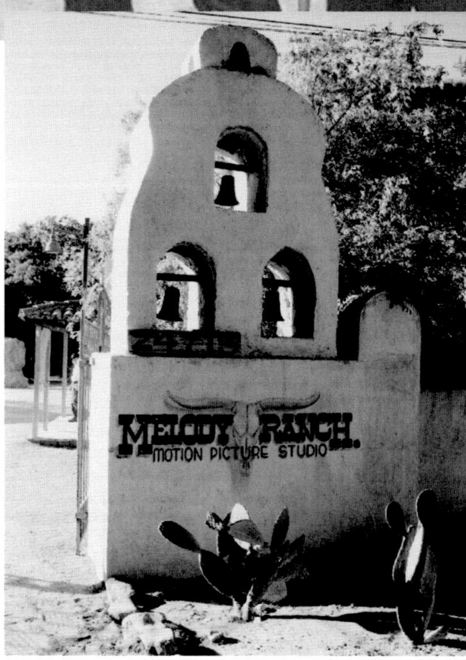

Paul Veluzat
He lived to be 101, but that hardly seems enough time to accomplish all the things that Paul Veluzat did in his life. As a young man, he joined up with the Texas Rangers and rode for a time with Mexican revolutionary Pancho Villa. Moving to Los Angeles, he worked as a bodyguard for oilman J. Paul Getty and evangelist Aimee Semple McPherson. Veluzat settled in Saugus in 1939, where he raised a family that included three sons. His ranches became filming locales, and today, Melody Ranch and the Veluzat Motion Picture Ranch are owned by sons Andre and Renaud, and son Rene owns the Blue Cloud Movie Ranch in Saugus. Pictured above is Paul Veluzat (center), with sons Renaud (left), and Andre at Melody Ranch in 1997. At left is a 2011 photograph of the entrance of Melody Ranch.

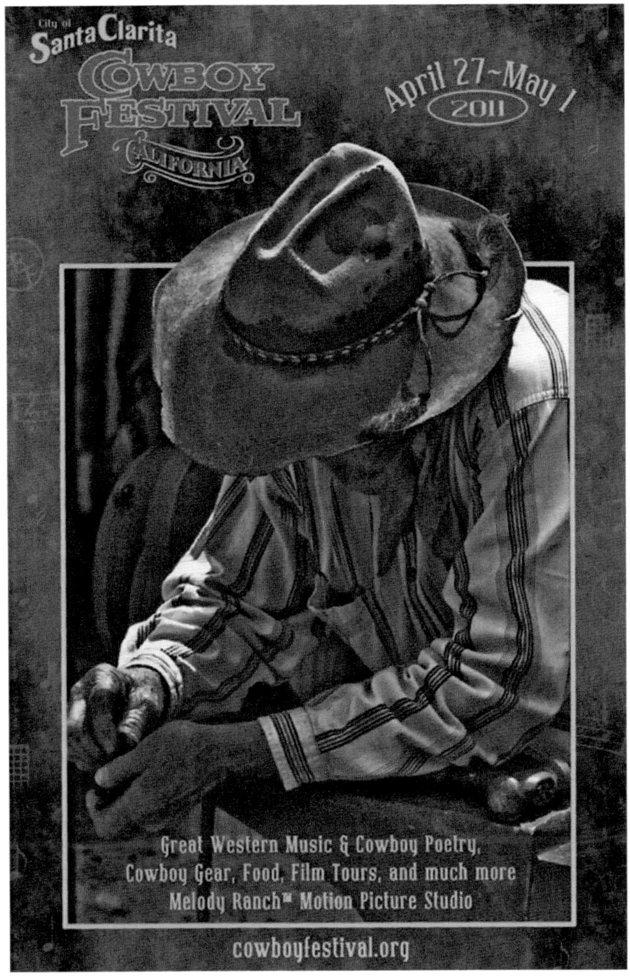

Andre and Renaud Veluzat
After his horse Champion died, Gene Autry sold the 21-acre Melody Ranch to brothers Andre and Renaud Veluzat, who painstakingly rebuilt the lot's former Western Town after conducting dozens of hours of research on the sets. Melody Ranch, which was the home of HBO's *Deadwood* (2004–2006), is open to the public on one weekend a year during Santa Clarita's Cowboy Festival in April. (Courtesy City of Santa Clarita.)

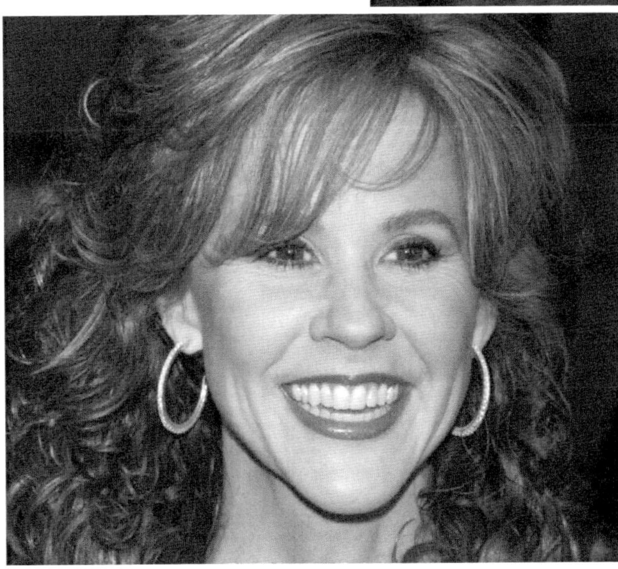

Linda Blair
Many remember Linda Blair (pictured in 2010) from her brush with the devil in *The Exorcist* (1973). Today, Blair is a guardian angel to abandoned pets through her Acton-based rescue, the Linda Blair WorldHeart Foundation, which is committed to the prevention of pet over-population. LBWF is one of the few groups that rescue newborn puppies and their mothers from substandard shelters, saving them from almost certain euthanization.

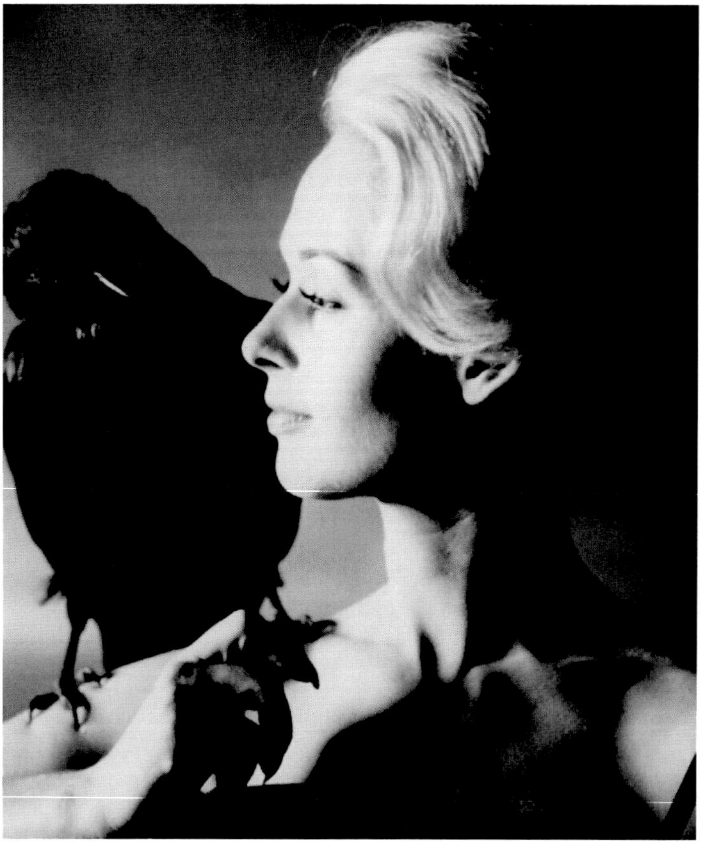

Tippi Hedren

The Santa Clarita Valley is filled with great neighbors, including a woman who, like many good neighbors, works a lot around the house, does a ton of volunteer work, and is famous for loving her cats. But in her case, the house she putters around is called the Shambala Preserve, and much of her volunteer work goes toward housing and feeding her cats—some of which weigh hundreds of pounds! You see, this special neighbor happens to be film legend Tippi Hedren (pictured in 1963), who rescues lions, leopards, ligers, tigers, and bobcats at her 73-acre Shambala Preserve near Acton. Tippi began rescuing large cats in 1970 and two years later purchased the property on Soledad Canyon Road that became the Shambala Preserve. It was here that she co-produced and starred in an early 1980s film called *Roar.* Today the Shambala Preserve is maintained by the Roar Foundation and provides lifelong sanctuary to abandoned exotic cats. It houses over 70 animals including Michael Jackson's Bengal tigers, which she acquired in 2006 when Jackson decided to vacate Neverland Ranch. Working around wild animals is a cakewalk compared to the stress Tippi must have felt making her film debut in *The Birds* in 1963 for legendary director Alfred Hitchcock. Before this, she worked as a fashion model and then appeared in television commercials. Hitchcock was first captivated by Tippi's striking Scandinavian beauty after seeing her in one of these commercials. A year after completing *The Birds*, Tippi starred again for "Hitch" in *Marnie*. While her days with Hitchcock are well documented, many forget that she also appeared in Charlie Chaplin's final film in 1967, *A Countess From Hong Kong*, which was filmed in London after Chaplin was exiled from the United States. Her *Countess* co-stars were Marlon Brando, Sophia Loren, and Chaplin's own son Sydney. In all likelihood, Tippi is the only female actor to have ever worked for both of these knighted English film masters. Today, she works tirelessly to support Shambala and to get federal laws passed that prevent the breeding of exotic cats as pets. She somehow still finds time to appear in the occasional film and television role. Tippi is the mother of actress Melanie Griffith, who is married to actor Antonio Banderas. The Shambala Preserve can be visited online at shambala.org.

Mark-Paul Gosselaar
To fans around the world, he is Zack Morris on *Saved By The Bell*, Detective John Clark on *NYPD Blue*, Jerry Kellerman on TNT's *Raising the Bar*, and Peter Bash on TNT's *Franklin and Bash*. But to his Santa Clarita neighbors, he is simply Mark-Paul. Mark-Paul Gosselaar (pictured here in 2011) first gained fame as a teenager in the 1980s and has seamlessly made the transition to adult starring roles.

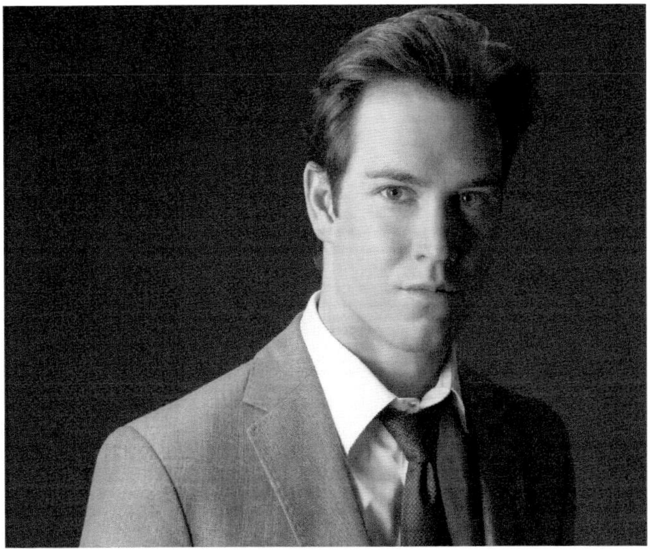

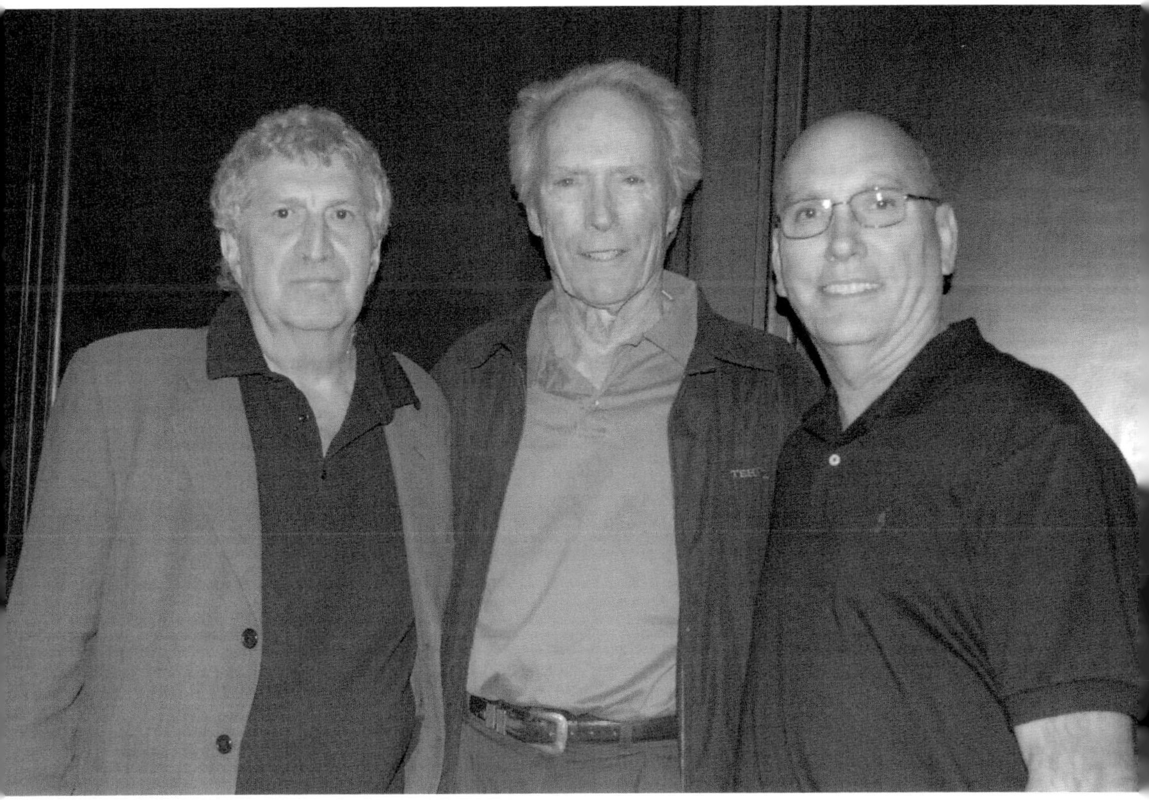

Joel Cox
Only a select group of Hollywood's film editors have won Academy Awards, and fewer still have worked alongside Clint Eastwood for 30 years. Both these things are on the resume of Santa Clarita Valley resident Joel Cox, who began his collaboration with Eastwood in 1976 and won an Oscar for *Unforgiven* in 1992. Pictured, from left to right, are Bruce Ricker, Clint Eastwood, and Joel Cox at the Paso Robles Film Festival in 2009.

INDEX